The

Alaskan

Bootlegger's

Bible

by

Leon W. Kania

Happy Mountain Publications
Copyright 2000

Happy Mountain Publications

3401 E. Naomi Ave
Wasilla, Alaska 99654
U.S.A.
Tel: 907-376-2610
Email: leon@happymountain.net

The Alaska Bootlegger's Bible

Printed in the United States of America

14th Printing - January 2012

Cover and Book Design - Scottie Kania
Photography - Scottie Kania
Illustrations - Scottie Kania

ISBN 0-9674524-0-6

"Muktuk Kania" AKA, He who tracks dried bone back to place of birth.

The Author

Shown with Eskimos butchering a whale. Got it on light tackle and a green pixie. Wudd'a thrown it back (not much bigger'n a greyhound bus) but it swallowed the hook.

My favorite fish story aside, this is a scene which few tonnicks or palefaces are privileged to witness. Incredibly brave Eskimo hunters have just killed and beached this gigantic whale on the shores of the Beaufort Sea. It will feed many families and they will waste practically nothing and share with other villages that in turn share their harvest of salmon, caribou, seal, walrus and whitefish. In this scene, portable TV sized chunks of meat and blubber are being removed.

All ages from the tiniest tyke to the elders are working in a well-orchestrated community effort to process this bounty. The meat, blubber, skin (muktuk) and blood are all consumed as food. The baleen (vinyl-like mouth brooms) and bone are made into artifacts for traditional use or sale. The whaling captains and their crews are highly respected by their people. Indeed, they are heroes and rightfully so. It takes incredible bravery and stamina to stalk these huge mammals in frail boats amid the ice floes. Though it's not common knowledge among outsiders, these hunters also become the hunted. Killer whales that kill other whales by ramming with their heads often mistake the bottom of a boat for a whale which in our frigid waters can mean death for an entire crew.

Ice cellars that are bottle shaped caves dug straight down into the permanently frozen ground (permafrost) are used to preserve the seasonal bounty of migratory fish and game. Fitted with an airtight lid or hatch and accessed via a ladder, these natural freezers have been used for centuries, just one of many ingenious inventions in use long before Christopher what's his name "discovered" America.

Table of Contents

Foreword 1

Introduction 2

Chapter One–The Naked Truth! 5

The Basic Concepts of Making Alcoholic Beverages 6
Facts and Fables for Success and Safety (or the good old days weren't so good) 9
Dynamite Whiskey 9
The Good, The Bad and the Deadly in Equipment and Materials 10
    Plastic 10
    Glass 11
Sterility, Hell, Holy Water and the Hobo's Friend 12
Universal Truths and Dark Secrets About Yeast and Fermenting 14

Chapter Two–Wine for the King, Wine for the Masses 17

Wine – From Apple to Zucchini 18
    The Bottling Process 19
    Secrets to Long-term Success 20
Wines – Doin' It (basic wine making steps, recipes and instructions) 20
Some Simple Wines 23
Sugar Wine 23
Mint Wine 24
Simple Dandelion Wine 24
Unorthodox and Stunningly Simple Wine Making 24
Universal Recipe Made With Store-Bought 100% Fruit Juice 25
Wine From the Vine, Fruit Trees and Berries 25
Basic Grape Wine Recipe (1 Gallon) 26
Second Wine Recipe (grape) 26
The Shape of the Grape 26
A Fresh Grape-Raisin Wine 27
Easy Grape Wine 27
Fruits and Berries 27
Cane Fruits – Blackberry, Raspberry, Salmonberry and all their Seedy Cousins such as
    Mulberries and Dewberries and More 27
Salmonberry Wine 27
Elderberry Wine 28
Blueberry Wine 28
Gooseberry Wine 28
Sweet Strawberry Wine 28

Dry Strawberry Wine 28
Fruit Wines 29
Mango Wine 29
Orange Wine 29
Apple Wine 29
Stone Fruit Wines 29
Peach, Plum, Prune and Apricot Wine 29
Cherry Wine 30
Alaskan Currant or Cranberry Wine 30
Currant Wine 30
Apple Sherry 30
"Beary" Berries 30
Feast and Famine Fermentation Method 31
Cider (Apples) and Perry (Pears) 31
Old Time Cider From Apples 33
Old Time Cider Recipe 33
Hard Cider 34
Great Cider 34
Vegetable Wines 34
Tomato Wine (red or green) 34
Corn Wine 34
Watermelon Wine (any type of melon is fine) 35
Rhubarb Wine 35
Root Wines 35
Basic Potato Wine 36
Naturally Improved Potato Wine (by starving the yeast and using malt enzymes to
    convert starches) 36
Simple Malting to Augment Wine 37
Parsnip Wine 37
Carrot Wine (Carrot Whiskey) 37
Beet Wine (red beets) 37
Sugar Beet Wine 38
Mangel Wine 38
Sweet Potato Wine 38
Grain Wines 38
Wheat Wine 38
Rice Wine 39
Barley Wine (Pearled Barley) 39
Cheating for Better Grain Wines 39
Blossom Wines 40
Simplest Flower Wine –Dandelion 40
More Full-Bodied Blossom Wines 40
Alaskan Fireweed Blossom Wine 40

Honey Wines (Mead) 41
Simplest Honey Wine 41
Flower and Honey Wine (sweet) 41
Honey and Fruit Wine (medium dry) 42
Honey and Fruit Juice Wine (Sweet) 42
Other Wines 42
Rose Hips Wine 42
Pea Pod Wine 43
Kvass (Bread Wine) 43
Kvass 43
Birch Sap Wine (one of my favorites) 44
Birch Sap Wine 44
Applejack 45
Applejack Recipe 45
Milk Wine (ALA Alaskan Engel Wine and Father Emmett Engel, the wine making
    priest) 46
Koumiss - Kefir Recipe #1 (the easy way) 48
Milk Wine Recipe #2 (the more traditional way) 48
Yogurt First (Miss Muffet's favorite) 48
Pruno – Jailhouse Wine 49
Pruno Recipe 49
Corn Squeezins 49
Modern Corn Squeezins 49

Chapter Three–From Prohibition-Style Homebrew to Gourmet Beers 51

Beer - From Alaskan Bush Beer to Gourmet Beers 52
  Cooking 53
Beer Making Steps 56
  I.Cooking 56
  II.Fermentation 56
  III.Racking and Fining 57
  IV.Bottling and Priming 57
  V.Storing 57
Making Beer With Malt Extracts 58
Prohibition Style Beer "Sneaky Pete" (a.k.a. Alaska Bush Beer) 58
Bush Beer 59
Al Capone Beer (Pilsner?) 59
Al Capone Speakeasy Beer 60
Steam Beer – All Grain 60
Steam Beer 60

Any Beer (Using Malt Extract Syrup) 61
Not Just Any Beer (Aromatic Hopping All-Malt Beer) 62
Light Beer and Dark Beer– What's the Difference? 63
Pale Lager Pilsner 63
Oatmeal Stout 64
Pilsner Style with Rice 64
Steam Beer 64
Barley Wine 65
Barley Wine Recipe 65
Smoked Beer (The Easy Way) 65
Smoked Stout 66
Wheat Beer 66
    Wheat Beer Tips: 67
Basic Wheat Beer Recipe 68
Making Beer From Malted Grain 68
Lager - Basic Recipe 68
    STEP 1. Gristing 69
    STEP 2. & 3. Cheating on Malt Grain Beers 69
    STEP 4. Boiling and Hopping 69
    STEP 5. Cooling/Pitching the Yeast 70
    STEP 6. Fermentation and Clarification 70
    STEP 7. Priming and Bottling 70
Other Beers 71
Chicha – Corn Beer 71
Chicha #1 (Corn Beer) 71
Corn Beer #2 72
Fruit Beers 72
Hot Pepper Beers 73

Chapter Four–Homemade "Poreboy" Equipment 75

"Pore Boy" Equipment (Making Your Own) 76
Fermentation Vessels 77
Fermentation Locks 77
Pruno 77
Pore Boy Homemade Bottle Capper 78
Making Your Own "Pore Boy" Capper 79
Unassembled Rapper Capper 80
Pore Boy Capper Head Parts and Assembly 80
"Poreboy" Scales 80
Holes to be Drilled for "Pore boy" Capper Parts 81
Homemade "Pore Boy" Scales 81
Bottle Cleaning 82

Grain and Hops Bags 85

Making Your Own Malt 85

Winnowing..87

Malt Roasting Temperatures 87

Other Tricks 88

The Iodine Test 88

Malting Wheat 88

Malting Tips 89

Making Your Own Malt Factory Out of an Old Refrigerator 92

Malting Your Own Sample Worksheet 92

Malt Factory 94

Sinkers and Floaters Test 95

Keggin' it (A Cheap and Easy Way to Naturally Carbonated Draft Beer) 96

Thermometers 98

The Hydrometer 98

U.S. Proof Spirit and Hydrometer Measurement 100

Use of the Hydrometer 100

Hydrometer Tips 101

Specific Gravity Temperature Table 103

Specific Gravity to Potential Alcohol Table 103

Chapter Five–Whiskey Makin' 105

Basics of Mashing for Distillation (And Dangers!) 106

Thin Mash Whiskey (Moonshine) 107

Thin Mash Whiskey 108

Bathtub Gin..108

Bathtub Gin #1 109

Bathtub Gin #2 109

Rum "White Lightening" 40 Rod 109

Corn Whiskey (Corn Likker, Moonshine, Splo, White Lightening, Tanglefoot, Mountain Dew, Loudmouth, and a lot of other names) 109

Real Corn Whiskey #1 – *With or Without Horse Turds* 110

Real Corn Whiskey #2 110

Preachers Whiskey (Also Free Whiskey or Sneaky Pete) 111

Distilling Theory (or Mother Nature is a Moonshiner) 111

Types of Stills and How They Work 112

The Retort Still 112

Retort Still–Operation 113

Traditional Pot Still 114

Traditional Pot Still–Operation 115

The Modern Pot Still (From a Pressure Cooker) 116

The Modern Pot Still Components 118

The Modern Pot Still Assembled 118

The Reflux Still, or Don't Lose Your Marbles (Reflux Column Still) 119

The Compound Still 119

Evolution of the Pot Still to the Reflux, to the Compound Still 120

The Two-Dollar Still or Get Crocked on Your Crock Pot 121

The Two-Dollar Still–Operation 122

The Disappearing Still or Two Woks and a Pot 123

The Disappearing Still–Operation 124

The Desk Drawer Still (No Home or Office Should Be Without One) 125

The Deskdrawer Still–Components 126

The Deskdrawer Still–Operation 127

Properties of Alcohol 128

Cold Weather Hazards of Alcohol 128

The Dead Trapper, Soldier, Miner, Bootlegger 128

Fermentation of Ethyl Alcohol 129

Basic Mash for Distilling Neutral Spirits 130

Distillation of Ethyl Alcohol 130

Cleaning the Still 133

Safety Factors During Distillation 133

The Devil, Vodka, Russian Bootlegging and Potatoes 134

Distilling For Reasons Other Than Whiskey Making 135

Chapter Six–Flavoring and Making Liqueurs 137

Flavoring and Making Liqueurs 138

   Steps: 139

Simple Syrup for Liqueurs 139

Homemade Recipes 139

Crème de Menthe I 139

Crème de Menthe II 139

Fresh Mint Liqueur 139

Bailey's Irish Cream 139

Irish Crème I 140

Irish Crème II 140

Creme De Cacao 140

Coffee Liqueur (Kahlua) 140

Coffee Liqueur 140

Drambuie I 140

Drambuie II 140

Amaretto 140

Cointreau No. 1 140

Cointreau No. 2 141

Anisette 141
Grand Marnier 141

Rum Shrub 141
Almond Shrub 141
Kümmel 141
Orange Peel Liqueur 142
Whole Orange Liqueur 142
Tangerine Liqueur 142
Tangerine Liqueur (made with peels or the zest) 142
Peach Liqueur 142
Peach Brandy (Canned Peaches) 142
Nectarine Liqueur 142
Apricot Liqueur 142
Apple Brandy 143
Apple Liqueur 143
Cranberry or Alaskan Watermelon Berry Liqueur 143
Plum Liqueur 143
Rhubarb Liqueur 143
Elderberry Liqueur 143
Raspberry Liqueur 143
Pineapple Liqueur 144
Blackberry or Other Cordial 144
Spiced Rum 144
Egg Nog 144
Noirot® Liqueur Extracts 144
Kirsch – Unsweetened, clear cherry drink. Also used a lot in cooking 145
Recipes for the Use of Flavors in the Preparation of Cordials and liqueurs 145
Anisette, Apricot, Blackberry, Creme de Cacao, etc. 145
Noirot® Flavor Per label instructions 146
Recipe Spirits (Brandy, Rum, Gin, Rye, etc.) 146
Any Cordial or Liqueur 146
Any Grain Alcohol (Using Noirot® Flavors) 146
Vermouth 146
Appendix A Tables 148
Appendix B Hops 150
Appendix C Tips 152
Appendix D Water 158
Appendix E Supply Sources 159
Appendix F Brewing Log 161
Glossary 162
Index 165

Foreword

After its heyday during Prohibition, "makin' your own" practically died out in the lower-48. Most Americans found it more convenient to buy it than make it. Alaska, however, was and still is a frontier where a trip to the store might be an annual event involving a trip of several hundred miles by anything from dogsled and river boat, to ATV's and airplanes. Your trip to the store might include coping with grizzly bears, belligerent moose, and onions freezing harder than cue balls. If you are really unlucky like a good friend of mine who grew up on an island near Dutch Harbor, the boat delivering your annual supply purchases will sink. They were able to retrieve the goods but not before all the labels on the canned goods had washed off. Every meal for that year was a surprise.

The challenges of shopping being what they are, our Alaskan life-style includes a lot more homemade goodies, be they bread, pies, wine or beer because toting in ingredients and making your own often means the difference between have and have not. Additionally, Alaska tends to attract the pioneer types, the independent spirits (some might say wackos) who choose to live apart from the herd and be as self sufficient as possible. A classic example is the story of the toothless old sourdough who not only killed the bear, but also used its teeth to make a set of dentures to eat it with. I know a number of folk, both men and women that could put Robinson Crusoe to shame.

I don't mean to say that those who survive and thrive in remote Alaska are necessarily outlaws, but if a moose appears in someone's yard a couple of days before hunting season, chances are very good that by opening day, it will be steaks, roasts and burgers. Legal? No! Is it done? Sure! As you'll learn in this book, making your own booze is not all that difficult. Is it legal? Beer and wine, yes. Whiskey? No! Is it done? Sure! This book may not make you into another Robinson Crusoe, it will however, teach you how to be almost wholly self sufficient in making your own beverages and the equipment to do it with.

1

Introduction

There are few things so frustrating or irksome as buying a "how-to" book to learn a skill like brewing, only to find it was written by a pompous "expert" who is trying to impress you with his brilliance. Instead of presenting his subject in simple terms for the beginner, this type of author dwells on his academic credentials and uses technical jargon that only someone with an advanced degree in the same field can understand. Making alcoholic beverages is part art and part science, sort of like baking homemade bread. Grandma made great bread with no degree. She didn't understand the genetics of yeast culture or the chemistry involved, but she knew what worked.

Long before there were such things as degrees, people were making beer, wine and even spirits. It's only in the last few centuries that the function of yeast in fermentation began to be understood. Granted that science and technology gives us better quality control, safety and reproducible results, but you don't need a degree in science to turn out a good beverage. No one knows who brewed the first batch of beer or wine. We think the Romans were the first big time distillers and some think it was a major cause of the fall of the Roman Empire. It wasn't the alcohol that did them in, but supposedly the lead in the booze. The theory is that they distilled the alcohol from their wine in lead vessels. We know now that ingesting lead causes severe brain damage, but then it was mainly their politicians who drank the stuff, so who knows.

It was not my intent at the start of this book to include a position statement on anything. I am not by nature a zealot, a nature nut or any kind of radical. Homebrewing has been a lifetime hobby, sometimes a necessity. Having started out long before it was in vogue, I had to improvise a lot of equipment and methods and it is my intent to pass on some of my sometimes unorthodox, or poor boy trove of lore and tricks. This book forced me to blow the dust off a lifetime's accumulation of reference material and to do some research into a present-day, state-of-the-art homebrewing and I am appalled! I knew many commercial breweries relied heavily on chemical additives and the wineries did so to a lesser degree, but homemade beers and wines are supposed to be wholesome, natural beverages. Such, apparently is not the case. The more recent "how-to" books and current catalogs seem to advocate what I consider a witch's brew of additives that are not necessary in making a quality, wholesome beverage.

The best beers and wines did not evolve from laboratories and chemical treatment. To the contrary, some of the worst beers and wines are the product of science and commercialization. I use campden tablets for sterilization of must or wort, gelatin for clarification, diluted chlorine bleach to sterilize my equipment, citric juice and tea for fermentation aids and that's it. It is wonderful to have all the superb yeast, malts, wine extracts and equipment available through the various suppliers. The books and magazines strengthen the fraternity and advance the art, but who needs all the chemicals?

Caution: While you can make your own beer and wine legally, it is illegal to distill your own spirits in the USA Even possession of the non-permitted still is illegal. Also, distilling is very dangerous with very real hazards of fire, explosions, scalding and poisoning. If you think you'd like to run off a batch of your own mountain dew, think again. You will be breaking the federal law and the "revenooers" will get

you. Don't do it! Much of the distilling infor-
mation in this book came from people who
worked in remote overseas areas and is included
as an example of "Yankee" ingenuity, rather
than a blueprint for crime.

Federal law permits an adult to make 100 gallons each of beer and wine for personal consumption. A two-adult household may make 200 gallons each. No fees, permits or paperwork are required.

Chapter One

The Naked Truth!

In This Chapter

➤ The basic Concepts of Making Alcoholic Beverages

➤ Facts and Fables for Success and Safety

➤ The Good, the Bad and the Deadly in Equipment and Materials

➤ Sterility, Hell, Holy Water and the Hobo's Friend

➤ Universal Truths and Dark Secrets About Yeast and Fermenting

Making alcoholic beverages is a simple and natural process practiced since condominium meant cave, but for safety and best results, there are some things the novice must know and understand about making everything from champagne to corn squeezins. This book will first give you a grasp of the basic principles of making all types of alcoholic beverages in nontechnical language, then we'll go on in easy stages until you know not only how to make them all, but also the equipment to do it with.

The Basic Concepts of Making Alcoholic Beverages

The CO_2 gas that yeast produces is heavier than air and this is probably the key factor in the discovery and development of all forms of brewing. At the risk of alienating all the picky little wine makers, arrogant brewmasters, distillers and associated scientists of the world, I'd like to take you back to the real basics of any kind of brewing, the discovery of this mysterious art. So pack a lunch and bring your bug spray, we're going back in time.

We exit the time machine just as two cavemen named Dork and Mork are heading out to harvest shoo-shoo berries. Dork has a basket and a shallow wooden bowl. Mork has one of those newfangled clay jars with a lid. The harvest is good and on the way back to the cave, they manage to mash their berries up pretty badly. A few days later, Dork's basket of berries is rotten. The ones in the shallow bowl have turned into a sour mush, but Mork and his wife are laughing it up outside of their cave drinking out of that big jar and doing the shoo-shoo boogie. What happened? They picked their berries side-by-side, off the same bushes. Here's what happened in the discovery of brewing. All the berries had natural yeast and bacteria on them. The ones in Dork's woven basket with lots of air rotted like berries normally do. The ones mashed in the shallow bowl soured or turned to vinegar because airborne vinegar bacteria had access to the

pulp. On the other hand, Mork's newfangled jar (or crock) was deep enough that as the natural yeast on the skins produced heavier than air CO_2 it formed a cap over the berries, excluding air and forcing the native yeast on the fruit to produce alcohol and more CO_2. The lid kept out vinegar making bacteria, wild yeast and bugs. That my friends, sums up the basis of the art and science of brewing and is the foundation of all distilling, jacking and squeezins too. Mother Nature does most of it. You just need to learn to work with her. Oh, by the way, Mork never did get a degree, but he founded Shoo-Shoo Valley Beverage Company and in his old age, set up a scholarship foundation to turn out picky little wine makers, brewmasters and scientists. Sad to say, his son didn't follow him in the business. He went into fire making research and got burnt real bad.

Granted, the preceding is an extremely simplified explanation of the brewing process. You can really make wine with such primitive methods. In fact, my Dad and some his buddies made a lot of wine and beer back in the good old days using material and equipment not much more sophisticated than Mork's. It wasn't bad either.

Since you now know the basics of brewing wine, let's move on to the rudiments of beer making. In essence, brewing beer is making wine out of grain, rather than fermenting the fruit sugars in fruits and berries. Some very high alcoholic content beverages made the same as beers are called bar-

In 1933, after cleaning up Chicago, the FBI transferred Elliott Ness to Cincinnati tasked with cleaning up the dangerous "Moonshine Mountains" of Kentucky, Tennessee and Ohio. Shot at many times, Elliot later said, "Those mountain men and their squirrel rifles gave me almost as many chills as the Capone mob."

ley wines, rather than beer. Again, Mother Nature does the hard part if you work with her. The chief difference in the beer making process from wine making is malting. Our food grains or cereals as we normally use them, are composed mainly of starch, which the yeast can't digest readily, but when a seed such as barley or wheat is moistened and starts to sprout, the enzymes in the seed begin to convert the starch to maltose, or malt sugar which brewers yeast thrives on. The trick is to allow the grain such as barley to sprout just enough to convert all its starch to sugar, then stop the growth by drying or lightly toasting the seeds which are then called malt, i.e., malted barley. Pale or barely toasted malt is used for pale beers. The more you toast it, the darker the husk gets and also the sugar inside it caramelizes.

The darker the malt, the darker the beer. For some reason, virtually none of the home-brewing books even touch on making your own malt. Malting is always treated as a complex art that the homebrewer can't hope to succeed at. Maybe there's a conspiracy to keep this mysterious art out of the hands of the common man by a secret group of gnome-like brewmasters. Vun day vee vill rule der vorld!

This is a bunch of hooey partner. In my youth, I knew an old time moonshiner from the hills of West-by-God-Virginia. He was a wonderful old guy and loved to tell me how they did things in the old days. You need malt to make whiskey too.

In fact, the fermented liquid is also called beer. He regaled me with lore about still making, muzzle loading rifles, etc. When I asked him about malt, he said, (This was for corn whiskey, mountain dew, white lightening, sonny.) they put about 40% of the corn they needed for a batch in sacks and would bury it in a manure pile for a

Typical Old-Time Still

couple of days. That ain't exactly high tech, is it? Now vee know der secret. Keep it quiet. If word leaks out, we'll have to register manure piles. I can see it now, a shiny car roars up to a poor old dirt farmer's barn and a couple of steely-eyed suits flash their badges to old Zeke and say out of the corner of their mouths, "You got a permit for that buddy?"

We're going to delve into it a lot deeper later (malting, not the manure pile), but let's move on to two more arts, one that we all know a bit about. Distilling, (illegal) and another jacking (illegal too) that somehow seems to have been forgotten and it's hard to understand how or why. Distilling has been practiced at least as long ago as those Romans fried their brains with lead-laced grappa (distilled grape wine.) The principle is simple. If you heat any fermented fluids containing alcohol and water judiciously, the alcohol that has a lower evaporation temperature will separate from the water as a vapor. If you can capture those vapors and condense them by cooling, you have made distilled spirits and all entail separation of alcohol from a fermented mixture of water, sugars and yeast. There are more types of distilling apparatus or stills than you can shake a stick at. We're going to cover a broad spectrum of these devices, ranging from the very conventional, to the very unorthodox, such as the desk drawer still and the now you see it, now you don't type that used different principles and literally disappears before your eyes. So far, we have covered in brutal basics, the fine arts of wine making, beer brewing and distilling. You should at this point, understand the concepts of the three related arts or science. Our next leap is almost a leap backward because we're going to look at a practice or process that was so common and is so simple; I can't understand how it has vanished.

Applejack! We've all heard of it, but we don't know what it is. It has connotations of colonial times when Ben Franklin and George Washington sat around in the town tavern drinking rum flips (whatever the heck that was) with an old manual typewriter on which the "s" key didn't work. (Aw, I know they didn't have typewriters then, but it makes for a good story.) So they used the "f" key and pecked out the Declaration of Independence saying, "The perfuit of happineff…" Perhaps if they'd had a word proceffor, thingf would have been different, mebbe.

Anyhow, jacking is sort of distilling in reverse. Alcohol evaporates at a lower temperature than water. Water freezes at a higher temperature than alcohol. Our forefathers in funny hats and stockings knew this and used it routinely to make knock-your-socks-off beverages. No heat, no coil, no still. The result is basically a brandy. Apple, pear, peach or cherry, it all worked the same. They fermented their fruits and grains, but instead of distilling them with heat, they concentrated the spirits by putting them out on the back porch when the weather got cold and they jacked them. As the fermented fluid froze, they removed the ice that formed,

thereby separating the alcohol from the water. This removes only the water so the applejack or whatever will be cloudy unless it's filtered or settled carefully. Some fortified wines are made this way.

A note of caution is in order here regarding this process. Distilling is regulated by law mainly because distilled spirits are a source of revenue for the federal government as are all commercial alcoholic beverages. We are permitted to make wine and beer in limited amounts for home consumption, but it is illegal to sell or even barter these products. As I mentioned earlier, even possession of an unpermitted still can get you in a lot of trouble. I don't think you'll get raided by BATF if you put a gallon or two of hard cider in your freezer for your own consumption, but I can't guarantee it either. Remember that this is a "how-to," not a "have-to" book and you're responsible for your own actions.

Now bear with me for one more leap. We leapt back in time to prehistoric brewing, then forward to distilling, then back to colonial times and jacking. Now, let's take a jump sideways to another traditional American alcoholic beverage that seems to have been forgotten except for its name, corn squeezins. Most people think it refers to corn whiskey or distilled moonshine, but in truth, it's a uniquely American innovation in a class all by itself. First, let's start by gnawing on a piece of sugar cane. Sweet and juicy, huh? We make rum out of the juice. Next, try nibbling on a piece of fresh corn stalk. Not much difference is there? Our ingenious forefathers used to make potent joy juice out of those succulent corn stalks, almost without breaking stride in their farm labors. Here's how they did it.

First, you need a silo; the big tall tank-like structure used to hold chopped up green vegetation (which fermented) for stock feed. When sugar laden corn stalks were chopped up and packed into the silo, it was time to make some corn squeezins. The bottom of the silo was covered with a layer of those sturdy old crockery jugs we normally think of as moonshine jugs. Each jug was corked with a section of dried corncob from last year's crop. Remember that these cobs were saved as heating fuel, for smoking meat and for use as toilet paper before they had toilet paper. A corncob makes a really tough cork for a jug, but it also has a soft porous center that worked admirably as a filter to let the sugar laden fluid squeezed out by the tons of silage stacked into the silo, fill the jugs with fermenting fluid.

The few old timers I knew that had made the stuff spoke fondly of it. I've never tried it, but I intend to. Lacking a silo, I think a press on the order of a cider press should work to extract the juice. Now you know what corn squeezins is. My problem is that I've lived in Alaska for the last twenty-three years and It's taken me almost that long to learn to grow corn here, but look out Zeke, next year we'uns goin' to have some corn squeezins.

Facts and Fables for Success and Safety (or the good old days weren't so good)

Years ago, the Lil' Abner cartoon strip had two characters who were always mixing up a vat of a potent brew called kickapoo joy juice. The ingredients they used were hilarious, an anvil to make it strong, a grindstone to make it smooth and a dead mouse to give it body, of course. Fact is stranger than fiction though, as illustrated by an old-timer I know of who complained to visitors that he had a horrible headache from some moon-shine he'd drunk the night before. His wife then shook her head sadly and said, "Too much dynamite." She was serious!

Dynamite Whiskey

Anyone who has used dynamite knows the fumes from expended nitro will give you one of the most awful headaches imaginable, but in this case, the old fellow had actually drunk moonshine laced with dynamite. You see, winters got darned cold in Alaska and the yeast in the barrels of mash hidden out in the woods would stop working if it got too cold. Today, we know nitroglycerin is a heart stimulant. Back then the old timers knew that a quarter stick or so of dynamite mixed in a barrel of mash jump started the yeast that had stopped working because of the cold. Another cure for a stuck ferment was to toss a piece of raw chicken or ripe meat in the brew. This remedy dates back centuries, long before Dr. Nobel blew up his laboratory with his first and second batches of nitroglycerin. The first batch he heated in a beaker, the second, he hit with a hammer. What a scientist! He should have won a prize. Forgive me for digressing. The meat provided nutrients, mainly nitrogen to a brew that lacked vigor. Nowadays, you can get nutrient tablets from any brewing supply firm, so put that dynamite down Clem, easy, and let go of that chicken.

Beware any old handed down tales, recipes or equipment. Some of this stuff is harmless, such as starting a brew by piling bakers' yeast on a slice of toast, topping it with a grape and floating this raft in the middle of your brew. Some of it's funny like the bootlegger who delivered right to your door with a milk wagon in white painted milk bottles. A lot of it's dangerous, even deadly, such as my old friend telling me it's okay to make a still out of a galvanized kerosene can, as long as you don't use it more than once. Chances are you would only live to use it once, which brings us to the next subject.

The Good, The Bad and the Deadly in Equipment and Materials

Metals and vessels used in any brewing or cooking and all related utensils and equipment must be benign or not toxic and not contaminated by anything harmful or detrimental to the success of your endeavor or your health. First, forget about using any old wooden kegs, casks, tubs or churns you may have on hand. Use them for planters. Most wooden vessels will be deteriorated and difficult or impossible to repair or maintain. At best, old wooden vessels will not be sterile. The wood will be permeated with bacteria that will turn anything you put in them into vinegar. Most likely you'll have an old whiskey barrel and the reason the whiskey companies get rid of them is that the wood, particularly the charred inner surfaces, absorb the nasty stuff out of raw whiskey. This nasty stuff is mainly fusel oil, a light form of alcohol that is the wicked stuff that gives you hangover headaches and is also a potent *laxative* used on livestock.

The wood also contains a lot of alcohol and hard core old drinkers used to get these barrels fresh from the whiskey companies, pour a gallon or two of water in them and slosh it around for a few days. They would get some of the cheapest, vilest, skull-split-

The Private's Revenge

A civil war private took horrible revenge on an officer notorious for confiscating and drinking his men's whiskey. He obtained a bottle of pure fusel oil and arranged for it to be "confiscated" too. Years later in his memoirs, he gleefully recalled that when the captain finally returned to duty several days later, he was "about as plump as a hoe handle."

ting, head for the outhouse and throw up on the way booze imaginable. Remember that they age whiskey in wooden barrels to soak the nasty stuff out of it. That's the best case scenario. If somebody at sometime put something else in that wooden vessel such as DDT maybe, you don't have a barrel, you have a death trap. Make some planters.

Metals come next and there is only one metal you should use. STAINLESS STEEL. Copper was the old metal of choice, but lead solder was used in the joints. Iron and aluminum react with the fermenting material and acids involved. Zinc-coated or galvanized metal containers are worse yet. We all know about the Romans and their lead vessels, but even a little bit of any kind of lead anywhere is poison and it ain't all obviously metal either. Lots of the old crocks and enamelware utensils or pots, even pewterware, used lead in the glaze or manufacturing process and some of the more recent imported stuff is as bad or worse than anything you pick up in a secondhand store. The newest U.S. made enamelware is safe and cheap, but it cracks easily and will rust through quickly. STAINLESS STEEL. Stick to stainless steel, or use plastic.

Plastic

When we talk about plastic, we are only talking about food grade plastic. Most new plastics are benign, nonpoisonous. Lots of people use new, well scrubbed plastic garbage cans as fermenting vessels or even double thickness garbage bags in cardboard boxes as fermenting containers. I don't, because some of the plastics can give a bad taste to things put in them. I've used the plastic buckets (food grade) that I got directly from caterers and knew what had been in them with great confidence and success, but many identical appearing containers have held things like paint, lubricants and solvents.

I live in Alaska where brining and smoking fish is part of the lifestyle. At one time while working for an oil company at Prudhoe Bay, I barely managed to stop a really shady surplus dealer from selling a bunch of plastic barrels to an Eskimo village. The villagers wanted the drums for salting fish, but they had originally held one of the most potent biocides known to man. The results could have been disastrous and it made a believer out of me in knowing exactly what kind of containers I use. Take heed, the food grade plastic containers are without doubt excellent vessels for fermenting, but make darned sure you know what was in them before using.

The clear plastic tubing sold under several brand names at most hardware stores is excellent for siphoning. It's transparent so it's easy to inspect for cleanliness and you can monitor the siphoning process without pulling the end out of the lower vessel continuously to check the flow. Buy the $3/8$" or $1/2$" inside diameter and about eight feet long for siphoning. Later, I'll show you how to make your own fermentation locks out of the smaller diameter stuff.

One precaution: the tubing will turn cloudy if left in contact with a bleach solution more *than the few minutes it takes to clean and rinse it.*

Glass

Of all materials we use in brewing and storing our beverages, glass is the one we most take for granted. It's nontoxic, strong, cheap, easy to clean and doesn't deteriorate, but there are some things you need to know about glass for both safety and success. Big glass containers are great for fermentation and storage. That's why some beer companies use glass-lined steel tanks with hundreds of barrel capacity. The biggest safe glass vessels you'll probably have access to are the big bottles called carboys that go on the office type water coolers. These hold 5-7 gallons and the small neck makes them easy to fit a fermentation lock to. On the negative side, they can be hard to clean and are heavy, clumsy and fragile when full. The best way to use these is to make a protective case for them with two plastic milk crates, which I'll cover later.

Stay away from the big glass containers such as aquariums and battery cases, mainly because of the danger of lead contamination from soldered seams or previous contents. When it comes to bottles, the three main considerations are color, strength and method of sealing. The brown or green colored bottles are best for beer and wine because they protect your product from the adverse affects of light. I admit I usually use a few clear bottles for each batch because it's easy and yes, fun to monitor the color and clarification of your creation. Regardless of

---

The Plains Indians relied on horses for transportation and christened the steam locomotive "The Iron Horse." In some quarters in Alaska, a snow machine is still called an "Iron Dog."

the color of bottle, always store your filled bottles in the dark, even if it's only by covering them with a black plastic trash bag.

The type of cap or cork a bottle is designed for, not only determines the practicality of reusing the bottle, but also is an indicator of the strength and safety of the bottle. Safety, the last factor, is no small matter, as bottles can explode with awesome force like a hand grenade. At best, you get a heck of a mess and wasted beverage. At worst, somebody can get hurt really bad. Glass soft drink and beer bottles that take a crimped on metal cap that must be removed with a bottle opener are strong and desirable. The crown caps and capping tools to re-use those bottles are readily available.

Next best, is the European style beer bottles with a wire clamp, porcelain top and rubber gasket usually called "flip-tops." These have a certain appeal initially because of their old-world, old-time appearance, but once the novelty wears off, you'll find they're a pain to work with, both for difficulty of cleaning and the extra work to sterilize and replace those little rubber gaskets. Gathering, cleaning, storing and sterilizing bottles is the real down side of making your own beer or wine. It's probably the main reason most beginners quit, but some of the shortcuts I'll show you will lessen the pain and increase the gain.

Champagne bottles are the strongest available and you should never miss a chance to beg, borrow or steal every one you can get. Granted, you may have to buy some new corks and a few tools to re-cork them, but they're still worth the effort and add class and safety to your wines. Better yet, many of them have a lip on the mouth that will accept the good old standby crown caps.

All of the bottles that take a twist-off cap should be shunned. These bottles can be re-

capped with a crown cap and I know people that have re-used them, but they are dan-

Crown Caps

gerous because they are made of a much thinner glass and can't take the pressure the older style bottles can. I say don't use them. How would you feel if you gave a friend a six-pack of your finest and a bottle exploded in his hand, cutting him badly? Not good. Another not so good feeling, mainly a dumb feeling, can come from bottle size or height. I once scrubbed and sterilized five cases of bottles in preparation of bottling up a batch of nectar. Just when I started to boogie, I made the awful discovery that about half the bottles I'd so laboriously cleaned were too short to be re-capped with the junk store special capper I had. In summary, be it bottles, fermenting vessels, cooking pots or other utensils; make sure they are strong, wholesome and safe.

Plastic beverage containers with screw caps can be used in lieu of glass bottles. Some, such as the two-liter Japanese beer containers work well. Others tend to leak under pressure. They can't stand heat, so must be sterilized with a bleach or campden tablet solution. Glass is better.

Sterility, Hell, Holy Water and the Hobo's Friend

Wholesome and safe also means sterile and here you have a leg up on your predecessors for a couple of thousand years. That means people had been making good, wholesome wine for a long time without benefit of modern science and technology for sterilization. How did the ancients make things sterile? The same way they made holy water. They boiled the hell out of it, an old poor joke, but hard science.

We still rely upon it as evidenced by our use of the autoclave to sterilize surgical instruments by boiling and steaming. But there

Glass Carboy With Stick-on Thermometer

are problems when it comes to delicate things like fruits juices, blossom wines, cider apples, plastic hoses an other things we use in our art that can be ruined by excessive heat. Until recently, sodium bisulfate was the ultimate weapon in sterilizing equipment. Dissolved in water, it makes a solution that sterilizes without boiling, inhibits growth of bacteria and was the magic sword for the homebrewer. Unfortunately, it's fallen out of favor and has become difficult to obtain, apparently because it caused health problems with people handling it in large volumes. Some, if not all the homebrewing supply companies have stopped carrying it. If you can find it, go ahead and use it. The problems as I recall, only involved persons that were handling large amounts of the stuff and inhaling the dust or powder in the process. The homebrewer will only be using it by pinches and spoonfuls.

But do not despair, you can always fall back on the "hobo's friend." During the Depression, a lot of destitute men roamed the country in search of work and a whole hobo culture sprang up. Part of that culture was the use of empty chlorine bleach jugs as canteens for drinking water. That tiny bit of bleach that remained in the jug was sufficient to chlorinate the creek or pond water

these poor guys often had to use. What worked then, works just as well today. Using unscented chlorine bleach, mix one tablespoon of bleach per gallon of cold water and rinse, soak or scrub all your equipment with this solution, then rinse again with cold water before it comes in contact with the materials to be fermented. If you're really picky, you may want to rinse the chlorine solution off with water that has been boiled, but unless you have reason to suspect your rinse water might be full of microorganisms, normal potable tap water should work fine. The only two drawbacks I've found with bleach is that if you're naturally sloppy like me, you should not wear your Sunday go to meetin' clothes because it will make bleach spots on them. Also, if you don't flush it out of the clear plastic tubing used for siphoning, it will make your hose cloudy. Other than that, the "hobo's friend" is also the brewer's friend.

So far we've covered sterilizing your equipment and water. The next and final part of the sterilization game, is treating the fruit juice vegetables and grain you'll be fermenting to make your product. Boiling or graduated heating of fermentables ranges from necessary to disastrous. With some products such as beer, grain spirits and root wines, heat properly applied is necessary to the conversion of starches to sugars and sterilization. In regard to tree fruits, blossoms and berries, heat is the enemy. Apply excessive heat to fruits and it works changes on the complex natural chemistry that will prevent Ma Nature from turning them into clear and delicious wine and cider. In the old days, it was a gamble that the natural yeast (good guys) on the skins of the fruit would start a ferment as soon as the juices were extracted. Hopefully they would be strong enough to overcome the other air-

Assorted Yeast Packets

borne yeast and vinegar bacteria (bad guys) that would turn it into vinegar or worse. So, when the grapes or other fruits were ripe, the young folk picked it and dumped it in a vat. At the same time, Uncle Guido and Aunt Rosa kicked off their shoes and boogied on the fruit. If the (good guys) were victorious, you got wine. If not, you made lots of salads with vinegar dressing. So long Uncle Guido. Arrivederci Aunt Rosa. Now we hava da campden tablet.

Campden tablets are potassium metabisulfate that is the magic bullet for wines and ciders. It suppresses wild yeast and bacteria while letting the carefully bred and tailored store-bought yeast run like racehorses through your precious fermentable. This stuff is to sterilizing about like strike-anywhere matches are to flint and steel and rubbing sticks together were to fire making. They are cheap (about 5¢ each) and are effective. One tablet treats about two gallons. They produce a gas, which evaporates out of your fermentation vessel quickly and leaves you with a wholesome, pure "good bugs" only wine or cider. Buy them from any homebrew supply store.

Universal Truths and Dark Secrets About Yeast and Fermenting

In the late 1800's, Louis Pasteur unraveled the mysteries of what functions yeast per-

formed in making beer and wine. He also discovered that most brewers and vintners were actually using a mixture of several strains of yeast. Other scientists then developed methods of isolating a single yeast cell and then nurturing a pure culture from that cell, thus giving us the pure strains of yeast we take for granted today.

Today, there are probably more specialized and identified strains of yeast available than there are varieties of tomato seeds. You don't need to know more than the general types and that they all work in the same basic manner. Nowadays, it's wonderful to be able to pick up a packet of yeast specially bred for the type of wine or beer you want to make for less than a buck. Having a known strain or type to start out with certainly eliminates a lot of failures and guesswork. In the good old days before science, they learned to save a sample of the fermenting liquid as a culture just like a sourdough starter. Like sourdough starters, these yeast cultures got handed down through the generations and the ones that gave the best results with local ingredients, gave rise to regional and proprietary or brand name products. You need never buy another pack of yeast again once you find the ones you like because I'll show you how to reproduce your own. But keep it quiet, or the yeast companies enforcers might come around to get the 80¢ you've gypped them out of. Bakers' yeast is the one we're all most familiar with and officially you can't make good beer or wine with it. Unofficially, many people make good, maybe not great, but nonetheless good beer and wine with it everyday. The main problem with bakers' yeast is it doesn't settle out well and if you shake the bottle a bit in pouring the beverage, it's cloudy and unappetizing. If you're so cheap you begrudge the yeast companies the initial 80¢, go ahead and use it. Just drink the stuff with the lights out and no one will ever know.

If you're a high roller like me, blow the 80¢ on a packet of real wine or beer yeast. You'll be glad you did, believe me. Wine yeasts come in all the flavors that wine does and generally have two main characteristics. They impart a winey flavor to your product and they are more alcohol resistant, so they'll live and work in a higher content medium. Wines are normally stronger than malted beverages (beers) but remember I mentioned barley wines earlier? Beer is usually 4-8% alcohol, wine around 14%. Fortified wines have alcohol; usually cheap brandy added and are the ones drunk in alleys in a paper sack. You'll learn that stronger is not necessarily better. I've made some real no walkin,' dumb talkin,' think a train hit you brews. I've had two of my neighbors taken home by their wives in wheel barrows and the Geneva Convention has threatened to ban some of my stuff along with dumdum bullets and sawtooth bayonets. Take it from me, please, it is best to make a reasonably strong product you and your friends can enjoy a glass or two of or on real special occasions, a couple forty mugs.

Beer yeast comes in many varieties also, but only two main types, bottom fermenting and top fermenting. There is not a whole heck of a lot of difference in the end product, they both make beer. The top fermenting stuff forms a cap of suds and expended yeast on the brew, which you skim off and call the product ale. The bottom fermenting stuff forms a layer of expended yeast on the bottom of the fermenting vessel. You siphon the brew off this stuff and call it lager.

Lager means stored or aged beer in German and the original product was stored and aged in cold, dark caves in the goode olde days. For the novice homebrewer, the main

consideration is the type of vessel you ferment in. If you use a large open vessel such as a crock or plastic bucket, you can skim the top fermenting yeast off. If you plan on using the carboys or water bottles, you'll have one heck of a time getting that cake of old yeast out of that jug.

Now we'll sing the Girl Scout song, "Sing Around the Campfire" because fermenting is just like a campfire. First you get the "blaze" or vigorous initial ferment, then you get the secondary or "'glowing embers" phase where everything is dying down. Yeast and solids are settling out and your wine or beer is starting to clarify. Then we get to the nearly out or "latent spark" stage that can be good if you want to start up just a little fire or ferment to carbonate your beer or bubbly in the bottle. It can also be bad in that if you put too much "sparks" and fuel or live yeast and unfermented sugars into a capped bottle, your product will geyser like a fire extinguisher when uncapped or worse yet, it will blow up. A few war stories are in order here to illustrate the divorce potential and real hazards of those "glowing sparks" or latent ferment.

First, let's revisit a good family friend, Stanley Zelinski and a Polish wedding reception, circa 1965. The dinner was over and in good Polish tradition, everybody was dancing the polka and getting smashed. Ziggy (Stanley) was an accomplished wine maker and insisted that as a special treat we all try his latest batch of red wine. Well, Ziggy wasn't too stable and the wine wasn't either. Now mind you, this was a Polish wedding. That means that his wife had repainted the dining room, the dog had been shampooed and manicured, new carpet was laid and her best china was set out. The priest was there and everybody was in their finest.

Well, Ziggy pulled the cork! The accordion player went down first. I think the cork caught him between the running lights. Ziggy lost his cool. If he'd just let the damned thing go, we would have had a big wine stain on the rug and in a month or so he might have been out of the doghouse. But no, Ziggy had to be a hero. He stuck his finger in the bottle which just increased the range to encompass not only newly painted walls and ceiling, but bride, bridesmaids, flower girls and little old ladies, most of them in pastel silk gowns. It was a stampede! Ziggy was up! Ziggy was down! Old ladies, flower girls and what was left of the band kept running over him! Then his wife went nuts. She did things to poor old Ziggy that would have made a karate instructor green with envy. I left early.

This brings us to homemade beer, hand grenades and wives. For years I worked on Alaska's North Slope oil field. I'd go north for a week or two, come home and make a batch of homebrew and then go back up above the Arctic Circle and get another paycheck. Once and only once, I bottled a batch of beer a bit early and stacked it in my wife's sewing room. Big mistake! It had to be a spontaneous detonation. One bottle set off another. Sixteen bottles of highly charged foamy sticky went off like hand grenades in a room filled with yarn, fabric and a sewing machine that never worked right afterward.

It was scary because it embedded glass fragments in the walls. Somebody could have been hurt badly. I caught hell for a long time. The message I'm trying to convey is the latent ferment in the bottle is necessary for sparkling wine, champagne or beer, but you really have to be careful when bottling, that you don't over carbonate. Remember the campfire. The little "sparks" of ferment are what makes bombs. Later, we'll get into priming, carbonation, use of the hydrometer and how to avoid a divorce.

Chapter Two

Wine for the King
Wine for the Masses

In This Chapter

➤ Wine – Basic Wine Making Steps and
   Recipes

➤ Feast or Famine Fermentation Method

➤ Cider (Apples) Perry (Pears) and
   Vegetable Wines

➤ Root Wines & Simple Malting
   (to augment wines)

➤ Alcohol Content of Wines

➤ Blossom Wines

➤ Other Wines (Birch Sap, Milk, Rose Hips
   and Jailhouse Wine)

Basic steps and a slew of recipes for everything from snob wines to rustic Alaska-style beverages for every pocketbook.

Wine – From Apple to Zucchini

Fine wine, fruit of the vine, plus tubers, taters, tree fruit, berries, honey, blossoms, grains and wines out of damned near anything except old sneakers.

Whether it's playing chess, dancing, safe cracking or brewing, the novice has to learn the basic steps before they can master the art. I'm going to talk you through making a simple batch of wine. At first, we won't deal with recipes. You'll get lots of them later. At this point, you need to know basic procedures and common pitfalls. A few tips and personal experiences will be thrown in for illustration.

Wine making is mostly all Mother Nature at work, so it's the simplest of all alcoholic beverages to make. We'll follow the bonfire sequence here. Blazing ferment, glowing coals with fermentation lock to clarify and burn down secondary fermentation and if desired, the final "sparks" or slow ferment in bottles to make bubbly, carbonated or sparkling wines or champagne.

The first secret to success in any type of fermentation is a good strong yeast culture that can hit the deck running like a bunch of tough gung-ho Marines. You will literally be conducting an invasion of a rich fermentable medium with your "good guy" yeast competing with any of a variety of "bad guys" that might be lurking on your fruit or come in via airborne invasion. To ensure that your side wins, a day before you start your batch, fill a sterilized bottle 2/3 full of boiled sugar water. Plug the bottle with a wad of cotton until it cools to room temperature, then add your yeast, re-plug it and let it work in a dark place until you're ready to add it to your fermenting vessel. This rejuvenates the yeast

that has been in a dormant state and lets it make millions more lively little "good guys" for your invasion.

Like any good general, you'll also establish a reserve. When you add the bottle of this strong, active yeast culture to your fermentables, reserve a few spoonfuls to start another bottle of culture for future batches, or to restart this batch in case the fermentation stops. Keep this culture in the refrigerator and nurture it about like a sourdough starter with sugar and water. Then in the primary fermentation or "bonfire stage," you'll put all your fermentables in a sterilized container such as a crock or food grade plastic bucket with at least ¼ more capacity than the volume of the brew, then add campden tablets and your vigorous yeast culture.

Remember Mork and Dork the cavemen now. Exclude all the airborne bugs with either a loose fitting lid or better yet, slip a plastic trash bag over the vessel to keep out the airborne bugs, exclude the air and retain the CO_2 produced by the yeast. You'll make this a simple pressure vessel by linking a bunch of rubber bands into a chain and stretching it around the bag and vessel like a shower cap. This will keep air and bugs out, but let the excess CO_2 produced by the yeast escape.

This initial ferment, especially with fruit pulp, will be vigorous to volcanic. Be patient, in a couple of days it will all calm down to simmering ferment, similar to an Alka-Seltzer tablet in a glass of water. This is the time to siphon and strain all the liquid off the lees or dregs of your primary fermenting vessel into a secondary fermenting vessel fitted with a fermentation lock. A fermentation lock in all the various styles and configurations is just a water barrier between the CO_2 gas trying to get out and the air trying to get in. This makes the yeast bugs get their oxygen from breaking down the sugars in your fermenting liquid and they produce CO_2 and alcohol. By making them exhale through a container of water, they get no air, thus continue to eat sugar to breathe and produce more CO_2 and alcohol.

When all the bubbling stops, you have reached the bottling point of your wine. Wine that all the sugars have fermented out of will be dry or tart wine. If you want to make sparkling wine or champagne, you'll add a small amount of sugar and let it ferment and naturally carbonate in the bottle. On the other hand, sweet wines remain sweet because your yeast has committed suicide so to speak. Alcohol is an antiseptic. It kills bugs. Your yeast eats sugar up until the fermenting medium reaches around 14% alcohol, then it dies because the antiseptic strength of the alcohol has become too strong for it. There may still be a lot of sugar in it; thus we get the strong, sweet desert wines. This fermentation process should take about two weeks. Remember, this is a natural process and will continue until all the sugar or fuel is consumed or the yeast dies.

The bubbles are the main indicators to watch. When the bubbles stop and your new wine becomes still, it's safe to bottle and will be a noncarbonated wine. Making bubbly or sparkling wines and champagne is a lot more tricky because it entails bottling the new wine with just enough unfermented sugar for the yeast to generate enough CO_2 to carbonate it. Care must be taken not to put enough in to explode the bottle or give you the runaway fire extinguisher effect when you open the bottle. I recommend that you start out with still or noncarbonated wines, then if you must live dangerously, risk a batch of bubbly. There are three ways to make bubbly.

First, there's the "wild guess" method, in that the mildly deranged wine maker waits until just a few bubbles are popping to the surface, then bottles his product and lays awake nights waiting for the explosions. He is seldom disappointed. The more rational amateur waits until all the bubbling stops, puts a tiny bit of sugar in each bottle, bottles his product and also lays awake nights waiting for the explosions. The real pro has mastered the use of the hydrometer and by checking the specific gravity of his brew before and during fermentation, is able to calculate confidently at what point to bottle. He sleeps peacefully until rudely awakened by the explosions. I'm not saying the home wine maker can't do it, just that it is very tricky to get just the right amount of carbonation in sparkling wines and champagne.

The Bottling Process

The bottling process is best kept simple at first. For the novice, use crown caps and strong re-capable beverage bottles. Sterilize your bottles and caps. Eyeball the depth of the lees or dregs in the bottom of your secondary fermentation container. You don't want to siphon the dregs into your bottles, just the good wholesome wine. With string, wire, fishing line or rubber bands, attach your clear plastic tubing to a thin wooden skewer or similar rod, so it will suspend the hose about an inch above the lees. With the big vessel up on a table and bottles arranged on the floor (a funnel sure helps) begin siphoning your new wine into the bottles. Fill each bottle to about three inches from the top, pinch or bind the end of the siphon hose to stop the flow and move on to the next bottle. When you're all finished filling, then cap the bottles with a crown cap or have someone help you by capping as you fill to reduce the risk of airborne contamination.

Note: I, contrary to other schools of thought, always leave about three inches of air space in all bottles as a safety factor. Air (oxygen) can degrade the quality of the beverage in the bottle. On the other hand, if the bottle blows up or the contents spew all over the kitchen, you'll be in deep gumba with the wife. I know! The air space in the bottle is a safety factor, sort of a pressure chamber for any additional CO_2 from latent fermentation.

Additional Note: Handle any new, untried batch with a towel wrapped around the bottle in case it blows up in your hands. Chill it in the refrigerator a couple of days and enjoy the fruits of your labor.

Secrets to Long-term Success

Two of the key factors in long-term success are records in the form of a diary or logbook to record what you've done for each batch and labels to identify and cross-reference the product. The best beer I've ever made or tasted is lost to me. It was lousy when bottled, but six months later, it was pure ambrosia and I didn't record the recipe. *If you don't keep records, everything you do will be guesswork.* If you do, you will become a pro, an artiste, improving with each batch.

Wines – Doin' It (basic wine making steps, recipes and instructions)

The rule of six p's applies from here on: prior planning and preparation prevents poor performance:

1. Pick the recipe you want to try first. Gather all the materials and equipment

you'll need then rehearse. Don't just go over the project in your mind, but assemble and inventory everything and walk through it on a dry run; all the way from start to bottling. Get your record book out and record each step you take from here on.

2. Start your yeast culture one to several days before you intend to start your batch. Plan on starting the batch on the weekend or when you have lots of time to do things right. Use a large bottle that will fit in your refrigerator to start your yeast culture in. Don't forget you're going to save some of this culture for future use. Boil four parts water to one part sugar by volume, let cool and add a couple spoonfuls of an acid fruit juice (frozen concentrate is okay) yeast and if you have it, yeast nutrient. Put this mixture in the sterilized bottle and plug loosely with cotton or better yet, fit with a penny bubbler. (See chapter four.) Only fill the bottle ¾ full because this will be a vigorous, "blazing bon fire" ferment. Keep it in a warm 60° F to 70° F location to get your yeast working vigorously. You'll use all but a few spoonfuls to start your batch, then refill the bottle with the sugar solution and save the culture in the refrigerator.

3. Sterilize all your primary fermentation vessels and equipment. Use a diluted chlorine bleach solution to sterilize everything that will come in contact with your fermenting wine (must.) Then rinse everything thoroughly because even a tiny drop of bleach will kill off the good yeast in the must.

4. Per the various recipes that follow, place the fermentable mixture and yeast in the primary fermenter. Yeast nutrients, campden tablets and other additives are optional, desirable perhaps, but not necessary. Cover or seal the mixture (now called must) to exclude air but let excess CO_2 escape. Now Mother Nature takes over.

   Note: We'll cover making wine out of everything from sugar water and fruit, to carrots, honey, potatoes, flowers and grain.

   When you're dealing with a lot of pulp, grain, unorthodox or nontraditional wines, it will require other steps that will be covered in the recipes.

5. Secondary fermentation is important in wine making for quality or taste. As the fermentation slows down, a lot of gunk or sludge accumulates on the bottom of the primary fermenter. This gunk or lees is dead yeast and vegetable matter that will impart bad tastes to your product. In ten days to two weeks, the fermentation should have slowed to the "glowing embers" stage. Now is the time to gently siphon the fermenting wine into the secondary fermenter, leaving all the gunk behind.

   Note: Siphoning works by a combination of atmospheric pressure and gravity flow. Your primary fermenter should be higher (on the table) than the secondary fermenter (on the floor.) You put your hose in the upper vessel, suck on the hose like a long straw, keeping the end as low as you can and when you get a mouthful of fluid, stick the end of the hose in the lower container.

The siphon effect will suck the fluid from the higher container to the lower. You don't want to transfer the gunk on the bottom, so you'll attach a skewer, wire or similar standoff to the intake end of your hose, so it doesn't stick into the gunk, but only transfers the good wine. Siphoning of beer and wine won't hurt you, but with gasoline and other fluids, there's real danger of inhaling or ingesting these substances. If you are not familiar with the process, practice siphoning water from one container to the other.

6. Racking means transferring your wine from one container to the other, leaving the gunk behind. With some batches it seems that you'll do this until hell freezes over and still have a murky product. Fining, or clarifying applies to both wine and beer and means adding something to the fermented fluid that will cause the gunk to settle out and make it clear. Various additives have been used over the ages to include bull's blood, beechwood chips, egg whites, ground up eggshells, gelatin and proprietary mixtures. We'll stick with gelatin. Liken this to a delicate gelatin parachute that you'll pour onto your cloudy brew. As the parachute floats slowly to the bottom of your vessel, it will entrap most of the murky stuff and carry it to the bottom. Just pick up a package of unflavored gelatin that is sold in any grocery store. One ounce is enough to clarify ten gallons of wine or beer at the end of the secondary fermentation stage. Dissolve it in hot water and when it cools to about body temperature, sprinkle it gently into your secondary fermenter, reseal the container and wait for the liquid to clarify.

7. The cap of choice is the plain old crown cap. It's simple, cheap and easy to apply. A screw cap container has one theoretical advantage because if you age your wine upside down, the yeast accumulates in the neck of the bottle and by cracking the seal, the yeast can be bled out, leaving only clear wine in the bottle. I've tried this the same as I've tried making fire by rubbing sticks together and I can only say, gotta match buddy? I have had no joy with either technique. Assuming you've chosen the crown cap route, a look at cappers is in order. All cappers press and crimp a crown cap over the lip of the bottle. The simplest and cheapest is the hammer type that only costs a couple bucks and does everything a capper is supposed to do. They're a forming device similar to a cookie cutter. You put the new cap on the mouth of the bottle, tap the capper down over it and it squeezes the cap on. They're slow, but cheap. All other cappers use some sort of lever system to squeeze the cap on. The main differences are speed and cost. *(Refer to Chapter Four, Making Your Own Capper.)* Don't forget your caps have to be sterilized too. Do this by dumping them in a sterilizing solution, using chlorine bleach or a campden tablet. Just fish them out and shake them off as you bottle. If using bleach, it's best to transfer them to a container of plain water first to preclude getting any of the solution in the bottle and stopping the final fermentation for carbonation.

8. Bottling homemade wine means either corks or caps. Corks are traditional and have snob appeal. Corks are also expensive (about 25¢ each) and require a couple of extra tools to compress them and drive them into the neck of the bottle. They can be self-defeating because your homemade wines will have a yeast deposit in the bottle. By the time you're finished worrying the cork out and tilt the bottle a couple of times to fill a few glasses, the yeast will be stirred up and the wine you worked so hard to clarify and age will look like bilge water. Better to use metal caps and invest in a classy decanter and some nice glasses. Chill the wine well, remove the metal cap gently and carefully pour it from a low class bottle to your aristocratic decanter.

9. Filling your bottles with wine or beer can influence the quality of your product because oxidation can downgrade the quality and "bad bugs" are lurking everywhere. You want to bottle the fruits of your labor as quickly as you can and with as little exposure to air as possible. The siphon hose and funnel method works, but it's sloppy, risky and a lot of work. You can pick up a little wand-like bottle filling device for less than five bucks. They fit into the siphon hose and have a little spring operated valve on the tip so you can flit from bottle to bottle, filling each bottle precisely and quickly. You don't need most of the gadgets on the market and you can make many of them yourself. The bottle filler isn't a necessity either, but in my opinion, it's a very worthwhile piece of equipment and well worth the nominal investment. There are also little plastic clamps that slip on your hose and enable you to control the flow. They're a little bit messy,

but the flow rate is so much faster that you can bottle 10 gallons in about an hour.

Common Inexpensive Hand Capper

10. With all your wine or beer finally bottled remember that how you store or age it can be just as important to its quality as the methods and material used in brewing it. Wines can be drunk as soon as they're clarified, but may continue to mellow and improve for as long as forty years. We know we want to keep it dark and cool as in a wine cellar, but most of us don't have that luxury. We also want to make effective use of limited storage space to avoid moving the bottles unnecessarily and thereby stirring up the yeast and last, but not least, safeguard the bottles. Pick up some empty wine boxes from your local liquor store with the cardboard dividers in them. By stacking them, you'll be able to store the maximum amount of wine in the minimum space; all nice and dark with the individual bottles nicely cushioned. It's the next best thing to digging a wine cellar.

Recipes

The ten steps we just covered are universal steps that will apply to all of the following wine recipes. We'll proceed from the most Spartan, simplest wines imaginable, up to the conventional wines from fresh fruit, then cover some less orthodox ones, such as root and vegetable wines. Finally, we'll look at some of the more exotic wines like honey wines blossom wines and milk wines.

Rather than repeat the same instructions over and over again, we'll only go into detail where it's germane to success or safety. These recipes will be middle of the road recipes, which will be forgiving to give you good results, but let you vary the main fermentable ingredients by plus or minus one third and still make good wine. Less fermentables should yield a dry wine, more fermentables, a sweet wine. You'll also begin to note the similarities in types of recipes that will give you a far better feel for the art and developing your own wines, rather than slavishly buying and following someone else's recipe. Last, but important, this is not a chemistry or science textbook. I advocate not using a bunch of chemical additives or sophisticated paraphernalia. Campden tablets and yeast nutrients are okay, they help your yeast get off to a good start and that's good. As for the rest of it, just buy your kids a chemistry set with the money and keep your wines natural.

Some Simple Wines

Sugar Wine

3   Lb.   Sugar

In California, a jury was indicted for drinking the evidence in a moonshining case.

1	Gal.	Boiling water
1	Pinch	Yeast

Note: 2-½ Lb. sugar per gallon yields maximum strength semi-dry wine, less equals dry wine, more equals sweet wine. This is the simplest wine possible. It has no body, bouquet, color or other qualities that any connoisseur is going to pay big bucks for. It's very similar to the basic thin mash recipe we'll look at for distilling that yields a bland alcohol and water product. It is very valuable however, as a basic learning wine. If you're a novice, this is the one you should try first, because it will give you a wealth of experience at practically no cost. I suggest you rig two one-gallon milk jugs with the penny bubbler fermentation lock *(See Chapter Four.)* Start ½ gallon of this mixture in each jug using a pinch of bakers' yeast in one and wine yeast in the other. Plan on bottling this in a couple of small screw cap plastic beverage bottles. This exercise will give you practical experience with fermentation locks, stages of fermentation, advantages of using special yeast, clarification, priming and aging. You can even drink this stuff, but don't expect to impress your true love with it during a romantic candlelight dinner.

Mint Wine

3	Cups	Fresh mint leaves
1	Gal.	Boiling water
3	Lb.	Sugar
1	Pkt.	Wine yeast

Pour hot sugar water over mint leaves, let cool, add yeast and cover or fit with fermentation lock. After the "blazing bonfire" stage of the fermentation dies down (about two weeks) strain into a secondary fermenter.

Bottle after fermentation is complete.

Simple Dandelion Wine

½	Gal.	Dandelion petals
1	Gal.	Boiling water
3	Lb.	Sugar
1	Pkt.	Wine yeast
1	Ea.	Campden tablet (optional)

Be sure the dandelions you pick have not been treated with any herbicides or exposed to lead-bearing exhaust fumes such as those picked along a freeway. Remove all the green parts and bugs that might be hitching a ride. In a large container, pour the boiling water over the dandelions, cover and let steep for about 5 days. Strain the fluid into a pot. Warm, don't boil and dissolve the sugar. Add yeast to cooled fluid (now called must) and place in your fermenting vessel. Campden tablets are optional. Since you're really not boiling the flowers, there's a chance of getting wild yeast or mold started when the flowers are steeping. If you see mold or detect a vinegar smell, skim the fluid off and blast the invaders with a campden tablet. Fermentation, racking and bottling should take about two weeks. This wine is a traditional favorite that will improve with age and is supposed to have tonic properties.

Unorthodox and Stunningly Simple Wine Making

Here we throw away the book of conventional wine making and all the specialized expensive gadgets. The first step is to clean and fit two one-gallon milk jugs with the Penny Bubbler (See Chapter Four) fermentation locks made out of flexible straws, balloons and modeling clay. Next, you'll need a gallon of 100% fruit juice, 3-½ pounds of sugar and a wine yeast starter. You can use grape, apple, cranberry, orange or other juices, that come in sealed jugs, so they're sterile and ready to make wine out of.

Wine yeast requires 2-½ lb. Sugar per gallon to make 14% alcohol (maximum strength) wine. Any more than 2-½ lb. per gallon will make a sweet wine. Recognizing that the fruit juice you purchase will have a lot of natural sugar in it, if you want to make a dry wine out of it, reduce the amount of sugar you'll add to this recipe to 2-½ pounds.

Universal Recipe Made With Store-Bought 100% Fruit Juice

1	Gal.	Fruit juice
3-½	Lb.	Sugar (for semi-dry wine)
1	Gal.	Water
1	Pkt.	Wine yeast

Boil water and 3-½ pounds of sugar, then pour into primary fermenter, cover and let cool. Add juice and yeast to cooled sugar mixture and cover. Transfer to milk jugs for secondary fermentation vessel. You shouldn't need a campden tablet for this recipe because both the juice and the sugar mixture are sterile. If you keep a yeast culture going in your refrigerator, you can make wine indefinitely without ever buying anything else but juice and sugar. This method also lends itself to blending some interesting wines.

If you want to live dangerously and try your hand at making sparkling wines or champagne, there's a field expedient way to do it, not foolproof mind you, but simple using the dry wine (2-½ lb. sugar) recipe. When your wine has fermented down to the bottling or "latent spark" stage, taste it. If it is completely dry, meaning no taste of sweet-

ness at all, you have fermented all the sugar out and have no more than 14% alcohol. If you add 1 oz. of sugar dissolved in one pint of boiled water uniformly mixed into your two gallons of wine, you should have a safe amount of sugar to carbonate the wine in the bottle. If your wine is at the 14% or 28 proof level, the sugar won't ferment out and you'll have a slightly sweet wine. This recipe gives you two gallons or ten bottles (fifths) of nice wine for the price of a gallon of juice and 3-½ pounds of sugar. If you use a bit of imagination, you can get pretty exotic too by making spiced wines or adding some blended fruit to the sugar wine recipes or juices, e.g., kiwi/brown sugar, cinnamon/apple, etc. (Makes 2 gallons)

Wine From the Vine, Fruit Trees and Berries

When we think of wine, we think of grape wine because most wine has traditionally been made of grapes and for good reason. A grape is a little wine making kit to itself, having all the necessary ingredients packaged by Mother Nature. A good variety of wine grapes will have natural yeast on its skin for fermentation and the right combination of water, sugar, acid and tannin to make wine with just a little luck. Our ancestors got by for centuries just by stomping on their grapes in vats. We help things along now via sterilization, selectively bred strains of yeast and excluding air.

The two main classes of grape wine are white and red. White wine is made from white grapes or the juice only of red grapes. Leaving the red skins in the fermenting mixture makes red wine. Let's proceed with a time proven grape wine recipe, but being Americans just brimming over with Yankee ingenuity, we'll plan on making a "second wine" to extract all the goodness from the pulp and also double our production

These steps apply to all subsequent wine recipes:

Basic Grape Wine Recipe (1 Gallon)

14	Lb.	Plus or minus 2 Lb. fresh grapes
1	Ea.	Campden tablet
1	Pkt.	Wine yeast

Using ripe grapes, remove stems and all old rotten or moldy grapes. Mash the grapes in the primary fermenter. Go ahead, get violent, work off your savage impulses, then add one campden tablet per gallon and plenty of good active yeast culture or bought wine yeast. You'll get a volcanic pulp cap that you should push down daily to aid extraction. After about a week, fermentation should have slowed sufficiently for you to siphon the fluids in the secondary fermenter. Squeeze the fluid out of the pulp with a jelly bag and add it to the secondary fermenter and fit a fermentation lock.

Note: At this point you should be all prepared to start your second wine from the grape pulp. Having ladled the pulp into your jelly or extraction bag, you should rinse the yeast deposits out of the primary fermenter. Save some of this residue in a sterile bottle to use as a yeast culture. Start your second wine as follows:

Second Wine Recipe (grape)

1	Gal.	Boiling water
2-½	Lb.	Sugar
10	Oz.	Grape juice concentrate
		Leftover grape pulp

Dissolve sugar in boiling water and cool. Add the rest of the ingredients. If you've taken reasonable care to keep things contamination free, you shouldn't need campden tablets or yeast. The pulp will be teeming with yeast to start an overwhelmingly strong fermentation. If you have doubts, mash up a campden tablet in warm water, add to the must and after an hour or so, give the mixture a shot of the yeast residue you saved. Process this second wine just like the first batch, but be sure to record and label everything you've done.

The Shape of the Grape

The next best thing to a fresh grape is a preserved grape and they come in several forms. The earliest sun-dried grape or raisin has an important role in home wine making, both as the prime ingredient and as a supplement to other fruits and vegetables. In bottles, cartons and cans, we now have juices, frozen concentrates and even canned concentrates made especially for building your own wines. As a general guide to interchangeability of various forms of grapes, you can use the following formula:

14 lb. fresh grapes = 1 gal. 100% juice = 32

Forbidden to legally make beer, some of our national breweries survived Prohibition by making malted milk. Others made soft drinks, which were in great demand as mixers for illegal alcohol. Sometimes there is more power than light.

oz. frozen concentrate =10 oz. canned concentrate = 6 Lb. raisins = 1 gal. Wine

A Fresh Grape-Raisin Wine

9	Lb.	Grapes (red or white)
2	Lb.	Raisins
1	Lb.	Sugar
1	Gal.	Water
1	Pkt.	Wine yeast

Easy Grape Wine

3	Lb.	Grapes (red or white)
3	Lb.	Sugar
1	Gal.	Water
1	Pkt.	Wine yeast

This is a quick and easy one because you only have to process three pounds of fresh fruit. With these recipes and the conversion formula, you should be able to make wine out of any form of grape you can get your hands on, so let's move on to fruits and berries.

Fruits and Berries

Generally all edible fruits and berries are made into wine in much the same way as grapes. Stone fruits are those with big pits such as plums, prunes, peaches and cherries and should have their seeds or pit removed. The pits, pips, seeds or whatever you want to call them, have excessive tannic acid and other properties that can impart a bad taste to the wine. With the cane fruits such as raspberries, blackberries and elderberries, don't get heavy handed in mashing them because if you crack the seeds, you'll be extracting the undesirable stuff.

Also, be darned sure of what you're mak-

ing wine out of because not all berries are edible. For example, pokeweed has a poisonous root, a delectably edible sprout and big juicy berries that will make you sick. In Alaska, we have beautiful baneberries that look very much like a cranberry, but they're toxic enough to make you sick, if not dead. A friend and I once amused ourselves in Korea by chasing and catching a bunch of little garter snakes. A few days later, we learned our "garter snakes" were actually the dreaded Mamusi Viper, about as deadly as coral snakes! The point I'm trying to make is you should know your local flora and fauna before you start foraging.

We can't hope to cover all the fruits and berries that you can make wine out of, so we'll cover a cross-section with forgiving recipes that you can adapt to what you have available. One additional point we can't go into detail here is preservation of fruits and berries. When you have an abundant harvest, you may be just too busy or too tired to play little old wine maker or berry picker. Be smart, employ the local kids to harvest for you and freeze or dehydrate the local bounty for later. With that, let's make some berry wine.

Cane Fruits – Blackberry, Raspberry, Salmonberry and all their Seedy Cousins such as Mulberries and Dewberries and More

Salmonberry Wine

5	Lb.	Berries (your choice)
2-½	Lb.	Sugar
1-½	Gal.	Water
1	Ea.	Campden tablet
1	Pkt.	Wine yeast

Again, use different types of yeast to make different varieties of wine with each batch. This recipe is similar to those for grapes, but the juice bag is more important to corral all those little seeds and stuff. This should yield a dry or medium dry wine. If you want a sweet wine, taste it and as the ferment slows down, add ½ lb. of sugar dissolved in as little water as possible. If the must tastes tart or dry when the fermentation nearly stops again, repeat the process. By adding sugar in increments and tasting, you are creeping up to the point where your yeast dies off and your wine becomes sweet, rather than dry.

You should at this time, begin to appreciate the hydrometer (in proper perspective.) The hydrometer is not a magic wand with which you can make infallible predictions. A hydrometer can bring you very close to the bull's eye on your first shot, rather than working entirely by guess or feel. If we liken it to hunting, the most expensive rifle money can buy will not guarantee that you bag a moose. Indeed, our Alaskan Eskimos, probably the best hunters in the world, provide for their families with some really motley firearms. It's not their tools but their understanding of nature that makes them so proficient. This is why I stressed earlier that you are better off without a hydrometer until you become attuned to nature. Otherwise, you'd just go crashing through the woods with your shiny new hydrometer cradled in your arm, scaring all the yeast away.

Caution: Do not use native Alaskan wild elderberries! Sambucus Racemosa – Pubens. They are inedible, toxic and cause nausea, diarrhea or worse. Use only domesticated "Lower-48" elderberries.

Elderberry Wine

3	Lb.	Elderberries
2-½	Lb.	Sugar
1	Gal.	Boiled water
1	Pkt.	Wine yeast

Make sure you remove all stems, as they can impart a bitter taste. Also drain, but don't mash the fermented pulp, or you'll squeeze a lot of nasty stuff out of the seeds.

Blueberry Wine

2	Lb.	Blueberries
2-¼	Lb.	Sugar
1	Gal.	Boiled water
1	Pkt.	Wine yeast

Gooseberry Wine

4	Lb.	Gooseberries
2-¼	Lb.	Sugar
1	Gal.	Boiled water
1	Pkt.	Wine yeast

Sweet Strawberry Wine

3-½	Lb.	Strawberries
2	Lb.	Sugar
1	Gal.	Boiled water
1	Pkt.	Wine yeast

Dry Strawberry Wine

5	Lb.	Strawberries
2	Ea.	Lemons
1	Lb.	Sugar
1	Gal.	Boiled water
1	Pkt.	Wine yeast

Add only the juice of the lemons to the must.

Fruit Wines

Mango Wine

6	Lb.	Mangoes
3	Lb.	Sugar
2	Ea.	Oranges
1	Ea.	Lemon
1	Gal.	Boiling water

Add juice and squeezed halves of citrus fruit to must. Boil mangoes until tender, mash and add to must, minus skins.

Orange Wine

1	Doz.	Oranges
1-½	Gal.	Water
4	Lb.	Sugar
1	Pkt.	Wine yeast
1	Ea.	Campden tablet

Grate orange part of peel and use in must. Discard white portion of peel. Chop and mash fruit pulp, discarding seeds. Pour boiling water over oranges, cover and let soak 2-4 days. Use a campden tablet after the water cools for safety, then strain out fluid. Warm, do not boil fluid and dissolve the sugar in it. Return to primary fermenter, add yeast when cool and proceed with basic wine making steps, see page 20.

Apple Wine

8	Lb.	Apples
4	Lb.	Sugar
1	Gal.	Boiling water
1	Pkt.	Wine yeast

Remove seeds from apples, then chop, mash or blend with peel. You may mix several varieties of apples to add character to your wine. Apple wine differs from apple cider, primarily in the amount of sugar used (alcohol produced.) Cider is just fermented apple juice and is comparable to beer in strength (around 6% alcohol.) Apple wine is much stronger (up to 14% alcohol.) Proceed with basic wine making steps on page 20.

Stone Fruit Wines

The traditional stone fruits, those with big bitter stones or seeds are peach, plum, and apricot. We now have a number of crossbred fruits such as nectarines, plumcots and of course, the humble dried prune. The seed from all such fruits should be removed or they'll impart a bitter taste to your wine. It's best to pit cherries, but if you're using small cherries or are a tad bit lazy, mash them in a bag and soak the pulp for 2-4 days. Just don't get so heavy handed you crack the seeds and use a campden tablet to keep the natural yeast on the skins from starting to prematurely ferment.

Peach, Plum, Prune and Apricot Wine

3	Lb.	Fruit (your choice)
2	Lb.	Sugar
1	Gal	Boiling water
1	Pkt.	Wine yeast
1	Ea.	Campden tablet

There is no need to peel the fruit, just halve it, pit, chop and mash in a bag. Pour only three quarts of boiled water over fruit and let soak for 2-4 days. Use a campden tablet to play it safe. Dissolve sugar in one quart boiling water. Let cool, then add sugar solution and yeast.

Cherry Wine

4	Lb.	Cherries (sweet
		or
3	Lb.	Cherries (sour)
		or
2	Lb.	Choke cherries
3	Lb.	Sugar
1	Gal.	Water
1	Pkt.	Wine yeast
1	Ea.	Campden tablet

Add 3 quarts of water to mashed fruit and one campden tablet. Soak 1 or 2 days, mashing pulp daily. Dissolve sugar in one quart boiling water; add to must when cooled along with yeast. Proceed with basic wine making steps on page 20.

Caution: The Alaskan baneberry can be deadly! It looks like a low bush cranberry, but grows on a much smaller plant and usually has only a single berry per plant.

The following recipe can be used with a variety of edible berries that may be unique to your region or be known by a colloquial name.

Alaskan Currant or Cranberry Wine

2	Lb.	Currants or cranberries
3	Lb.	Sugar
1	Gal.	Water
1	Pkt.	Wine yeast
1	Ea.	Campden tablet

Crush and soak berries in 3 quarts of water for two days. Boil sugar in one quart of water. When cool, add to must with yeast. Proceed with basic wine making steps on page 20.

Currant Wine

1	Gal.	Currants
1	Lb.	Raisins
1	Lb.	Sugar
1	Gal.	Water
1	Pkt.	Wine yeast

Proceed with basic wine making steps on page 20.

Apple Sherry

6	Lb.	Fresh apples
2	Lb.	Dried apricots
1	Lb.	Raisins
1		Biscuit Shredded wheat
2	Lb.	Sugar
1	Gal.	Water

Chop and mash apples. Boil apricots in 1 gallon of water. Pour hot fluid over apples and add yeast when cool. Ferment for two weeks, then rack to another container. Add shredded wheat, sugar and chopped raisins, and then ferment for approximately three more weeks. When fermentation stops, rack and bottle. Proceed with basic wine making steps on page 20.

"Beary" Berries

In most regions wild berry pickers have to worry about snakes. Happily, we have no snakes in Alaska, but we do have lots of berry loving black bears and grizzly bears. Both are dangerous, especially mothers with cubs. A number of Alaskans are killed or mauled by bears every year, so it pays to be prudent.

Making noise so you don't surprise a bear

is a good idea and many people wear bells for this reason. Pepper spray may discourage an aggressive bear, but then again it may not. Packing a suitable firearm with which you are proficient is a good idea. Most people packing hip howitzers couldn't hit a bull in the butt with a bass fiddle and this may lead to a false sense of security. At least be careful or the score may be Bear 1, Visitors 0.

An old timer once told me how he almost stepped on a sleeping grizzly in a blueberry patch. He was wearing chest waders because it was a rainy day and the panicked bear defecated explosively with purple blueberry scat at point blank range when he surprised her. As he put it, "She crapped all over the outside of my waders and I crapped all over the inside.

Feast and Famine Fermentation Method

Yeast bugs tend to work like little kids who want to eat their dessert and push the carrots to the side. This method isn't high tech. It's a natural way to promote a stronger fermentation and aid clarification without a bunch of chemical additives. If your must is too rich with sugar, it may actually retard fermentation and clarification. If you withhold about ½ the sugar and ¼ of the water and remove the pulp from the must after a few days, up to a week you will push your yeast to the brink of starvation. You'll keep your yeast bugs hungry enough to clean their plate, consuming more of the haze producing, less fermentable food in the must than might otherwise be the case. After you've finished starving your yeast bugs, reward them for cleaning their plate by transferring them to the secondary fermenter and feed them the remaining sugar and water.

Synopsis

We've covered making wine out of a good cross-section of vine, tree fruits and berries, but before we move on to cider making, a recapitulation is in order. You've probably noticed there is a good bit of similarity between the recipes. The ones I've presented are aimed at a medium dry wine and can be adjusted for dryness and sweetness by adding or subtracting up to one third more or less sugar. The amount of natural sugar in your fruits will be influenced by species, weather, ripeness and so on, which means the properties of your wines will vary also. You can get more predictable results by mastering the use of the hydrometer, but even great vintners of the world have the same problem and often blend different wines to produce a more uniform product from season to season.

With that disclaimer, let's summarize that with the exception of pure grape wine (14 lb. per gallon) and apples (about 8 lb. per gallon, plus water and sugar) you can use a basic recipe for just about any other fruit. The basic formula is 3-½ lb. fruit, plus 2-½ lb. sugar, plus 1 gal. Water, plus yeast, equals wine, plus or minus $1/3$ sugar = dry or sweet wine.

Cider (Apples) and Perry (Pears)

These are two of the most traditional beverages and simplest to make. In days of old, the juice was squeezed from apples and pears and allowed to ferment from the natural yeast on the skins. That's it! Of course, the product varied greatly according to sugar content of the fruit and it could range from 9% knock your socks off, to about 5% beer-like strength. Unless it's fermented carefully and bottled quickly, chances are good that vinegar bacteria will get to it and ruin the batch. My Uncle Bill kept a wooden barrel of apple cider in the basement of his house and when the coast was clear, Cousin Bob and I would flit down the stairs, check the status of the keg right from the spigot, purely in the interests of science, of course. It was great! Then, after our families hadn't visited for several weeks, Bob, being absent but I, knowing the way, made another scientific expedition to the basement. Lordy! You can't appreciate how strong natural vinegar can be until you gulp it greedily in the dark! The wages of sin, I guess. I learned my lesson. Since then, I always let the other guy drink first.

Cider and perry are good and easy to make. Sterilize the juice with campden tablets and use a wine or champagne yeast to take some of the guesswork out of it. Add sugar and you're upping the alcohol into the wine league. But there's a trick to it. If you want to make dry semisweet, or really sweet cider, rather than let the runaway fermentation continue, taste and even sweeten the must until it's just the way you like it, then zap it with three or four campden tablets per gallon, crushed and dissolved in a little boiled water. In this concentration, you should overpower even your "good guy" yeast. There is no set recipe for cider or perry, but you should only use good quality fruit, nothing rotten and if at all possible, blend a variety of fruits, some sweet and some tart to add character or balance to the must.

Lacking a cider press or press bag, the field expedient way of extracting the juice is as follows. Sort, wash and chop your fruit, then put it in a large sturdy vessel and mash it with a homemade wooden masher. You can extract the juice first by squeezing the pulp through a cloth bag or ferment pulp and all, then extract it later. Remember that you can get a second batch out of this pulp, using the second wine steps we covered earlier, cider and wine out of the same apples. That's hard to beat. Since cider and perry are so similar, we'll just say cider in the following recipes and talk about apples. If you want perry, just substitute pears. With either (so you'll have some aiming points) a starting specific gravity of 1.040 will yield about 5% alcohol, 1.060 about 8%, the sweeter the cider, the less alcohol, the dryer or harder the cider, the more alcohol. Commercial sweet cider is basically slightly fermented apple juice in which the fermentation has been arrested at a very early stage via pasteurization or chemical additives and contains no appreciable alcohol.

Cider vinegar as we buy it here in the US, has been greatly diluted to 5% acidity. The natural full-strength vinegar can be dangerously strong. I was really lucky because my Uncle Bill's keg wasn't yet full strength. I speak from experience because I seriously burned my mouth and lips by merely tasting a tiny sip of full-strength vinegar I bought from a Russian street vendor. If you, through mischance or intent, end up with natural vinegar, treat it with extreme respect and

---

Judge John Knox ruled that prescriptions for whiskey were not limited under Prohibition, making physicians an important source for those seeking alcoholic beverages. An average of 10 million prescriptions were issued each year during Prohibition.

keep it out of the reach of children.

Old Time Cider From Apples

Ideally, several varieties of apples, some tart, some sweet, should be used to yield a more balanced cider. If you only have one variety, that's okay too. Sort your apples and wash them in a sterilizing solution using campden tablets or a bleach solution. This is important not only to kill all the wild yeast, but also because people have become seriously ill from cider made with unwashed apples. The culprit has been the e-coli bacteria from the droppings of deer, livestock and other critters that had been dining on fallen apples.

Using only good unspoiled fruit, wash it, then chop or mince it finely. In a large sturdy vessel, mix your fruit with one campden tablet crushed and dissolved in a little warm water per each three pounds of fruit, then mash the fruit to a pulp with a clean wooden masher or pestle. You can hack or cobble a serviceable masher out of a tree limb or scrap lumber, but remember to use untreated lumber and to sterilize it before each use.

Juice extraction in the old days, was done by ladling the pulp into strong cloth bags and pressing it in a cider press. Assuming you don't have a cider press handy, you have two options. You can add yeast and/or water and sugar directly to the pulp and plan on straining it through a cloth when you rack it. The second and better option is to extract all the good stuff from the pulp by straining and wringing it through a cloth bag first. The second method is better even though you'll discard some fermentable material. Working with juice alone, you'll be able to take a hydrometer reading and ad-just specific gravity by adding sugar, honey, water, etc. and it will be a heck of a lot easier to get a clear product when you rack.

Your finished product can be sweet, hard (dry and higher alcohol) and still un-carbonated or sparkling (carbonated like beer or champagne.) For sweeter cider, let it ferment until it suits your taste, then blast it with three campden tablets per gallon, dissolved in a little warmed cider. This *should* stop the fermentation, but it's best to keep it in loosely capped jugs in the refrigerator. If capped tightly, the chances are good that you'll get a latent ferment with exploding bottles. Letting the cider ferment completely, a flat, dry alcoholic (hard) cider that can be safely bottled will result. This flat, dry cider can be bottled as is, or it you desire carbonated champagne-like cider. Prime it exactly as you would beer, adding either ¼ cup of sugar per gallon in bulk or adding ¼ teaspoon per 12 ounce bottle.

There is an alternative method to achieve a sweet, but not excessively alcoholic cider by using beer, rather that wine yeast. The theory is that beer yeast dies off at 9-10% alcohol therefore, any residual sugars will not ferment out, yielding a sweet cider at a beer, albeit a strong beer strength. As I've said before, the brew spirits sometimes pee all over the pillars of science, but if you're full of the spirit of adventure, give it a try.

Old Time Cider Recipe

		Juice from 3 lb. apples
		Water to make up 1 gal.
1	Ea.	Campden tablet
1	Pkt.	Wine yeast
1	Gal.	Water (additional to above gal.)
2		
2	Lb.	Sugar

Combine ingredients in primary fermentation vessel. Do not heat the apple juice. Heating apple or any other fruit juice may result in a murky beverage, due to the presence of natural pectin in the juice. Rack to secondary fermenter when vigorous ferment dies down and fit with a fermentation lock. You may add dissolved gelatin as a fining agent after a day or two.

When the fermentation dies down to the point that your fermentation lock is no longer bubbling, you may bottle your hard cider. It will clarify in the bottle in about a week. This will be the same stuff our colonial forefathers drank as a common beverage and also jacked into applejack.

Note: Basic wine making steps on page 20 covered earlier, apply to making cider and perry.

Hard Cider

5	Gal.	Sweet cider
3	Lb.	Brown sugar
3	Lb.	Honey
2	Pkt.	Champagne yeast

Strain 3 gallons of cider into a 5-gal. carboy. Strain 2 gal. into a pot and heat enough to allow sugar and honey to thoroughly dissolve. Pour into a carboy and finish filling to the neck. Pitch yeast and seal with airlock/fermentation lock. When fermentation stops, bottle and prime with sugar to add carbonation.

Great Cider

1	Gal.	Pasteurized apple juice
12	Oz.	100% apple juice concentrate

1	Cup	White sugar
1	Pkt.	Champagne yeast
1	Gal.	Water

Proceed with basic wine making steps on page 20.

Vegetable Wines

Any normally edible part of a vegetable can be used in wine making. Not all parts of all vegetables are edible though. Rhubarb leaves have a high enough concentration of oxalic acid to be deadly poisonous. I've read that a number of people actually died in Britain during WWII from cooking and eating rhubarb leaves. If it grows above the ground in the garden, I call it a vegetable. If it grows below the ground, I call it a root and we'll cover them in the next section.

Proceed with basic wine making steps on page 20 and any special instructions given in the specific recipe.

Tomato Wine (red or green)

3-½	Lb.	Tomatoes
2-½	Lb.	Sugar
1	Gal.	Boiling water
1	Pkt.	Wine yeast

Proceed with basic wine making steps on page 20.

Corn Wine

2-½	Lb.	Sweet corn kernels
1-¾	Lb.	Sugar
1	Gal.	Boiling water
1	Pkt.	Wine yeast

Sweet corn is full of sugar that begins to turn

to starch as soon as it's picked. You'll use less sugar in this one, but make it in a different sequence where speed is important.

Step 1

First start a sugar wine, page 23 in your primary fermenter. This will be just boiled water, sugar and yeast. When you have a vigorous ferment working, your blender plugged in and everything in place, you'll proceed to the next step.

Step 2

Proceed to the garden. Rip ten ears of succulent sweet corn off the stalks and dash madly back into the kitchen, shucking the corn as you go.

Step 3

Cut the quivering kernels from the cob and feed them into the blender. It's brutal, I know, just like cooking lobsters or missionaries, best fresh.

Step 4

Feed the flashing, thrashing pool of yeast the gory mixture, then fit with a fermentation lock or cover with a plastic sheet.

Watermelon Wine (any type of melon is fine)

3-½	Lb.	Melon (your choice)
2	Lb.	Sugar
1	Gal.	Boiling water
1	Pkt.	Wine yeast

For watermelon, use pure juice, plus yeast. May use blender, but remove seeds. For most hard melons, use melon flesh, plus water and sugar, then learn the tune, "Old Dogs, Children and Watermelon Wine." Proceed with basic wine making steps on page 20.

Rhubarb Wine

5	Lb.	Rhubarb stalks (no leaves, they're poisonous)
4-½	Lb.	Sugar
2	Gal.	Water
1	Pkt.	Wine yeast
1	Ea.	Campden tablet

Chop, crush and soak rhubarb in 1 gallon of water with 1 campden tablet for about a week. Boil remainder of water and sugar. Add to must and then remove the rhubarb pulp (best to use a cloth bag to retain the rhubarb.) When this cools down, pitch your yeast and proceed with basic wine making steps on page 20.

Note: Rhubarb is to wine making what baling wire is to repair. It just seems to work no matter how you use it. I have a friend who violates just about every rule in the wine making books, of which he has read nary a one. I've cringed when he described his methods of cooking, blending, fermenting, etc., yet his wife's garden club has made an annual event of tasting his rhubarb wine. Chuck the rule book, if the ladies like it, make a big old batch.

Root Wines

Root wines are surprising. They sound horrible, but turn out far better that you'd expect. Most of the roots, potatoes, parsnips, carrots, beets, etc. are plumb full of fermentables that by now you know are starches and/or sugar. Potatoes make vodka, the drink of choice of the old "Evil Empire" and a large part of the world's sugar comes not from sugar cane, but from sugar beets.

Root wines pose a greater challenge to the homebrewer because the starches and sugars they contain are less digestible to yeast than the fruit and malt sugars we usually work with. There are a couple of tricks to the game that will enhance your wines if you know them. First, let's use the lowly potato as our example. If for no other reason than we know the Russians turn them into alcohol routinely and anything they can do, we can do better, right? The starch and sugar levels in a potato can change dramatically in storage due to light, temperature and other factors. They start to sprout just like barley seeds when we malt them. So if you use older potatoes or other root vegetables that are wrinkled and past their eating prime, you'll not only be saving food that might otherwise be wasted, but you'll craftily be using them at their prime fermenting stage.

Second, you'll be dealing with a high starch content. When you rinse freshly cut potatoes, the cloudiness in the water is due to starch. It's important to use the feast and famine fermentation technique on page 31. You want to breed a hoard of healthy little yeast bugs initially and then make them positively ravenous so they eat all the starch haze in the must.

Third, unlike the noble grape and lesser fruits, root vegetables are lacking in acids, tannin and enzymes that aid starch conversion and fermentation. You can add chemicals of course, or you can call 1-800-Mother-Nature. I prefer to augment with natural ingredients to help things along. White raisins, white grape concentrate or citrus fruits will provide desirable acids. Just a bit of tea will provide tannin and you can buy malted grain if you like, but if you'll pick up a few

pounds of wheat berries or non-treated barley, you can begin learning the art of making your own malt and improve your root wines at the same time.

Basic Potato Wine

2	Lb.	Potatoes
2-½	Lb.	Sugar
1	Lb.	Raisins
4	Ea.	Oranges and/or lemons chopped
1	Tsp.	Tea
1	Pkt.	Wine yeast
1	Gal.	Water

Note: While the potato is the staff of life for much of the world, the vines, sprouts, eyes and green flesh that results when the tuber grows exposed to sunlight, not only tastes bad, they are poisonous! Old wrinkled spuds are best for wine, but remove the nasty stuff. You don't have to peel the potato or other roots. A good scrubbing is enough, but be sure to skim off any scum that rises to the surface when you boil them. I suggest you peel them and avoid the scum. Peel and pare, then grate the old potatoes. Bring to a boil in one gallon of water and then pour potato water only over sugar and raisins. When cool, add juice from citrus fruit, tea and yeast. Proceed with basic wine making steps on page 20.

Naturally Improved Potato Wine (by starving the yeast and using malt enzymes to convert starches)

4	Lb.	Potatoes
2-½	Lb.	White raisins
		or
½	Pint	White grape concentrate
4	Ea.	Oranges and/or lemons

		chopped
1	Lb.	Cracked malted grain
1	Tsp.	Tea
1	Pkt.	Wine yeast
1	Gal.	Water

Clean and grate the spuds. Boil in 1 gal. of water and strain fluid into another bigger pot. This pot should be stainless steel or enamel. Simmer the potato water with the cracked-malted grain for 20 minutes, then strain the hot fluid on to all remaining ingredients except the yeast in the primary fermenter. When cool, add yeast, preferably a big batch of vigorous culture. Remember the feast and famine trick on page 31. If you hold back a part of the sugar and water, you'll force the yeast to clarify your wine. It will take three or four days to malt your wheat or barley. Remember that you must not use chemically treated seed grain, only untreated grain intended for human or animal consumption.

Simple Malting to Augment Wine

Soak grain (barley, wheat or corn) for 1-3 days in plain water, then drain. Change water daily. Spread the grain on a tray or plastic sheet no more than one inch deep and keep it moist, turning daily until the sprouts are one half the length of the seed. Dry the sprouted seed in an oven at the lowest temperature until the sprouts and roots will crumble and the seed is dry enough to crack. Rub the roots and sprouts off the malted grain with your hands. To winnow the grain or separate it from the chaff or debris, just spread a plastic sheet outdoors and pour the grain on it from about waist height, using the breeze or an electric fan to blow the chaff away.

Crack the malted grain with a rolling pin. This completes the malting process. The malted grain will taste distinctly sweet.

Parsnip Wine

4	Lb.	Parsnips
3	Lb.	Sugar
1	Lb.	Raisins
4	Ea.	Oranges or lemons chopped or sliced
1	Gal.	Water
1	Pkt.	Wine yeast

Process as basic potato wine or augment as with Naturally Improved Potato Wine on the previous page.

Carrot Wine (Carrot Whiskey)

4	Lb.	Carrots
3	Lb.	Sugar
1	Lb.	Raisins
4	Ea.	Oranges or lemons chopped or sliced
1	Gal.	Water
1	Pkt.	Wine yeast

Process as basic potato wine or augment as with Naturally Improved Potato Wine on the previous page. See Applejack page 46. If you jack this stuff even though it's not distilled, it's called carrot whiskey.

Beet Wine (red beets)

4	Lb.	Red beets
2	Lb.	Sugar
1	Lb.	Raisins
4	Ea.	Oranges or lemons chopped or sliced
1	Gal.	Water

1	Pkt.	Wine yeast

Scrape the skin of the beet to remove the rough outer layer, then slice, chop or grate. Soak the beet flesh in one gallon of water for an hour or two, then bring to a boil and simmer for ten minutes. Pour hot fluid only over all other ingredients except yeast. When cool, add yeast and proceed with basic wine making steps on page 20.

Sugar Beet Wine

4	Lb.	Sugar beets
1	Lb.	Sugar
4	Ea.	Oranges or lemons chopped or sliced
1	Gal.	Water
1	Pkt.	Wine yeast

Sugar beets, as their name implies, are rich in natural sugar, therefore much less cane sugar is required. Grate the beets and soak in a gallon of water for two or three hours, then bring to a boil and simmer for twenty minutes. Pour hot strained fluid only, not the grated beets, over all other ingredients, except yeast. When cool, add yeast and proceed with basic wine making steps on page 20.

Mangel Wine

5	Lb.	Mangels
3-½	Lb.	Sugar
4	Ea.	Oranges or lemons chopped or sliced
1	Gal.	Water
1	Pkt.	Wine yeast

Scrape mangels clean, then chop, slice or grate. Bring to a boil in one gallon of water,

then simmer twenty minutes. Skim the fluid, then pour over other ingredients. When cool, add yeast and proceed with basic wine making steps on page 20.

Sweet Potato Wine

4	Lb.	Sweet potatoes (not yams)
2-½	Lb.	Sugar
4	Ea.	Oranges or lemons chopped or sliced
1	Gal.	Water
1	Pkt.	Wine yeast

Peel and grate the sweet potatoes. In one gallon of water, bring to a boil and simmer twenty minutes. Pour hot sweet potato fluid over other ingredients, except yeast. When cool, add yeast and proceed with basic wine making steps on page 20.

Grain Wines

The following wine recipes are not for malt beverages. Remember in the earlier part of this book when we compared the various types of brew? We said that some very strong brews using malted barley, hops and wine yeast were called barley wines. Since they use hops and malts and are brewed like beer, we'll cover them with the beer making recipes. The ones in this section are more wine-like than beer-like. With that precise scientific explanation, let's move on to the recipe.

Wheat Wine

3	Lb.	Wheat (wheat berries)
3	Lb.	Sugar
4	Ea.	Oranges or lemons chopped or sliced
1	Gal.	Water

| ¼ | Oz. | Unflavored gelatin |
| 1 | Pkt. | Wine yeast |

Plan on using a jelly bag or homemade muslin bag to contain the grain in the primary fermenter, otherwise you'll be chasing wheat seeds around throughout the whole process and straining your wine through your teeth when you drink it. Put the wheat in another pot of boiling water about 10 minutes with the heat off, using a bag to contain the wheat, raisins and fruit pulp. As in the previous recipe, add the ingredients to the primary fermenter except the yeast. Once the must has cooled, add the yeast and proceed with basic wine making steps on page 20.

Rice Wine

2-½	Lb.	Rice (brown preferably)
1	Lb.	Raisins
2-½	Lb.	Sugar
1	Gal.	Water
1	Pkt.	Wine yeast

You will have far better results if you use brown or unpolished rice for reasons that I'll explain at the end of this section on grain wines. Don't confuse brown rice with wild rice that is a Native American plant that grows wild in the Everglades.

Boil the sugar in 1 gal. water. Chop the raisins and scald them with the rice in another pot of boiling water. To make things easier, use a sterilized cloth bag and marbles to contain and submerge the grain, raisins and squeezed out citrus fruit. Add this bag to the 1 gallon of boiled sugar in your primary fermenter.

The scalding sterilizes the rice and raisins and helps convert the rice starch to sugar.

When everything cools down, add the yeast and proceed with basic wine making steps on page 20.

Barley Wine (Pearled Barley)

2-½	Lb.	Pearled Barley
1	Lb.	Raisins
2-½	Lb.	Sugar
1	Gal.	Water
1	Pkt.	Wine yeast

Proceed exactly as with the rice wine recipe preceding this recipe

Cheating for Better Grain Wines

To make better natural grain wines we need to take a look at two enzymes, diastase contained in wheat and barley seeds and koji contained in rice. These two substances convert starch to sugar.

The wheat seed has an easily removable husk so those little light brown wheat seeds have an outer covering of bran that contains the diastase around a white center of starch. A wheat berry will sprout and grow just as you buy it from a health food store. Rice and barley have far tougher husks, so to make them easier to cook and eat, we grind off the husk and bran, giving us nice white polished rice and pearled barley.

These won't grow because the essential stuff of life has been ground off them to make them more attractive, including the bran containing koji and diastase respectively. All we have left is the starch. Brown rice simply hasn't been ground down as much as polished rice, hence it has some koji in the remaining bran to help convert starch to sugar. You can buy extracts or artificial versions of either enzyme to make your grain wines or you can wing it and go the natural way. If you substitute one third pale cracked barley malt for the grain in any of these recipes, you will take a giant step toward converting the starch in your must and getting better, clearer wines.

Blossom Wines

Blossom, or flower wines are just nice. You can't buy them. Gathering the flowers is good for the soul and some of them at least, are supposed to be very good for you and they are very easy to make. Blossoms you can use to make wines are: *dandelion, rose, hawthorn, carnation, lime, woodruff, honeysuckle, primrose, cowslip, nasturtian, violets, and Alaskan fireweed.*

Now before you go hog wild, let me tell you a story. Back when I was a Boy Scout, I and the other country boys of Troop 293 (Beaver Troop) camped among a bunch of city boys. The city boys were impressed with our rustic frontiersman ways, to include using a handful of leaves for toilet paper. They did too, but they used poison oak. The message is clear. Know your flora and fauna, or it will bite you, well…you know where. *Not all blossoms are safe to use for wine.*

Simplest Flower Wine –Dandelion

2-4	Qt.	Blossom (petals only, no leaves, stalks, etc.)
2-½	Lb.	Sugar
1	Gal.	Water
1	Pkt.	Wine yeast
1	Ea.	Campden tablet

The more blossoms you use, the more of the essence you'll have in your wine. If you scald the blossoms with boiling water as some ad-

vocate, you'll have a sterile must of boiled flowers. Just as with aromatic hops, if you boil them, you'll destroy or lose the most delicate oils and scents. You might as well make boiled cabbage wine and forget about the flowers. Boil the water and dissolve the sugar in it. When the solution is well cooled, mix the blossoms and one well-pulverized campden tablet in the primary fermenter. Add no yeast at this point. Instead, seal the primary fermenter to exclude all air (a plastic sheet with rubber bands around it will do) and let the essence of the blossoms soak into the sugar solution for 4 or 5 days. When it feels right, add a good strong yeast culture and proceed with basic wine making steps on page 20 of primary and secondary fermentation, racking, fining and bottling.

More Full-Bodied Blossom Wines

The previous recipe is fine, but for more body and less blossom picking per gallon, we'll use a few more ingredients. It's not too hard to come up with a gallon of dandelion or clover blossoms, but unless you raid the local botanical gardens or park, it may be hard to come up with all the flowers you need for some of the others.

Alaskan Fireweed Blossom Wine

1	Pint	Blossoms (petals only, no leaves, stalks, etc.) Other blossoms listed can be used.
2-½	Lb.	Sugar
½	Lb.	White raisins chopped or
4	Oz.	White grape concentrate
1	Gal.	Water
1	Pkt.	Wine yeast

1	Ea.	Campden tablet

Boil the water and sugar. Turn off the heat and add the chopped raisins, if used. Put this mixture in the primary fermenter and when it's cool, add the blossoms, chopped citrus fruit and one pulverized campden tablet. Cover securely and let soak for 3-4 days. (You may have chosen to use white grape concentrate instead of raisins.) Add the yeast and proceed with basic wine making steps on page 20.

Honey Wines (Mead)

In the days of old when knights were bold and sugar wasn't invented, they made their wine from honey, indeed. There wasn't much else that fermented. Before sugar, honey was about the only sweetener available and it was fermented in combination with a variety of ingredients encompassing fruits, blossoms, spices and herbs of every description. Depending on what went into it, it was called mead, sack, metheglin, melomel and pyment in English. Every other culture or language has its own terms as well for what we simply call honey wine.

Honey by itself has enough character to make a good wine and in fact, can be substituted in part or whole for sugar in any wine or beer recipe. Some of the old recipes, particularly those calling for pungent spices, amount to gilding the lily, for honey is after all, the pure essence or nectar of flowers and at the most, we want to complement, not overpower its character.

Before you look at the first recipe, you should know two important things about honey wines. Between 2-½ and 3-½ lb. of honey per gallon should yield a dry to medium dry wine, depending on the type of yeast and efficiency of your ferment. While rich in sugar, honey lacks the acids and tannin important to fermentation and clarification, so augmentation with citrus and tea is recommended to increase the speed and efficiency of the brewing process.

Simplest Honey Wine

2-½	Lb.	Honey
1	Gal.	Water
1	Pkt.	Wine yeast

Dissolve the honey in one gallon of boiling water and pour into the primary fermenter. When cooled to room temperature, add the yeast and proceed with the basic wine making steps of primary and secondary fermentation, racking fining and bottling on page 20.

Flower and Honey Wine (sweet)

4	Lb.	Honey
4	Pints	Blossoms (fireweed blossoms, but other blossoms as listed will work as well.)
1	Gal.	Water
4	Ea.	Oranges and/or lemons
4	Oz.	Tea (discard leaves)
1	Pkt.	Wine yeast

Boil honey in one gallon of water until dissolved. Put the blossoms, chopped and squeezed citrus fruit and tea in your primary fermenter and pour the hot fluid over all. When cool, add yeast and proceed with Proceed with basic wine making steps on page 20.

Honey wines are notoriously slow in fermenting and clarifying so plan on leaving this in the secondary fermenter fitted with a fermentation lock for weeks or even months. Try to keep it at around 70º F and shielded from sunlight. On a long-term project like this, it's a good idea to fit some additional glass jugs with fermentation locks, so you don't tie up key equipment such as big expensive carboys that you could be using for other quicker projects.

Honey and Fruit Wine (medium dry)

3	Lb.	Fruit
2-½	Lb.	Honey
1	Lb.	Raisins
1	Gal.	Water
1	Pkt.	Wine yeast
1	Ea.	Campden tablet

We'll vary our methods here to increase your expertise. We'll rely on the raisins and fruit to provide the desirable acids and tannin and soak the ingredients without yeast to extract the good stuff from the fruit. First pit, chop or mash the types of fruit you've chosen and place it and the chopped raisins in the primary fermenter. Dissolve the honey in one gallon of boiling water and pour it over the fruit. Stir in one pulverized campden tablet, cover and let soak one or two days. Add yeast and proceed with basic wine making steps on page 20.

Honey and Fruit Juice Wine (Sweet)

4-½	Lb.	Honey
½	Gal.	Water
½	Gal.	Fruit juice
1	Lb.	Raisins
1	Pkt.	Wine yeast

Boil and dissolve the honey in ½ gallon of water. Pour the hot fluid over the chopped raisins in the primary fermenter. Add ½ gallon of fresh squeezed commercial 100% or reconstituted from concentrate juice to the primary fermenter. When the mixture, or must cools, add yeast and proceed with basic wine making steps on page 20.

Tip: Plain old off-the-shelf cranberry and red currant juices are excellent choices for this type of wine. They lend tartness and a nice rose color without an overpowering flavor.

Other Wines

You can make wines out of, or flavored with lots of other things like coffee, tea, onions, parsley, jams and jellies. I've no doubt you can make wine out of leftover mashed potatoes or hot peppers, but who the heck wants to? Don't get too carried away because some flowers can have harmful effects and I purposely have steered away from herbs for similar reasons. Some other wines that don't fall into any other category are:

Rose Hips Wine

3	Lb.	Rose hips
1	Lb.	Raisins
2-½	Lb.	Sugar
1	Gal.	Water
1	Pkt.	Wine yeast

Break the rose hips up with your fingers so you don't break open the bitter seeds and put them with the chopped raisins. Dissolve the sugar in boiling water and pour it over the rose hips and raisins. When cool, add yeast and Proceed with basic wine making steps on page 20.

Rose hips are interesting because they contain far more vitamin C than citrus fruits.

They're an important source of vitamin C for Alaskan Eskimos, but they have one drawback. Rose hips are covered with microscopic spines which if you eat too many, can cause a miserable anal irritation. The Eskimo term for this ailment is really apt. It translates as "itchy butt disease." Enjoy your wine.

Pea Pod Wine

4	Lb.	Pea pods
2-½	Lb.	Sugar
1	Gal.	Water
2	Ea.	Oranges or lemons chopped or sliced
1	Ea.	Campden tablet
1	Pkt.	Wine yeast

Wash thoroughly and bruise the pod. Chop and squeeze the citrus fruit. Soak or marinate the pods and citrus fruit in a gallon of water with one campden tablet overnight. Strain and boil the water with the sugar, then pour it back over the pods and fruit. Add yeast when cooled to around 55° F and proceed with basic wine making steps on page 20.

The new Sugar Snap peas with the thick edible pods are ideal for this wine, but more traditional garden peas are fine too. Use fresh green pods and eat the peas as you shell them. Older peas tend to be starchy and bitter, so use only the freshest pods.

Kvass (Bread Wine)

Kvass is a mildly alcoholic drink, popular in Russia and Central European countries. It falls somewhere between a wine and a beer. It's fermented from grain (old bread) but uses no malted grain, hence, we'll cover it under

other wines, rather than malt beverages (beers.)

Kvass in my Russian dictionary means simply fermented beverage. My mother however, who is always right, says it also means sour. I think Mum's right again because kvass is a tart, thirst-quenching beverage traditionally sold by street vendors, much like we sell lemonade. It's kind of like buttermilk in that you either like it or hate it, no middle ground. It's a thrifty peasant's drink that recycles crusts and ends of bread into a wholesome, nutritious drink.

Kvass

1	Loaf	Dry rye bread (about 2 lb.)
3	Cups	Sugar
¼	Cup	White raisins chopped (optional)
1	Pkt.	Ale yeast
2	Gal.	Water

Crumble bread into a cloth bag and place it in a primary fermenter. Boil sugar and water. Pour over the bread, then add raisins. When cool, pitch yeast. After 24 hours, remove bread bag. After two more days, transfer your kvass to loosely capped containers to refrigerate and settle it. It is ready to drink.

If you want to bottle and cap a few bottles of kvass, treat it like beer by transferring it to a secondary fermenter with a fermentation lock. When fermentation is at the "dying ember" stage, prime each bottle as with beer. Bottle and cap.

You can either add chopped raisins when you add the yeast or wait until bottling time and add 1 to 3 raisins to each bottle, or if you feel adventurous, add a couple of berries such as strawberries or raspberries for a unique thirst quencher.

Birch Sap Wine (one of my favorites)

I once demonstrated to two little neighbor boys that birch sap was sweet by dipping my finger in and tasting some fluid flowing from a fresh cut birch stump. They loved the demo, but declined the taste test because they informed me Ralph, their big yellow dog had just peed all over the stump.

Birch sap is sweet. You can make syrup out of it, similar to maple syrup, but you need to boil down eighty gallons of birch sap for a gallon of birch syrup, compared to a mere forty gallons for the maple syrup. What I'm leading up to is that it takes an enormous amount of sap to get a significant amount of sugar and you can kill a lot of trees in the process. In fact, Russian peasants devastated vast tracts of their forests by rapaciously tapping birches to make wine. I'm not advocating anything of the sort, but you can judiciously harvest a few gallons of sap, enough to give you delicately flavored wine without harming the tree. This is best done in the springtime when the sap is flowing profusely. Merely clip one or two low branches at a point where they are about as thick as your thumb. Use pruning shears or a saw to make a nice clean cut that will heal quickly. If you're squeamish about this, you shouldn't be because moose routinely dine on birch limbs this size and it doesn't seem to hurt either the moose or the birches.

Attach a plastic milk jug to the ends of the limbs and harvest the sap daily. It's a good idea to fit a mesh fabric such as cheesecloth or a piece of nylon hosiery to keep out bugs and debris. As you accumulate the sap, store it in the refrigerator and treat it with campden tablets because it has definitely been exposed to airborne yeast and vinegar bacteria.

Birch Sap Wine

1	Gal.	Birch sap
2	Lb.	Cane sugar
2	Ea.	Oranges or lemons chopped or sliced
1	Pkt.	Wine yeast
1	Ea.	Campden tablet

Warm, but do not boil the sap to dissolve the sugar in it. Pour this fluid over the squeezed halves and juice of the citrus fruit in the fermenter. Add yeast when cooled to 55° F and proceed with basic wine making steps on page 20.

Note: This recipe is based on the sap of the white or silver birch prevalent in northern regions. The red or sweet birch, native to more temperate regions is the one used in old-fashioned soft drink extracts and I think it should have more wine making potential, but I've never used it in brewing. We used to chew the bark of the twigs like candy when we were lads, but we also used to curl up inside truck tires and roll down hillsides for amusement (before TV.) I

Prohibition did not criminalize the possession, purchase or use of liquor, only its manufacture, transport, or sale. Medicinal use was legal, which made for millions of prescriptions being written for "medicinal purposes."

won't recommend either practice here, but will attest that the fair sport of tire riding will do more to your equilibrium than any bottle of wine ever brewed.

Special Note: Birch sap contains a natural antiseptic called xytol. Depending on the whims of Mother Nature, sap from the same tree may ferment vigorously one year and very slowly another. Just be patient.

Applejack

Applejack is about as American as apple pie and easier to make. Heck, it's hard not to make applejack. As a bunch of my ne're do well friends once found out the hard way. In its simplest form, applejack is simple apple cider (about 6% alcohol maximum) which by purpose or accident has been frozen which separates the water from the alcohol.

We were teenagers at the time, had gotten access to a barrel of hard cider, filled a bunch of bottles and hidden them in a shed. When the weekend rolled around, they retrieved their cider and proceeded to the weekly record hop. Unfortunately, the stuff had frozen or jacked in the unheated shed, so when they started sampling the contents, it was about like drinking straight whiskey. Nobody got killed or hurt, but a few got to meet their proud parents at the local police station that night. Just like adding antifreeze to your car radiator as the concentration or strength of alcohol increases in your jack, ever-lower temperatures are required to freeze more water out of it.

I have an impressive, but worthless table that professes to show precisely what strength or proof of alcohol will be produced at progressively lower temperatures. To illustrate, once while living in a dry camp (no booze) a

couple of hundred miles north of the Arctic Circle, a couple of gallons of cooking sherry appeared in our food shipment. This stuff was 28 proof, or 14% alcohol and it was unanimously and enthusiastically decided to jack the stuff into something more potable. With the temperature hovering at a balmy -60° F, this appeared to be no problem. It proved impossible however, the salt content and suspended solids were such that it froze to a briny slush that was undrinkable. The teaching point here is that jacking, unlike distilling, removes only the water. The alcohol, salts, solids and fusel oils are concentrated. The end product of jacking will be murky, so racking and clarification before freezing is important and settling and filtration of the end product will vastly improve its quality.

Applejack Recipe

8	Lb.	Apples (mixed varieties if possible)
		or
1	Gal	Apple juice
4	Lb.	Sugar, cane or brown
1	Gal.	Water
1	Pkt.	Champagne yeast

Wash apples and remove seeds and mash fruit, no need to peel. Dissolve sugar in 1 gal. boiling water and pour over apple pulp in primary fermenter or mix with juice. When cool, add champagne yeast. Champagne yeast yields the highest percentage of alcohol, but any wine yeast will work. When the vigorous fermentation dies down, rack the must to a secondary fermenter fitted with a fermentation lock.

You may want to rack this several times to

eliminate all the lees you can. Remember, jacking concentrates not only the alcohol, but also the solid material so the clearer you make the wine ,t he clearer and more appetizing your applejack will be. Also, as with cooking sherry, the more salts or other stuff in the fluid, the harder it will be to freeze. You may use gelatin as a clarifying agent if you wish. Just dissolve an ounce of unflavored gelatin per five gallons of wine and mix it in when you rack to another vessel. Wait until fermentation stops.

Now the jacking begins. At the coldest temperature you can manage, you want to freeze your brew. Remember, it doesn't have to be apples. You can jack anything that ferments in wide mouthed plastic container. They have to be wide mouthed so you can extract the ice and flexible so the expansion of the ice doesn't break them. At first you'll be able to remove and discard the ice in cakes or sheets. As the fluid becomes more concentrated, you begin skimming out slush. Remember that jacking is a fractional crystallization process. This slush doesn't freeze solid because it contains some alcohol. If you drain this slush through a fine mesh (nylon hose) at a slightly warmer temperature, the alcohol will drain out of the ice crystals. This is a tedious process requiring a separate collection vessel and the gain is small, so you might not want to bother with it. When you reach the point that ice crystals will no longer form in your jack, you've reached the maximum strength, unless you can make things colder, you're jacked out.

Milk Wine (ALA Alaskan Engel Wine and Father Emmett Engel, the wine making priest)

Most cultures, including the Chinese, had some form of milk wine, i.e., kefir in the Balkans and koumiss (fermented mare's milk) in the Mideast. The challenge in making milk wine is in the conversion of the milk sugar (lactose) into a fermentable sugar like the fructose (fruit sugar) and malt sugar (maltose) we commonly use in wines and beers. We'll go into the recipes, but not the chemistry. Just accept the fact that we'll be dabbling in enzyme action to convert sugars just like we do in mashing grains to convert starch into sugar.

Now, the way the ancients got their enzymes and bacteria was pretty gross. They used calves intestines to kick off their brews. Rejoice! Far more appetizing modern ingredients are readily available. There are dairy digestive supplements for lactose intolerant people, those who have problems digesting dairy products. You just add a few drops per quart of milk and it breaks the lactose down into fermentable sugars. Freeze-dried yogurt starter separates the milk solids from the liquid whey and wine or bakers' yeast does the rest. No calf guts. Aren't you glad?

Alaska has had many colorful characters, but few to match Father Emmett Engel, the bootlegging priest. Until his death in 1986, the fiery Father defiantly operated an illegal milk winery at Big Lake, Alaska and pursued his dream of establishing his Casa De San Josè Monastery. Father Engel was quite a man, a retired priest from the Diocese of Whitehorse, Yukon Territory. He professed to follow a divine directive to produce his milk wine and not only ignored and defied secular laws which interfered with his mission, but on occasion was known to tap a trooper on his snot locker.

He derived his inspiration from a visit by the Holy Mother when he was 28 years old. He was told through another priest that he must make wine from whey. He quotes her as saying, "I have chosen this young man to make wine from milk whey which contains no fusel oil. I choose it as my very own wine." Father Engel explained that the devil reigns unchallenged in alcohol's containing fusel oils, but without them, favorable effects would follow. Interestingly enough, the BATF tests of Father Engel's product showed fusel oil present, but only in minute amounts. The good Father did not accept the lab's conclusion.

Now Father Engel was not our run of the mill, sneak in the night bootlegger. Heavens no! He had an enormous yellow sign on the Parks Highway proclaiming his milk winery. He put out flyers saying:

Engel wine! Super fine! No hangover! Yes, moon over! Wine four years old! Much different!

He gave the authorities fits and ulcers. One enforcement official said that in 32 years of service, Engel was "the most difficult person I have ever dealt with." When the cops and the revenuers raided him for everything from licenses, to taxes and sanitation, the good Father apparently lacked tact, using phrases like, "Where are your cloven hooves? Where is your tail?" and calling the troopers Roman soldiers. When verbal communications failed, Father Engel apparently reverted to nonverbal communications and on at least one occasion, "kicked ass" on a raiding party of revenuers and troopers sent to confiscate four barrels of his product. The case was settled in local court with a fine of $500 over the protest of certain officials who apparently felt that they had received well over $500 worth of nonverbal communication. The good Father continued making and selling wine.

It was good wine. I bought it and drank it. Maybe the dogs did pee on the dried milk sacks occasionally. I don't doubt that some mouse turds and an occasional mouse found its way into the vats. Adds body. Father Engel was not one to get along with authority, a bit eccentric and by his own admission, "I'm unusual, even to myself." But he made a good and wholesome milk wine with motives that warrant thought, not ridicule. It was a honey colored wine, hard to define or describe. It had a full body, not like any fruit wine, not quite like a sake either. It had a wholesome, this is different and it's good for me taste. When Father Engel left, he seems to have taken his recipe with him. He probably has set up on some cloud and is knocking a few halos loose on celestial revenuers. The recipes which follow are not divinely inspired, but when you try them, do so in memory of Father Emmett Engel, the wine making priest.

Milk is sweet, full of lactose, milk sugar. Lactose does not ferment like the other sugars we work with. In fact, it is added to some stouts as a sweetener because it will not ferment into alcohol. Some people get sick from milk because their systems are not attuned to breaking down lactose. Various ancient cultures however, have been making wine out of milk for centuries, all using pretty disgusting stuff, ranging from saliva to calf guts to start the breakdown of lactose via enzymes to glucose and other fermentable sugars. Puke not fair maiden, barf not young feller, there are ways to make milk wine without hurling. Modern science and the local pharmacy come to our rescue here. Recognizing the problems many people experience with dairy products, there is now a variety of products that break down lactose into more digestible and fermentable sugars; some you swallow, some you add to the milk.

Koumiss - Kefir Recipe #1 (the easy way)

2	Qt.	Commercial lactose-free milk
2	Lb.	Cane sugar, corn syrup or honey
2	Qt.	Water
1	Pkt.	Champagne yeast for high alcohol, but even bakers' yeast works all right

The lactose-free milk has been enzyme modified to break the milk sugar down into easily digestible/fermentable sugars. It's noticeably sweeter than conventional milk.

Dissolve the sugar in boiling water and let cool to room temperature, then add to milk and pitch yeast. It is important to let the water cool so you don't scald the milk which alters its chemistry. It's best to use a fermentation lock from the start. Ferment at room temperature about 70° F. After about a week your milk wine will separate into three distinct layers, a curd or cottage cheese on top, the fluid or whey, and on the bottom, a fine yogurt-like layer. It's now time to rack the wine by straining it through a colander lined with cheesecloth to separate the solids from the whey. Put the liquid into a secondary fermentation vessel with fermentation lock and proceed with fermentation, racking and bottling as with other wines. This process will yield about one quart per gallon of cottage cheese (curds) when you strain it. It is wholesome, good for you, but will hammer you into the ground like a tent peg because it's high in alcohol content. If you don't want to go on a cheese bender, rinse it and strain it through cheesecloth to remove the kick.

Milk Wine Recipe #2 (the more traditional way)

1	Gal.	Low-fat milk or reconstituted milk
4	Lb.	Cane sugar, syrup or honey
30	Drops	Lactaid® enzyme
1	Gal.	Water
1	Pkt.	Champagne yeast

Note: Any equivalent commercial additive sold in most health food stores as a digestive aid for lactose intolerant people can be substituted for Lactaid.

Warm milk in a basin or sink of warm water, add and mix lactose conversion drops. Let stand overnight at room temperature. Proceed as with Recipe #1. Father Engel ran his milk winery entirely with dried milk.

Yogurt First (Miss Muffet's favorite)

1	Gal.	Low-fat milk
30	Drops	Lactaid enzyme
1	Gal.	Water
1	Pkt.	Champagne yeast
1	Pkt.	Yogurt culture
4	Lb.	Cane sugar or honey

Note: an equivalent commercial additive sold in most health food stores as a digestive aid for lactose intolerant people can be substituted for Lactaid. Warm the milk and add yogurt culture per instructions. Save the whey. Dissolve sugar in water. When cool, mix with whey, Lactaid and yeast and proceed as with Recipe #1 and #2.

I won't attempt to explain or profess to understand the chemistry of this one, but it works. You make the yogurt first (nonalcoholic) then make the wine out of the whey. I'm sure Father Engel could explain it. I can't.

Pruno – Jailhouse Wine

Homebrewing is not encouraged in penal institutions, but it goes on nevertheless. Clandestinely, of course! The product may not have much snob appeal, but the ingenuity employed is remarkable. A one-quart milk carton is used as a fermentation vessel and a disposable latex glove is pulled over the top as an improvised fermentation lock. Fermentables vary according to whatever can be smuggled from the kitchen, so "Pruno" may be anything from a simple sugar wine through a range of wines similar to those covered in this book.

Pruno Recipe

1-²/₃	Cups	Sugar
1	Qt.	Water or fruit juice
1	Pinch	Bakers' yeast and/or a couple of raisins or grapes

Dissolve sugar in carton of water/juice and add yeast/raisins or grapes. Slip the glove over the carton, ferment until the glove deflates. Then invite your cellmates to a wine tasting. (Use milk carton and rubber disposable glove illustrated in chapter four, page 77.)

Corn Squeezins

Traditional corn squeezins were the fermented juice from green corn stalks. Farmers filled their silos with chopped green corn to feed their livestock in the winter. As tons of corn was piled in the silo, the sweet sap or juice from the corn stalks accumulated in the bottom along with natural yeast that caused it to ferment. Jugs corked with corn cobs were placed in the bottom of the silo first and as juice accumulated, it filtered through the porous core of the cobs, filling them with what was basically a corn stalk wine. When the silo was finally empty, the jugs of corn squeezins were recovered.

I'm sure you'll see the similarity to apple cider, just natural juices and yeast and if you have access to a cider press, you can make old time corn squeezins with it too. If you're one of those unfortunates that doesn't have a silo or a cider press, you can still make a batch with the following all corn recipe.

Modern Corn Squeezins

6	Ears	Fresh or frozen sweet corn
6	Ears	Dried red corncobs
1	T	Citrus fruit
1	T	Tea
1-½	Gal.	Water
1	Pkt.	Wine yeast
1	Qt.	Light corn syrup

Cook and eat the corn. Boil the red corncobs in the same corn-flavored water to add color and more flavor. Add tea and citrus juice. Remove cobs and dissolve corn syrup. Pour the fluid into a fermenting vessel. (The vanilla flavored syrup is okay. You won't taste the vanilla after fermentation.) When cool, add yeast and fit with a fermentation lock. Follow basic wine making steps on page 20.)

Chapter Three

From Prohibition-Style
Homebrew to Gourmet Beers

In This Chapter

➤ Beer

➤ Making Beer With Malt Extracts

➤ Light Beer and Dark Beer

➤ Making Beer From Malted Grain

➤ Cheating on Malt Grain Beer

The why, the how and then some of making your own brew and equipment. Closely guarded secrets revealed at great peril to make great (even organic) beer.

Beer - From Alaskan Bush Beer to Gourmet Beers

I've just walked and talked you through a variety of wines. I said at the outset that wine was the simplest beverage to make, because it's mostly a natural process. Beer making is not much different except instead of dealing with naturally occurring fruit sugars, we'll be converting the starch from grains to natural sugars. We'll use more complex, but natural processes to produce a wholesome and nourishing beverage that is classed as a foodstuff in Europe, rather than the "bladder wash" we've come to accept as beer in America.

Forgive me, but a bit of history is in order here, to explain the difference between "beer" companies. By German law, their equivalent of our pure food laws, nothing can be called beer unless its ingredients are only malted grain (barley and wheat) water, hops and yeast. That's all.

Such was the case in the good old USA prior to prohibition. We had many small breweries turning out wholesome, traditional beer. We also had developed American strains of barley that had more of the sugar conversion enzymes than the traditional European beer barley. Prohibition put most of the honest traditional breweries out of business. The big boys, meaning the bootlegging organized crime types found that using the high enzyme malted American barley along with corn and cane sugar, rice and other ingredients, enabled them to make a bootleg beer that had little body. It was cheaper and easier to make than a full-bodied all malt brew, so evolved what we Americans now call beer.

Until the resurgence of the many American microbreweries, there was little or no true beer in America. We had become accustomed to drinking the pale, bodiless, tart tasting product that had one redeeming quality for the US brewing companies. It was cheap to make. Commercial beers also used a lot of artificial additives like heading agents, artificial carbonation and coloring. The occasional dark beer on the market was usually the same old product with a bit of caramel food coloring added. We became a nation that drank our beer ice cold, because it had to be drunk this way to deaden the taste buds. Let me assure you that you can easily make beer that is far superior to most of the commercial products, the wonderful brave little microbreweries that are now springing up excepted and commended, of course.

First, I'll give you a detailed explanation of the brewing process so you understand each step, then you'll get a summary of beer making steps in an easy to use format. To begin your first batch of beer, first make a strong, active yeast starter, just as in wine making. Next, we'll want the starches in the grain fully converted to sugar. This can be done by filtering hot water through a container of slightly cracked-malted grain. The wet grain is called mash. The resultant liquid extracted is called wort. The temperature of the water is increased in graduated steps over a period of several hours. The whole process called mashing, gradually activates the various enzymes to convert all the starch to fermentable sugars and also extracts other natural substances from the grain, like proteins that will give the beer color, flavor and body. The resultant liquid, or wort, is similar to a thin molasses and water solution.

The mashing process is laborious and is not usually done by the novice or even the advanced homebrewer. Instead, most homebrewing is done using malt extracts bought from homebrewing supply firms. As your skills develop, you'll probably want to experiment with blending malted grain with malt extracts to develop your own personal favorite beers, but keep it simple at first and just use malt extracts.

In essence, the manufacturers make the wort and condense it for you, selling it in the form of syrup or powdered concentrated malt extract. If that sounds like cheating to you, just remember Grandma made good bread, but she didn't usually grow her own grain and mill her own flour. Grandma was no dummy and you shouldn't be either. Buy good reliable ingredients and later, if you wish, try working with malted grain. The most important thing is to understand the mashing and extraction process, so you'll be better able to transform amber waves of grain into amber mugs of good beer.

Note: In mashing, the temperature of the mash is gradually raised from 140º F to 170º F over a period of about 12 hours. In this chapter, I cover a simplified method in "cheating on malt grain beers."

Cooking

With your large primary fermenting vessel spiffy clean, sterilized, covered and standing by, we'll begin cooking your beer in the biggest pot you can lay your hands on, either stainless steel or enameled. Some people cook, but not ferment their beer in an aluminum pot. You may choose to also. There's a risk of getting "off" tastes from aluminum, so I discourage the practice. This cooking is the guts of the whole process, because it accomplishes several things necessary to successful beer making. Boiling sterilizes all the ingredients so that when you add your yeast culture to the cooled fluid, it will be the perfect medium for brewers yeast to thrive in with no undesired competition. Even if your pot is not large enough to hold your entire batch, you'll boil all the ingredients, adding boiled water to your primary fermenter until you meet the volume specified in your recipe.

Boiling also reconstitutes the concentrated malt extract you brought into the watery wort that was extracted from the grain. It not only completes the conversion of any residual starch in the wort, but it aids in the clarification of the beer in the following manner. The temperatures used in mashing or extraction are a bit below boiling to avoid cooking rather than converting the starch and destroying the natural enzymes. As your wort approaches boiling temperature, proteins and other suspended solids will be transformed into denser material. Called trub, this stuff will eventually settle out, giving you a clear beer. Don't worry about removing it. Increasing the boiling time to as much as an hour will improve trub separation, but is not necessary.

Caution: As your wort reaches boiling temperatures, it will reach a "break" or breaking point at which it will suddenly froth up to about double the volume of the liquid in your pot. This break may bring your marriage close to the breaking point, because your pot, if too small will overflow with a hot sticky foam that is miserable to clean up, especially if it gets cooked on to the stove top and sundry utensils. So, forewarned be standing by your pot with a big stainless steel spoon, or even a clean wooden paddle. When the break comes, stir the wort until it settles down to a rolling boil. You can also sprinkle cold water on the wort to settle it down.

Continue boiling for at least thirty minutes to cook out the solids, more is better, up to two hours for wheat beer. The other, and crucially important function of boiling is to infuse your wort with hops. Hops is the noble plant, without which we would not have beer. Other plants have been used in the past, like spruce needles, but nothing else performs so many good functions so well. Hops adds the bitter flavor that balances the malt flavor of the wort. It aids in clarifying the beer and acts as a natural preservative so the beer improves with age.

There are four main ways to put hops in your beer and of course, there are many varieties of hops. The simplest method is to buy hopped malt extract that the manufacturer has formulated to give you a good wholesome beer. The second method is to add all or additional hops yourself when cooking the wort for a more personalized beer. You do this by putting your hops flowers in a clean cloth bag and boiling it like a tea bag in the wort. The third method entails using hops extract, mainly oils that you buy in little bottles and add to the wort. All three methods have a marked advantage and a marked disadvantage over the fourth method in that they sterilize the hops by boiling, but they boil off the lightest most flavorful and aromatic of the hops oils.

The fourth method of adding hops, aromatic hopping, is very simple and enables you to make far better beers, even than the microbreweries because it's unsterile. All commercial breweries have to be fanatics when it comes to sterilization because the slightest contamination can ruin hundreds of barrels of beer. But in the boiling process, they boil off the finest, most delicate of the hops oils. You, the homebrewer, with only five or ten gallons per batch, can afford to

live dangerously, risking a small batch in order to obtain the absolute finest of gourmet beers.

Aromatic hopping is accomplished by adding a small bag containing a fraction of the hops specified in your recipe, of the most delicate aromatic hops, to your primary fermenting vessel and pouring the hot wort over it. Keep the wort covered until it cools down to room temperature, then remove the aromatic hops, add the yeast and let the vigorous primary fermentation proceed. If you can fit a fermentation lock to your primary fermenter, so much the better. Once the "bonfire" burns down to the "glowing embers" phase, transfer your brew to a secondary fermenter and use a fermentation lock for sure.

Unlike wine, when you bottle beer, you definitely want to make it bubbly, but again, not too bubbly. That is unless you're British, of course. I tend to judge a culture or a country by their beers and any American privileged to visit a few British pubs, will soon develop an appreciation for how really good a warm, flat beer can be. All brew that bubbles is not necessarily good, and a glass of bitters without a foaming head, drunk warm is one of the finer things in life.

We Yanks like our beer foamy and luckily, beer is far less fickle or treacherous in regard to carbonation than wine. With beer, you're dealing with far less complex fermentables than wine. Consequently, when our beer reaches the end of the "dying embers" stage, the fermentation is usually truly near its end, not playing possum to flare up inside your bottles. Most homebrewers wait for this stage and then add a small amount of sugar either to the bulk brew or to each bottle to rekindle just enough fermentation in their bottles to carbonate the beverage.

Bottling beer is the same process as we covered with wine, using strong beverage bottles with crown caps, but filling the bottles is the most tedious task in homebrewing, next to cleaning the blasted things. There are tricks and tools to lighten the labor in both tasks that I cover later, but remember, with beer, bigger is better. Happy is he who has a large supply of the old-style quart beer bottles. Twenty-four quart bottles will handle a five-gallon batch instead of cleaning, filling and capping sixty of the smaller bottles. If you are truly fortunate or crafty, you will have amassed a hoard of the two-liter plastic or aluminum containers with screw caps that some Japanese beers are sold in.

A good friend of mine, a fellow Polack and beer lover lives way out in the Alaskan bush and he has been using the same containers I gave him for years. Twelve containers hold a five-gallon batch. They don't break,

A Variety of Reusable Bottles and Containers to use in Bottling Beer

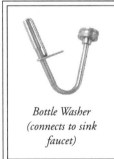

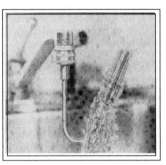

Bottle Washer (connects to sink faucet)

are easy to clean and the screw caps are resealable, so you can enjoy a glass or two and put the rest away for another day without wasting any. I've seen and read about a bunch of different keg setups people have devised and most of them are plumber's nightmares. I've devised a way of converting an old commercial keg to a naturally carbonated draft homebrew keg. You'll like it.

See chapter four for more information on cobbling up your own draft beer keg. It's cheap and simple. For now, with your new beer bottled and as good as you can make it, there are ways to make it much better. First, store your beer in a cool place. Second, keep it as dark as possible. Until you actually taste the difference, you will never appreciate the way a beer can improve by aging a few weeks, or how exposure to light adversely affects the taste of beer. The aging is particularly important if you've used the aromatic hops process. You'll make beer like money can't buy. Don't forget the record keeping. Both brewer's log and labels are very important to long-term success. In the short-term, making your own humorous labels with crazy contents and captions is a lot of fun and makes great (and low-cost) gifts. I actually made my own canned beer once using the equipment I had for home canning fish in metal cans. Using a Xerox machine or your computer, it's easy to make your own labels using your friends or relatives photographs, even your pets. The best label I made was, "Whoo-Whoo Beer," a drawing of a steam locomotive and then on the bottom, "You'll think a train hit you." I don't think any of those cans ever got thrown away. In fact, some of them are in beer can collections now.

The illustration on page 54 is the above-mentioned example of labels I've used. It was used on canned beer I made for Christmas gifts. I used the metal cans many Alaskans use for home canning salmon. A friend used a Polaroid photo of himself depicted as the brewmaster. Just make a master copy and Xerox it. This can be a lot of hoots, but make sure you state on the label that it is not to be sold.

Beer Making Steps

Back in the Gold Rush Days a German peddler in Seattle was selling eyeglasses to prospectors sailing for Alaska. He had one young fellow try on several sets of spectacles, but the lad still couldn't read the local paper. Finally he admitted to the German that he had never learned to read, whereupon the old peddler stomped off muttering, "Dot dumkoff vants un education vor tree dollars!"

Vell, ve giffs you der education here but it is very abbreviated. I'll hit the basic steps, designated by Roman numerals. These steps will be subdivided into BASIC for the novice, ADVANCED for those who want to make a more tailor made brew and GENERAL supplemental information to ensure success.

I.   Cooking

      Basic – Boil all fermentables such

as hopped malt extracts and sugar for at least ½ hour or more boiling, up to two hours with wheat beer is better.

Advanced – The use of boiling hops, aromatic hops, malted grain and adjuncts such as rice, oats, etc.

General – Everything used should be sterilized either by cooking or treatment with sterilizing agent.

Keep records. Your brewing log should record everything you use and do.

II.   Fermentation

Basic – Pour your boiled wort into a sterile fermentation vessel. When wort cools to 50° F, add a packet of yeast. Exclude air by means of a plastic sheet or fermentation lock.

Advanced – You should have made a strong yeast starter several days beforehand to ensure you start off with a vigorous fermentation. You'll save and nurture some of this culture as a backup in case you have a stuck ferment or for use in subsequent brews.

General – Optimum temperatures for fermentation are 50° F to 60° F.

Fermentation will progress from

vigorous and frothy (10-14 days) to just a few bubbles like the end of an Alka-Seltzer®. It's time to proceed to the next step.

III.   **Racking and Fining**

Basic – Carefully and gently siphon your wort to another sterilized container, leaving all the lees (gunk) behind. Fit a fermentation lock to this, the secondary container. This is called racking. When there is only the occasional bubble and the wort is starting to clarify and look drinkable, add dissolved gelatin or other settling agent to it. This is called fining.

Advanced – Lager, or store the wort at a near freezing temperature for weeks or months to further clarify and mature it.

General – Homebrew will settle or clarify in the bottle in a week or so. There will be a residue of yeast in the bottle, which means you merely pour the beer into a pitcher, leaving the residue behind.

IV.   **Bottling and Priming**

Basic – Your new made beer is now pretty flat and looking pretty clear, but it is still full of living yeast cells. What you want to do now is get it bottled while adding just enough sugar to let the yeast bugs give it carbonation, or a head before they croak and settle to the bottom of the bottle. This

is called priming. There are many ways of priming. The two simplest ways are to add ¼ cup of sterile dissolved sugar per gallon of wort and stir it lightly or to add ¼ teaspoon of sugar to each 12-oz. bottle before filling.

Advanced – Using your hydrometer, you may bottle at a certain specific gravity if you dare and hope for the best. You may also try krausening, priming with just enough vigorously fermenting wort from another batch. Lots of luck! You may want to try your hand at smoked, hot pepper or fruit/berry beers. Just add the ingredients when you bottle.

General – Priming is best done with corn sugar. Cane sugar is okay, but may impart a cider taste to your beer. Frankly, I use Karo® syrup; even the vanilla flavored stuff. It's cheap, easy to get and not even my most persnickety friends have ever detected any vanilla taste.

Bottling is a mechanical process that needs little explanation. Just make sure anything that touches the beer, caps, bottles and hoses is sterilized. I run my bottles through the dishwasher, soak the caps in a bleach solution and rinse them in a bowl as I bottle.

V.   **Storing**

Basic – Figure on storing your

beer in a dark cool place for 7-10 days before drinking. It gets better with age. The little stick-on stars or dots are convenient ways of labeling your bottles. Use with a good brewer's log and you'll improve with each batch.

Advanced – As you become more arrogant and egotistical about your brews, you'll want to design your own labels. When you give a friend some plain ol' homebrew, you're an okay guy. When you give him a six-pack of "Ol' Stump Blower, Pile Driver," etc. you become a legend in your own time and can borrow his tools anytime you want.

Making Beer With Malt Extracts

Brewing your own beer has always been fun and it's even more so since its popularity has increased and fine ingredients and equipment have become so readily available. We have covered the basic steps and equipment in previous sections and they are identical to wine making with two exceptions. Since we are dealing with malt extracts, we'll boil the raw beer or wort for sterility, conversion of starches, removal of suspended solids and getting the good stuff out of the hops. We'll also add sugar, or prime our beer before bottling or kegging it.

I admit to grossly, brutally simplifying or omitting entirely, segments of the science of brewing. Instead, we have and will continue to focus on the art of beer making. We'll pick up a few nuggets of knowledge as we go, but this is "Brewing for Fun," not "Brewing 201."

We'll stick to traditional, natural ingredients without the exotic or chemical additives so many advocate. The recipes will be representative of different techniques in brewing and can be adapted to your own tastes as your skills develop.

Prohibition Style Beer "Sneaky Pete" (a.k.a. Alaska Bush Beer)

3	Lb.	Can Blue Ribbon Malt Syrup (hops flavored)
4	Lb.	Cane sugar
5	Gal.	Water
1	Pkt.	Bakers' yeast

In the biggest pot you can get your hands on, boil and dissolve in a total of 5 gallons of water, the malt and sugar. Put this wort in a primary fermenter (a crock in my younger days) and when it's cool, crumble in a cake of bakers' yeast. When almost all the little bubbles stop, bottle it, adding ¼ teaspoon of sugar to each bottle.

This is the recipe I worked with in my youth, handed down from my Grandmother. Blue Ribbon Malt was available from any grocery store, ostensibly for cooking and baking purposes. I'm sure that's why it was hops flavored. You went to the store with a well-rehearsed alibi for why you wanted it. "Aunt Aggie is making gingerbread cookies," and you sneaked home with it like a thief in the night.

Nobody had ever heard of a fermentation lock, or secondary fermenter, etc. If you'd shown us a hydrometer in those days, we'd have thought it was something the veterinarian used on cows. As a "star student," you already see several weaknesses in this recipe, i.e., no fermentation lock, bottling the murky wort before it clarified, using bakers' yeast and not much hops. All true.

How was it? Well, you had to chill the hell out of it to settle the bakers' yeast and pour it into a glass carefully to avoid stirring up clouds of yeast. Sometimes lots of bottles blew up. On the other hand, when I was making it, a glass of draft cost 15¢, and a bottle of beer 25¢ at Dugan's Tavern. I made it for 3¢ a bottle, cap included, which made it damned good beer.

There's probably been more of this beer made in Alaska than any other style. The ingredients are easy to get and when you're packing in several months of provisions to a remote homestead or mine, it can mean the difference between beer and no beer. Ketchup bottles and Mason jars were and are still used for bottling. One guy I know swears putting a raisin in each jar makes it extra fine. Also said to produce blue smoke when opened.

There are so many good canned malt extracts and yeast available now that for the price of a case of "Big Brewer Bladderwash," the novice brewer can make several cases of far superior beer. You must have a good fermentation vessel fitted with a fermentation lock. A large glass carboy is ideal, but if you're a struggling college student, a food grade plastic bucket with a snap on resealable lid, will work just as well. Make a hole in the lid with your trusty pocketknife, just large enough to squeeze a piece of plastic tubing through. Seal around the tubing with something that is not too unspeakably gross and drop the other end of the hose in a jar of

water. You're ready for business. This, by the way, is called a "bubbler," a simple homemade fermentation lock. Sterility is all-important and the vinegar bacteria can react with amazing speed. I've had wort turning sour on me and smelling like vinegar in less than an hour. If it happens, campden tablets can't save you, boil the whole batch again, re-sterilize your equipment, cool and get some yeast into the wort. This is another good reason to reserve some of your yeast culture.

Bush Beer

There are several reasons for this beer's popularity. First, many Alaskan grocers did and still do cater to "bush orders," meaning that folks in the bush mail, telephone or otherwise order their groceries which are then delivered by mail, freight forwarder or bush pilot. Second, up into the '70's, making beer or wine at home was against federal law, so the malt and yeast were ostensibly ordered for baking and cooking.

Additionally, many remote communities regulate or even prohibit the sale or importation of alcoholic beverages and just as during "The Great Experiment," this prompted people to make their own. You can be sure that "bush beer" is still widely made in Alaska, but with better mail ordered ingredients than the ones in this recipe.

Al Capone Beer (Pilsner?)

This beer is interesting not only because it

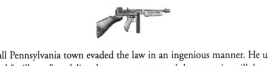

A bootlegger in a small Pennsylvania town evaded the law in an ingenious manner. He used a horsedrawn milk wagon and a uniformed "milkman" to deliver booze to customers' doorsteps in milk bottles painted white.

is supposed to be one that one of "Big Al's" breweries actually used, but also it's all grain with the exception of *soybeans*. I've bad-mouthed the prohibition era beer, but Al did employ some of the best brewmasters in the country and this is definitely not a thin bodied "sneaky Pete" recipe. It's doubly interesting because it deals with naturally carbonated keg beer. This is a pilsner recipe calling for soft water, low in mineral content. I suggest that you buy a couple of jugs of distilled water to mix with your tap water if you try this one. The following recipe is allegedly from the Sieben Brewery of 1924, which was owned by Al Capone at that time. It is supposedly a typical speakeasy beer with overtones of a German pilsner.

Note: All the following beer and barley wine recipes aim at 5 gallons of wort. You will lose some water in the boiling and mashing process, so plan on adding boiled water to the primary fermenter to make up for any loss. That means marking your primary fermenter at the 5-gallon level before you start brewing.

Al Capone Speakeasy Beer

6	Lb.	Six-row lager malt
2	Lb.	Rice (ground)
½	Lb.	Soy grits (from health food store)
1-½	Oz.	Hersbrucker 6% alpha-acid
½	Oz.	Hallertauer 5% alpha-acid
½	Oz.	Hersbrucker 6% alpha-acid
½	Oz.	Hallertauer
1	Pkt.	Red Star lager yeast
5	Gal.	Water (soft)

Cook rice in 1-½ gallons of water for 30 minutes. Preheat mash tun and add 1-½ gallons of 120° F water. Adjust rice temperature to 190° F with 1 gallon hot water. Add rice to mash tun and immediately mash in malt and soy grits. The temperature should end up between 150° F and 155° F. Hold at 150° F to 155° F for 1-½ hours.

Sparge with 165° F water to collect 5-½ gallons of wort. Boil wort for 1 hour using the follow hop schedule:

> 60 min. – 1-½ oz. Hersbrucker 6% alpha-acid
>
> 30 min. – ½ oz. Hallertauer 5% alpha-acid
>
> 10 min. – 1/8 oz. Hersbrucker 6% alpha-acid

Add ½ oz. of Hallertauer after turning off the boil and cover brew kettle. Cool to 55° F. Pitch with about 14 grams Red Star lager yeast. Remember that this was during prohibition! Ferment and condition at 55° F. Bottle with ¼ cup priming sugar per gallon.

Steam Beer – All Grain

Steam beer was developed for the hell raising "49er" gold miners in California. Demand was high and the cold temperatures for months of traditional lagering of European style beers couldn't be duplicated in California then. What evolved was a full-bodied relatively quickly fermented beer with loads of natural carbonation (steam.)

You'll need the biggest pot you can get your hands on and one or more muslin grain bags to cook (mash) and sparge (extract) 5 gallons of rich wort to make this beer.

Steam Beer

5	Gal.	Water

8	Lb.	Crystal malt slightly toasted, to the point that brown crystals like dried syrup or molasses have formed in the grains.
4	Lb.	Pale malt fully modified but floury and sweet. Crack the malt with a rolling pin and mix both types. The mashing or conversion of grain enzymes and starch to sugars is not a brutal boil, but a graduated heating of a grain and water mixture (mash.) As the temperature of the mash is increased in steps, strange and wonderful things happen to convert seeds into sweet wort which in turn, you turn into beer.
2	Oz.	Hops, Northern Brewer boiling
½	Oz.	Hops, Cascade, aromatic
1	Pkt.	Lager yeast
5	Gal.	Water (wort) when it's all over
1-½	Cup	Priming sugar

Heat the mash to 130° F and hold at this temperature for 30 minutes, then raise the temperature to 155° F and hold for 90 minutes. Drain all the wort and sparge the grain with more 155° F water to extract all the malt sugar.

Boil the wort for 1 hour with the boiling hops, adding the aromatic hops for the last 10 minutes. Remove the hops and transfer the wort to your primary fermenter. Add the yeast when the wort is cool. Prime, bottle or keg as with other beer.

Any Beer (Using Malt Extract Syrup)

5	Gal.	Water
1	Can (3.3 1b.)	Hopped malt extract
3	Lb.	Sugar (Preferably corn, but cane sugar will work.)
	or	
3	Bottles	Karo® Corn Syrup, plain preferably, but I have used the vanilla. (Light vanilla flavor is masked by the hops.)
1	Pkt.	Beer yeast (or start culture 1 or 2 days in advance.
1	Oz.	Hops
1-¼	Cup	Priming sugar (corn or cane)

1) Boil the water, malt extract, sugar and hops together for at least thirty minutes. Do this in several batches if you only have a small stainless steel or enamel pot. The goal is to sterilize everything going into the fermenter, and to let the malt boil for at least thirty minutes and do its conversion trick on the syrup. Pour the fluids, now called the wort into the fermenter, cover, and cool. Add yeast and then seal with fermentation lock in place.

2) *DO NOT GET SLIPSHOD OR CARELESS!* When the vigorous fermentation (blazing bonfire) slows to a steady effervescence (glowing embers stage) transfer (rack) your beer to a secondary fer-

menter, carefully, leaving the gunk (lees) behind. Fining is optional, should be done a day or two before bottling. (See Basic Beer Making steps, page 31)

3) With everything happily fermenting, get ready for the bottling and priming stage in about five days. When your fermentation lock quits bubbling, bottle and prime. The ¼ teaspoon of sugar in each bottle priming technique is slow and tedious. It's far easier and safer, contamination-wise, to boil 1-¼ cup of sugar with a cup of water and sprinkle the cooled mixture into the secondary fermenter 2-4 hours before you bottle. Stir gently to mix sugar, but not stir up gunk on the bottom. While you are sterilizing your bottles in the dishwasher and getting your bottling operation set up, the sugar will circulate through your wort.

4) Remember, with beer, bigger is better, so if you have 2-liter Japanese kegs or quart beer bottles, you'll be finished quickly. With small bottles, even with one of the bottle filling wands, it's a chore. Have at least 2-¼ cases of small bottles and caps sterilized and then do it.

5) Age your beer about ten days in a cool, dark place before you pop a top. A couple of weeks will improve things greatly. Don't forget your record book and labels. You should get better with each batch, not scratch your head and say, "How the heck did I make that batch?"

Not Just Any Beer (Aromatic Hopping All-Malt Beer)

You'll make excellent beers using the hopped malt extracts and sugar, but you'll probably want to experiment with more personalized brews and improve your product. No problem! If you dispense with the sugar, replacing it with malt, you'll get a much fuller bodied brew. Adding some hops after the wort has been boiled, called aromatic hopping, will add the delicate hops oils that are boiled out of commercial beers and hopped extracts.

1	Can (3.3 lb.)	Light hopped malt extract syrup
2	Lb.	Light malt extract (dry)
1	Oz.	Hops (bittering, or boiling hops)
1	Oz.	Aromatic hops
5	Gal.	Water
1	Pkt.	Yeast (ale or lager)
1-¼	Cups	Priming sugar

Put the bittering or boiling hops in a cloth bag with a couple of marbles. Put the aromatic hops (there's a hops table in the back of this book to help you select hops) in a smaller bag with a couple of marbles and place it in the primary fermenter. The game plan is to dissolve and simmer the malts for at least 30 minutes, with the boiling hops bag in the wort. This will take a big pot (18 qt.) or you can divide the malt up and boil several batches, using the same hops or dividing them also if you only have a smaller pot. Pour the boiling wort over the aromatic hops and keep adding wort, or boiled water until you reach the five-gallon mark on your primary fermenter. (You did mark it, didn't you?) When the wort cools down, fish the aromatic hops bag out with a sterile spoon. The one you used to stir your boiling wort should be just fine. Now add the yeast and if you've had the foresight to make a big vigorous starter a day or two before, you are well on your way to success. You can use either an ale or a lager yeast. Ale yeasts ferment faster, warmer 60° F - 80° F, form a cake on the top of the wort and are traditionally used for ales and stouts. Lager yeasts settle to the bottom, are slower, work colder (35° F) and are traditionally used for lagers and steam beers. Regardless of the type of yeast you choose, this recipe will give you an all malt aromatically hopped beer of superior quality and will serve as a base recipe for building the beer of your dreams.

Note: You can leave the aromatic hops in the primary fermenter for maximum flavor, but make sure they're in a bag so they're easy to remove.

Transfer your wort to a secondary fermenter when the "blazing bonfire" ferment dies down to the "glowing embers" stage and fine (add gelatin) a day or two before bottling. About 4 hours prior to bottling, dissolve the priming sugar in a cup of boiled water and when it cools, add it to the beer. Notice that we're sticking to natural ingredients without a bunch of additives. The priming sugar is a compromise for the homebrewer. German brewers, to comply with their *only malt, hops, yeast and water* laws use a trick called krausening to prime. They add just enough fermenting wort from a young batch of beer to carbonate one that is ready for bottling.

Being able to tell how much "just enough" is, is one of the things that separate us homebrewers from master brewers. Just stay with ¼ cup of priming sugar per gallon and you'll know you have "just enough."

Light Beer and Dark Beer– What's the Difference?

Burnt sugar is called caramel, used for food coloring and flavoring. The more you roast malted barley, the more you char the malt sugar, hence the malt extract becomes darker (caramelized) until some of the darkest malts are basically charcoal. As you burn the sugar, you decrease the amount of fermentable material in the malt, but increase the coloring and flavoring substances that are unfermentable and give dark beers their characteristic color, flavor and body.

With all malt beers, the color, body and flavor are determined by blending light and dark malts. Adjuncts are ingredients other than malt that are fermentable to some degree and add the characteristics like color, flavor and body to beers. Rice, corn, corn sugar, brown sugar, molasses and oatmeal are common adjuncts that can be used to build every thing from pale, light-bodied beers, to dark heavy-bodied stouts, that as the Irish say, "a mouse can run across the head without wetting it's feet." Let's look at some representative recipes using adjuncts and malt extracts.

Pale Lager Pilsner

| 2 | Lb. | Light malt extract syrup |
| 2 | Lb. | Pale malt extract dried |

1-½	Lb.	Corn sugar (hold 1-¼ cups) for priming.)
2	Oz.	Boiling hops
1	Oz.	Aromatic hops
5	Gal.	Water
1	Pkt.	Lager yeast

Boil all the malt extract and boiling hops for 1 to 1-½ hours at a rolling boil. Pour the hot wort over the aromatic hops and sugar in the primary fermenter. Saaz hops are traditional Pilsner hops with a distinctive flavor. When the wort cools, add (pitch) your yeast and proceed with standard beer making steps.

Oatmeal Stout

1	Can (3.3 lb.)	Dark malt extract syrup
1	Lb.	Pale malt extract (dried)
1	Lb.	Oatmeal
1	Cup (8 oz.)	Brown sugar
2	Cups (16 oz)	Molasses
3	Oz.	Hops
5	Gal.	Water
1	Pkt.	Yeast
1-¼	Cup	Cane or corn sugar (for priming)

You need a big pot for this one, because you need to let the malt work on the starches and sugars while gradually increasing the temperature. Put the oatmeal and hops in separate cloth bags. Bring two gallons of water to a boil, turn off the heat, add the oatmeal and let it steep for an hour. Remove the oatmeal and dissolve all the malt sugar and molasses and add the hops bag. Bring this wort to near boiling temperature and simmer it for one hour, more if convenient. Then bring the wort to a rolling boil, remembering it will froth up briefly when the

breakpoint is reached. Continue the rolling boil for one half hour, then pour the wort into the primary fermenter and boiled water to the 5-gal. mark. Add yeast when it's cooled. After going through the primary and secondary fermentation stages, add the priming sugar about three hours before bottling.

Pilsner Style with Rice

1	Can (3.3 lb.)	Light malt extract
2	Lb.	Sugar, corn or cane (reserve 1-¼ cup for priming.)
1	Lb.	Rice
2	Oz.	Boiling hops (Saaz hops is traditional for Pilsner beer)
5	Gal.	Water
1	Oz.	Aromatic hops
1	Pkt.	Beer yeast

Boil the rice in one gallon of water, then pour the rice and water into a cloth bag in your primary fermenter. Add your aromatic hops to the bag and tie it off. Dissolve the malt extract and sugar and boil with the other hops, also in a bag. Pour the hot wort over the bag of rice and aromatic hops. When cool, pitch your yeast in. Let the wort ferment about five days, then remove the rice bag. Continue with basic brewing steps to include priming with 1-¼ cups of sugar you reserved from the recipe.

Steam Beer

2	Cans (6.6 lb.)	Light malt extract syrup

1	Lb.	Crystal malt (malted barley seed.)
3	Oz.	Hops (Cascade)
1	Pkt.	Lager yeast
1-½	Cup	Sugar or priming

> *If you over prime (carbonate) your beer, it may geyser just like a fire extinguisher. I say just like, because CO_2 recovered from commercial brewing is used in, you guessed it, fire extinguishers.*

Crack the malted barley with a rolling pin. I usually use a beer or wine bottle as a rolling pin. Don't get too macho. The husk of the grain should just be cracked. If you pulverize it, you're liable to get a starch haze in your beer. Put it in a bag with some marbles and boil it with the malt extract. Keep the wort at a rolling boil for about a half-hour to get a good conversion. Don't forget the yeast starter trick either. If you start your beer with a large batch of vigorous hungry yeast, you are helping nature make better beer instead of adding a bunch of chemicals. Cool the wort and pitch in the yeast, then follow basic brewing steps (page 68.) Prime with 1-¼ cups of sugar dissolved in boiled water 4 hours before you bottle.

Barley Wine

This is the "make my day" magnum of malt beverages. I once donated ten gallons of a similar brew to the Mount McKinley Mountainmen for one of their rendezvous or parties. This is a semi-crazy club that thinks hunting grizzly bears with flintlock rifles and Bowie knives is a jolly pastime. They are not known for their refinement or moderation. They were unanimous that it was the best beer and the best party they'd ever had, but beyond a certain point, none of them could remember what happened.

Barley Wine Recipe

12	Lb.	Light malt extract

1	Lb.	Crystal, or partially caramelized grain for color and body.
2	Oz.	Cascade of Fuggle hops (aromatic)
2	Pkt.	Champagne yeast
3	Oz.	Bullion or Chinook hops (boiling)
5	Gal.	Water
¾	Cup	Priming sugar

Mash the grain malts for one hour in two gallons of water in a grain bag at 150° F. Remove and discard grain. Add malt extracts, boiling hops, remaining water and boil for an hour. Add aromatic hops, turn off heat and steep for 20 minutes. Strain wort into fermenter and pitch yeast when cooled to 55° F.

This brew is a crossbreed between normal malt beverages and wine. It may take over a month to ferment all the rich malt mixture via the champagne yeast. You'll use slightly less priming sugar because this is more of a sparkling wine than a foaming brew. Like wines, it requires aging for from 3 months to a year.

Smoked Beer (The Easy Way)

Traditional German style smoked beers are made by leaking some Beech smoke into the barley during the malting process. There's nothing terribly exotic about it. It's just a flavoring process. Smoked beers are usually dark, heavy bodied beer, but that need not be the case. Any beer recipe can be made into a smoked beer and you can even split a batch into several degrees of smoke flavoring.

If you've ever smoked meat or fish, you know it can be a tricky process, very easy to overdo and then your product tastes like the soot from your chimney. My easy method does away with the smoldering fire, smokehouse and most of the guesswork by using the Liquid Smoke sold for Bar-B-Queing. There's more on Liquid Smoke® in the tips section, so here let's just say that Liquid Smoke® is just natural smoke concentrate and water mixed at a uniform strength so you can tailor your recipes with far more precision than if you were smoking grain in the backyard. Let's do a heavy-bodied stout and then smoke it.

Smoked Stout

1	Can (3.3 lb.)	Dark hopped malt extract
1	Lb.	Crystal malt (cracked)
½	Lb.	Black malt (cracked)
4	Lb.	Brown sugar
2	Oz.	Hops (boiling, See hops table)
5	Gal.	Water
1	Pkt.	Beer yeast (to taste) Liquid Smoke® (See following instructions for guidelines.)
1-½	Cup	Priming sugar
2	Tsp.	Non-iodized salt

		(optional)
1	Oz.	Citrus fruit juice (optional)

Boil the malts, sugar, hops and optional ingredients for only a half-hour with the grain malt and hops in a cloth bag. Depending on your pot size, you may want to split the ingredients up to cook in two or more batches, then combine boiled wort and boiled water, if necessary to fill the fermenter to the five-gallon mark. Cool, pitch yeast and ferment as with other beers. This is a heavy-bodied beer that may take longer than lighter beers to ferment and age. The optional citrus juice and salt are to aid fermentation. You prime this beer in your normal manner, but add an additional step to the bottling process to smoke it. Taste preferences vary greatly. Some people like just a hint of smoke, others like a strong smoke flavor. To find just the right level of smoke for your tastes, using 12 oz. Bottles, divide your bottles into 4 equal groups and then add ¹/₈, ¹/₄, and ¹/₂ tsp. of Liquid Smoke® to 75% of your bottles. Bottle 25% with no smoke. Now bottle and label each sample and let it age for about two weeks. This may seem like a lot of work, but it is the easiest way to determine how smoky you like your smoked beers. Additionally, there is no waste, because if some of this batch is too strong for you when you try it, just tone it down by blending/mixing it in a pitcher with the un-smoked bottles. Once you've determined how smoky you like your beer you can add the liquid smoke during the boiling of the wort.

Wheat Beer

It is very difficult to get a clear beer using wheat, usually the more wheat, the more murk. Most commercial wheat beers are in fact murky, but still good. Beer can be made using malted wheat alone, no barley malt and as in most things related to beer, the Germans lead the pack. Most wheat beers however, use a combination of malted barley and wheat for several reasons.

First of all, malted wheat is more difficult and hence, more expensive to make than malted barley. This is because the sprouting wheat seed is far more delicate than barley and can't be turned and handled while sprouting as barley can.

Additionally, wheat has less of the diastase enzyme than barley and more proteins and stuff that won't ferment out. Consequently, it is far more difficult to get a complete conversion of starch and a haze-free beer when working with wheat. This is compounded by the fact that the wheat seed has no husk and hence, tends to cake up when mashing, unlike barley seed, which with its husks forms a porous filter bed, facilitating conversion and sparging.

Ground malted wheat is called brewers flour and is used as an adjunct or additional ingredient as are flaked or rolled corn, oats, rye and barley to add characteristics to beers, e.g., flavor, body and head. All these adjuncts pose similar problems to the homebrewer and there are several measures you can take to increase the quality (clarity) of your beer.

Wheat Beer Tips:

1. Boil the heck out of your wort. As much as two hours of boiling when using wheat or other adjuncts.

2. Use barley malt in the majority, wheat malt in the minority, e.g., 2:1, and 3:1 in mashing and boiling to take advantage of the conversion enzymes in barley.

3. This is one of the rare instances where I suggest you try commercial additives, e.g., diastase or koji, to improve the clarity of your brew.

4. The Germans use special yeast for wheat beer. You can do one of three things to make a clearer wheat beer in regard to yeast. If you can find a commercial source of wheat beer yeast, try it. If you can't buy a special yeast, use ale rather than lager yeast for wheat beer. The third alternative may not be entirely legal because commercial brewers understandably regard the processes and ingredients use in their beers as trade secrets and their proprietary rights may include the special yeast they use.

5. With that warning, you may, if you choose, try to bootleg a yeast culture from a wheat beer you wish to imitate. In brief, sterilize an unopened bottle of the beer you select in a chlorine bleach solution and use a fermentation lock that will fit the bottle. Pour out two thirds of the beer, trying to disturb any yeast sediment on the bottom as little as possible. Replace one third of the contents with a sterile sugar and water solution and fit your fermentation lock to the bottle. If the beer was not pasteurized and filtered sufficiently to kill or remove every one of the original yeast bugs, you may succeed in getting a starter going. This is not a surefire process by any means and requires careful attention to avoid contamination from airborne bugs and patience because you're trying to

resurrect a thriving culture from a few survivors. If you succeed, you'll want to keep a starter going and take insane precautions to avoid contamination. Even then, the culture may mutate or degrade over time. Then you'll have to "play it again Sam."

Basic Wheat Beer Recipe

1	Can (3.3 lb.)	Light malt extract
1	Lb.	Sugar, cane or corn
2	Lb.	Malted wheat berries
		or
		1 can malted wheat extract in lieu of sugar and wheat berries
5	Gal.	Water
2	Oz.	Boiling hops (Cascade or Hallertau)
1	Oz.	Aromatic hops (Saaz)
1	Pkt.	Gelatin
1	Pkt.	Ale yeast, commercial wheat beer yeast or bootlegged wheat beer yeast
1-¼	Cup	Priming sugar

Follow basic beer making steps (page 56) with the following special considerations. Make a large vigorous yeast starter to start you off with a bang. Start this about 3 days prior to boiling. Crack the malted wheat with a rolling pin. Boil malts, sugar and boiling hops for 2 hours to aid conversion of wheat. If you want to try the "feast and famine" fermentation method on page 31 to aid

clarification, reserve the pound of sugar and 1 gallon of water until you transfer to the secondary fermenter, then add boiled, cooled sugar solution.

Making Beer From Malted Grain

Why in Sam Hill anyone would want to make beer from grain with all the syrups and extracts available is a good question. There are multiple answers. Using commercial extracts is kind of like making instant add water beer or painting by numbers. You haven't really mastered the art until you do it the hard way. Quality is a debatable factor. The variety of superb ingredients available today makes it possible for the homebrewer to make beers that capitalize on centuries of experience in the malting arts. Economy may or may not be a factor. The commercially available malted grains are pricey if you go that route. You can buy fifty or a hundred pounds of barley or wheat for a few bucks and malt your own grain. Your malt may not measure up to the commercial product, but then again it may surpass it. Personal pride and satisfaction are probably the main reasons anyone brews with grain malts. I know that when I grew my own barley, malted it and made my own beer out of it, (some was damned good beer) I got a deep personal satisfaction out of it. Regardless of reasons, if you want to brew beer from grain malts, these recipes and instructions will get you started and a few tricks thrown in will make it easier.

Lager - Basic Recipe

10	Lb.	Light or pale malted barley
3	Oz.	Hops

| 5 | Gal. | Water |
| 1 | Pkt. | Beer yeast |

This is like making tea from grain malts. We want to extract the good stuff from the grain, convert it to sugar, then purify and flavor it with hops by boiling. The resultant wort or raw beer is what we'll add the yeast to in order to turn it into good beer.

STEP 1.
Gristing

Crack all the grain malt with a rolling pin. Your malted grain is now called grist.

STEP 2. & 3.

Conversion (mashing) and extraction (sparging) we first want to infuse the grain with hot water to dissolve the malt sugar and some of the starch. Then, by keeping the mixture hot for some hours, we want to let the enzymes in the malt convert the maximum starch to sugar. There are a horrendous number of ways advocated and proven to accomplish the conversion and extraction of the essence of malt. We're going to throw the book away and cheat.

Cheating on Malt Grain Beers

You will need an insulated beverage cooler of at least five gallon capacity and a cloth bag for the cracked grain malt. Put the bag of cracked malt in the insulated drink container and pour up to five gallons of 175º F

boiling water in it, then put the lid on. When this mash finally cools down, you will have converted most of the good stuff into malt sugar. Drain the wort and bring it up to five gallons by pouring boiled water over the grain bag to extract all the good stuff.

Using the insulated beverage container to keep the mash hot for several hours is a real shortcut over conventional methods of heating the mash in steps. The mash will tend to settle and cake up, blocking the drain on the containers. The cloth bag works as a big tea bag, but you need a false bottom in the container so the drain isn't blocked. A large colander or improvised strainer that keeps the mash bag above the drain hole is all you need. Don't stir the mash because the grain husks form a natural filter that lets mostly soluble sugars leach out rather than undissolved starches. It's best to let the mash steep overnight in the insulated container, then after you drain the extracted wort slowly dribble about a gallon or more of hot water through the grain to flush out the residual sugars. This is called sparging in brewer talk. If you end up with more than 5 gallons, no problem, just boil it down in the next step.

Note: Use 170º F water when you pour it on the grain. The temperature will drop to around 150º F as it heats the grain and container.

STEP 4.
Boiling and Hopping

By bringing the wort and the bag of boiling hops to a boil and holding them at a rolling

Bootlegging during Prohibition was so rampant in one northern city that the spent mash from the many stills and illicit breweries clogged the sewage system.

boil for at least a half-hour, you'll accomplish several things. The wort will be sterilized and become infused with the hops essence. Proteins and other suspended solids will coagulate, curdle or in simple terms, thicken, so they will settle out during fermentation. The hops will aid in settling out some of the organic material due to its astringent properties and impart its flavoring and preservative properties. India-style ales evolved because British Red Coat troops demanded beer and more hops were required to preserve their beer shipped via sailing ship throughout England's vast empire.

STEP 5.
Cooling/Pitching the Yeast

At this stage, the wort is very vulnerable to contamination, so you want to keep it covered. Cool it quickly and get a vigorous yeast culture started in it as quickly as you can. Put the pot of hot wort in a bath or laundry tub and fill the tub with the coldest water you can manage. Dumping some ice in the tub will speed the cooling a lot. When the wort is cooled down to about body temperature, pour it into the primary fermenter, add the yeast and cover or seal the fermenter. It's a good idea to always hold back part of your yeast culture in case you misjudge and kill the yeast by adding it to the wort when it's still too hot. If you keep a reserve you have a second shot at restarting a vigorous ferment if something goes wrong, e.g., a dead, stuck or vinegar bug contaminated ferment.

STEP 6.
Fermentation and Clarification

The feast and famine method (page 31) of fermentation is hard to apply when you're extracting your own malt because you're pressed to get it all done, sterilized and fermenting before vinegar bacteria develops. Dropping in a large vigorous yeast starter at the beginning is the best way to attack the starch you may have in your wort. A handful of beech or hazelnut wood chips sterilized with a campden tablet and added to the wort is a traditional method of clarifying beer. Adding one half ounce of dissolved unflavored gelatin when the fermentation is dying down is a simple method of clarifying without using exotic additives. Remember that your homebrew will also clarify as it ages in the bottle.

STEP 7.
Priming and Bottling

After going through the work of making an all grain malt beer, you may be reluctant to defile your noble beer with cane priming sugar. Compromise, use corn sugar that is the same type of sugar you extracted from the grain and prime the wort with ¼ cup per gallon dissolved in boiled water. Krausening, using sweet wort from a new batch of beer, is very tricky and a mistake at this stage. It can give you a flat under carbonated beer or explosions and geysers. The next batch you make, maybe you should invest in a hydrometer and put some science in your beer.

So long Cheechako, you'll have to paddle your own canoe from here. You should now know enough to build your own beer recipes from scratch. No more painting by numbers, you can create your own masterpieces (recipes.) Just remember that 8 to 16 pounds of malted grain of various colors and you can make anything from light pilsners to heavy bocks. If you want to get fancy in mashing, start out at 140º F and increase mash temperature gradually over 3 hours to 170º F. If you really want to get exotic, some-day try a batch of kriek. That's Belgian fruit-flavored beer. Just add a quart of cherries, raspberries, salmon berries or raisins to the wort with the yeast. Some like it. Most don't.

I'm gonna shove ya into the current now. Good luck! Paddle like hell and I almost for-got! *LOOK OUT FOR THE RAPIDS!* But for now, just enjoy the art.

Other Beers

Chicha – Corn Beer

Several forms of corn beer have been brewed in Central and South America for centuries. The Incas and even earlier cultures brewed a variety of beverages from salivated roots and grains. By salivated, we mean the ingredi-ents were chewed and the saliva provided enzymes and bacteria to begin the conver-sion of starches.

Happily, they also used a more appetiz-ing method, utilizing malted corn to make Chicha or "spitless" beer. This beverage was flavored with various spice, herbs and fruits. In some regions Chicha is still made as the beverage of local preference. It's drunk after a few days fermentation in what we'd con-sider the murky wort stage. The local variet-ies of corn used yield brews of various colors to include red and blue.

Modern homebrewers and commercial brewers often use flaked maize (corn) as an adjunct or additional ingredient in beer mak-ing, but this is merely corn that has been steamed, rolled and dried. If you want to try your hand at Chicha, you're probably going to have to malt your own corn. Here are a few tips to malting corn that will get

you off to a good start.

First, as always don't use any chemically treated seed corn in brewing. The type of corn you use is important. The colored In-dian or ornamental corn is the stuff used by the Incas. It malts beautifully, but if you use purple corn, you get purple beer. Plain yel-low, uncracked corn as used for feeding live stock is the best all round choice, but if you can't get it, popcorn will do.

You have to soak corn longer than wheat or barley to get good germination. Soak it at least four days, popcorn, six, then keep it moist while it's sprouting. When the corn sprout is about 1-1/2 inches long, it is fully modified. Taste it. It will be extremely sweet.

Dried corn, either before or after malt-ing is miserable stuff to grind, about like try-ing to grind marbles. Use the old moonshiner's trick and grind your sprouted corn before you dry it, when it's soft. This will give you an intensely sweet flour or meal, high in enzymes. You can if you like, use flaked corn or corn meal as an adjunct and mash it together. If you do so, mix the meal with cold water before you add it to the hot wort to keep it from forming lumps.

Chicha #1 (Corn Beer)

1-¼	Gal. (5 qt.)	Water
1	Lb.	Ground malted corn, any variety
1	Lb.	Brown sugar
¼	Cup	Yeast starter culture, ale or lager yeast
1-2	Tsp. total	Your choice of any of the following spices, fennel mint, mace, anise, cilantro, clove, All Spice, cin-namon, coriander

or orange peel. (If none of the ice creamy flavors appeal to you for a beer, I can only say that I concur.)

While we should pity the poor Incas because they didn't have hops, I question whether they could have had some of the above spices before the arrival of the Europeans. I suspect those that advocate some of this stuff are of the same type that like pineapple pizza. In the interests of authenticity, we'll not use hops. In the interests of drinkability, I'll use caraway seed. The Sun God forgives me, I am sure.

Mix the corn in one gallon of cold water, then heat gradually to 160° F. Don't boil it! Try to hold the temperature at 160° F for one hour. This should complete the conversion of the malted corn. Strain this mixture through a cheesecloth or muslin strainer into a larger pot. Return the grain to the initial pot and add one more quart of water and heat to 160° F again. Strain this fluid into the larger pot also, and discard the spent grain. This is called sparging to extract the last of the grain sugar and flavor.

Your large pot should now contain 1 gallon of wort, 1 quart being boiled off or discarded with the mash. Now combine the wort and brown sugar, bringing them to a boil for about thirty minutes, the flavorings of your choice toward the end of the boil. It's best to put the spices in a small cloth bag with a couple with a couple of glass marbles to make them easy to remove. Pour this wort into your primary fermenter and add the yeast when it's cool.

Chicha is normally drunk after five or six days while it is still fermenting and murky. You can however, rack, fine, bottle and prime it like conventional beer.

Corn Beer #2

This is a hopped beer similar to a wheat beer, in that the corn is malted and used in conjunction with barley malt to achieve complete conversion, rather than using corn (or other grain) merely as an adjunct.

4	Lb.	Malted and ground corn
5	Lb.	Pale malted barley, cracked
2-½	Oz.	Hallertau Hops
1	Pkt.	Lager yeast
5	Gal.	Water
1-¼	Cup	Priming sugar

In a grain bag, mash the barley and corn at 155° F and hold for 1-½ hours. Corn converts at a slightly higher temperature than barley (155° F) Drain the wort into your boiling kettle and sparge the grain with 160° F water to make up to five gallons of wort.

Boil the wort for 1 hour with 2 ounces of hops, adding the remaining ½ ounce during the last ten minutes. Transfer to a primary fermenter and add yeast when cool. Proceed with fermentation, racking, fining, priming and bottling as with other beers.

Fruit Beers

There are old traditional beers that incorporate fruits and berries and modern specialty beers that do so too. The older ones, traditionally made in Belgium and France, use raspberries and cherries as ingredients and in olden days at least, were fermented in open vats, relying on airborne yeast. Called kriek, framboise and lambic, they are tart tasting due to both the fruit and the wild yeast cultures used.

The present day specialty brewers seem to hold nothing sacred and are incorporating nontraditional fruits which some may find appealing, others and myself included, appalling. If you want to be a trailblazer, try things like apricots, currants, salmonberries, grapes and raisins. If you are weird enough to experiment with things like bananas and strawberries, do, but please, I beg you, don't tell me about it. Assuming you'll want to do this on an experimental basis, first get a batch of conventional beer started, using either ale or lager yeast.

Set up a separate secondary fermenter or two, using gallon jugs. Using campden tablets, sterilize one half pound of fruit or berries per gallon of experimental fruit beer, add to fermenters, top off with the fermenting wort and install fermentation lock(s.) Rack, fine, and bottle as with any beer, to include priming.

Since this will be a trailblazing experiment, you will definitely want to keep good records on this one. Also, since these are sort of a crossbreed between beers and wines and the European varieties often use several varieties of yeast, you may want to try a little crossbreeding too. If you do, add a bit of wine yeast when you mix the wort and fruit. You may or may not like the result, but it will be unique.

Fish Story

An Alaskan fisherman was bragging about Alaskan fishing to a Texan fisherman. When the Texan interrupted him with "What size do they get to?"

About 6-7 inches was the reply. "Hell," laughed the Texan, "We throw 'em back longer than that!" The Alaskan grinned and said, "Whadda ya mean, long? We only measure between the eyes."

Hot Pepper Beers

The hot pepper that makes one person wildly enthusiastic may make another just plain wild. Some people swear by these beers, others just swear profusely when they try them.

You build these beers like an anarchist builds bombs, gradually increasing the power until you have it just right. You should add the peppers to the brew late in the process, not cooking them, but letting them steep or marinate. The easiest way to build your recipe is to add slices of pepper (sterilized in campden solution first) to the bottles in varying amounts to determine the strength you like, then work up a bulk recipe for the next batch.

Actually, I've had 100% rave reviews on all of my pepper beers and this includes yanking the caps off a poor batch, dropping in some peppers and recapping the stuff. Sweet pepper or "Debil" peppers, all the same. A ½ inch slice of a pepper as thick as a wiener is a good start per 12 oz. bottle. All go good with pizza. Just like smoked beers or bringing in artillery fire, do a test shot, then adjust.

Happy Jalepeño!

Chapter Four

Homemade "Poreboy" Equipment
and Making Malt

In This Chapter

➤ Practical Application (making your own equipment) Draft Keg, Fermentation Locks

➤ Making Your Own Scales

➤ Making Your Own Malt

➤ Making Your Own Malt Factory

➤ US Proof Spirit and Hydrometer Measurement

For those of us who are "pore-to-do," rather than "well-to-do," or live in the bush. This chapter is all "can-do." Cheap!

"Pore Boy" Equipment (Making Your Own)

After all the distilling and bootlegging lore, war stories and caveman tales, you're probably beginning to feel like an anarchist or a "Thunder Road" whiskey running rebel. That has not been my intent, nor is it a result, if you've read this far. To the contrary, if you were a complete novice at page one, you should have progressed from the egg, to the flight feathers stage in the arts of wine making and beer brewing. You now know the principles and theory. Flap your wings and crow if you like. The next step is to throw your fuzzy little body off the limb of theory into the winds of practical application. Follow me and flap like crazy! Caw! Caw!

Practical application entails actually doing, or making something. Now whether we're building a chicken coop, making a cake or whatever, we upright walking critters use tools. I've only touched briefly on some of these tools and I promised to teach you how to make some of them. But there is a real pitfall in regard to paraphernalia and sophisticated gadgets, because you really don't need most of it. I've made good beer and wine for years in blissful ignorance with little more than a siphoning hose and a bottle capper. As I read more books and got more scientific, it was less and less fun, and it seemed like the quality of my product went downhill too With this in mind, let's start cobbling up some basic equipment and looking at some shortcuts.

A starter kit of basic beer and wine making equipment will run from $50 to $200 from the brewing supply companies. This "pore boy" chapter on making your own equipment is not intended to take business

Food Grade Plastic Container

Plastic Food Grade Bucket From a Restaurant Makes an Ideal Fermenter

away from the supply firms, which sell a wonderful array of excellent equipment and ingredients. Instead, this chapter is written for the aspiring brewer or wine maker who may never get started because of the initial expense or because they live in a remote area and neither the equipment, nor the advice to get them started on a lifelong hobby is available.

If you try it and like it, you'll start shopping for equipment at your local supplier or via the many mail-order catalogs. If you have the urge, but never get started, everybody loses. This section will get you off to a good start for about ten bucks, less if you're a good scrounger. So, let's get started.

Fermentation Vessels

Carboys and crocks aren't what they're cracked up to be. They are heavy, clumsy, fragile and expensive. A carboy will set you back about twenty bucks; crocks are even more expensive. They are outmoded. Don't mess with them. The *food grade* plastic buckets (5-7 gal.) that restaurants etc. get pickles and stuff in makes excellent fermentation vessels. It's child's play to fit a fermentation lock to the snap on lids. Even better yet are the 5-gal. Plastic jugs which the same folks get their cooking oil in. These jugs are light, unbreakable, have a handle, spout and large screw cap. Again, they're easy to fit a fermentation lock to or just put a disposable latex glove (surgical gloves) over the spout secured with a rubber band.

Best of all, both these containers are cheap to free! I've never paid more than 50¢ a piece for them. Remember; use only food grade plastic containers, no old paint or chemical containers! One exception to this is the 30-gal. Chlorine bleach container Laundromats use. With the tops cut out and well rinsed, these are just right for making a big batch for the keg you're going to rig up; Right? The food grade plastic buckets and cooking oil containers, you can get from restaurants for little or nothing are actually better fermentation vessels.

Fermentation Locks

Next, and undoubtedly man's most important invention in producing quality fermented beverages, is the fermentation lock. An airtight cover with some means of pressure relief is required on large mouthed bulk fermenting vessels. A plastic sheet secured

Pruno

If you choose to practice any of the distilling lore I cover, you may need this one because it's commonly used in prisons to make "Pruno," or clandestine hooch in jail. A disposable latex glove slipped over a milk carton and secured with a rubber band is a very effective fermentation lock. When I use them, I usually make a few pinholes in them. You can Scotch tape a few fingers down if you wish to make a political statement.

Pill Bottle Deluxe

Drill a hole in the fermenter lid and bottom of a plastic pill or spice bottle, then press a plastic straw into holes. Drill a tiny hole in the bottle lid for a vent. (A 15/64" or ¼" drill bit makes a perfect press-fit for most straws.) Use a plastic bottle cap on the top of the straw for a bubbler valve when bottle is partially filled with water. This works slick for converting plastic jugs into fermenters for small batches of wine or beer. So inexpensive! So easy!

Penny Bubbler

"Penny Bubbler" made from plastic straw and a balloon with a few drops of water in the bottom, a couple of pinholes in top secured with a rubber band. Drill ¼" hole through a plastic lid. A "Penny Bubbler" on juice jug, it's all you need to get started. It's especially good for small amounts, such as a gallon of your favorite wine.

The Bubbler

Just drop the end of the hose in the bottle of water. If I explain this one, I'll be insulting you.

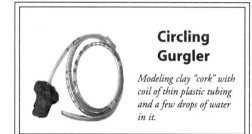

Circling Gurgler

Modeling clay "cork" with coil of thin plastic tubing and a few drops of water in it.

with an elastic band works very well for the "bonfire, or vigorous primary fermentation stage. As things settle down, your fermenting beer or wine becomes vulnerable to picking up bad tastes from all the dead yeast. Also, as the generation of a positive flow of protective CO_2 gas decreases, it's increasingly vulnerable to

Typical Store-bought Fermentation Lock

air and airborne organisms and the yeast gets weak too. Hence, the need for some kind of fermentation lock, all of which work as a snorkel in reverse, letting the yeast exhale CO_2, but not inhale air and bugs. We cover making a variety of fermentation locks in the Pore Boy chapter, but a common plastic trash bag is hard to beat for containers like crocks or open barrels.

There are a number of fermentation locks on the market, all of which work well and require tight fitting corks. Buy them if you like and as a convict said to his buddy walking the last mile, "More power to ya, Joe!" Joe didn't need that and you don't ever need to buy another fermentation lock. With a couple of feet of clear plastic tubing, some modeling clay and a bit of plastic wrap, some plastic straws and a few penny balloons, you can tailor make fermentation locks for years for pennies.

Referring to the photos, get out your modeling clay to make a cork or plug for your fermenting vessel. Use the plastic wrap to make a skin over a glob of modeling clay and then press it into the mouth of your fermenter. Next, poke a hole through the plug and press-fit the end of your fermentation lock through it. The simplest method is to just use a length of plastic tubing and immerse the other end in a container of water. This simple bubbler works well on large containers. A smaller version made out of a flexible straw and a rubber balloon is handier for smaller fermenting containers such as milk jugs.

A disposable latex glove like doctors use makes a good fermentation lock on a necked container such as a carboy or jug. Just slip the glove over the neck after you add your yeast. You may want to secure it with some rubber bands to keep it from blowing off during the initial vigorous ferment, but not too tight. Excess CO_2 forces it way out the wrist.

The Field Expedient Capper

Once you use this one you'll detest it! But if you are "pore-to-do," live in the bush and have broken your capper or only want to try

Metal Clamp

your hand at a few bottles of birch sap or salmonberry wine, this will get you by.

There's nothing to making this. It is just a common screw adjustable hose clamp, as used on a car heater hose. An unused crown cap is about 1-¼ inches in diameter; after it's crimped over the lip of a bottle, about 1 inch. You calibrate this precision instrument by tightening it on a used cap until it is a tight slip fit. Next you set a filled bottle on a padded surface (like old newspapers) place a new cap on the mouth of the bottle and with a soft piece of wood judiciously tap the hose clamp down over the cap, crimping or squeezing it on to the bottle.

After you're all done, it's a good idea to go over all the bottles a second time, giving each cap an extra squeeze by giving the screw a little twist. This is a tedious process and once you use it, you'll vow to get a "real" capper at first chance; crude as hell, but it works.

Making Your Own "Pore Boy" Capper
No Engineers Need Apply
(Plans on Pages 83-84)

A good capper is one of the most indispensable pieces of equipment and also one of the most expensive for the novice to acquire. I, being one of the worst carpenters that ever bent a nail, built this one for $2.11, plus some scrap lumber and a few nuts, bolts, screws and nails I had laying around. If you too are a maladroit rejoice! At last, here is a project suited for your talents because this gizmo operates on slop; if it doesn't wobble, it doesn't work. The guts and main cost of this is for a 1" copper pipe coupling, the solder on type, and about 4" of copper pipe. I used a 1"x ½" reducing coupling and about 4" of ½" I.D. pipe or tubing. The 1" I.D. (internal diameter) copper pipe has an O.D. (outer diameter) of 1-¹/₈", exactly the size of a crown cap when crimped on a bottle. The large end of the coupling will become the head of your capper. In the small end, you'll solder the short piece of ½" I.D. pipe, which

Pore Boy Homemade Bottle Capper

serves as the drive shaft.

You can cap a bottle just by tapping the fitting over the cap and bottle mouth, but it will be hard to extract the capped bottle. Fittings by different manufacturers will vary in shape, but all will be too deep and the capped bottle will tend to stick, so you'll have to hack, grind or file it back so it's just deep enough to fully seat the cap on the bottle. Don't do the final filing until you have the whole capper assembled, then file and test.

The rest of this device is cobbled together out of lumber scraps and the illustrations show how simple it is to build. I've used 1"x4" and 2'x4' scraps in building these with satisfactory results. There is enough material in an old wooden pallet to make a capper with wood to spare. In the interests of simplicity and strength, we'll use only 2"x4" scraps in this one. Obviously, if you can get your hands on hardwood like oak or maple, the end result will be stronger and more durable, but it's not necessary. There are no angles, bevels or fancy cuts to make, only

Unassembled Rapper Capper

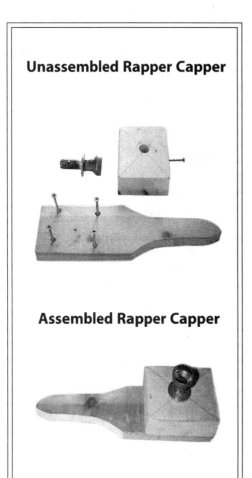

Assembled Rapper Capper

This capper was invented by an ape and not a particularly bright ape at that. It is club powered. You just hit it with a chunk of wood to seat the cap on the bottle. Materials cost came to a staggering $1.47. It's just a wooden paddle with a homemade capper head mounted in it (capper head as for the "Pore Boy" capper.) Cut and drill a square chunk of 2x4 to accept the metal head of the capper head shown on page 10, then run a screw into the side to retain the head. Whittle out a suitable handle and screw it on.

This capper is more fun to make than it is to use, unless you're an aborigine at heart, but it will do everything the $50.00 chrome plated model will do and is ideal for getting you started. If you only plan on making a gallon or two of wine or beer at a time, this and a gross of caps ($2.00) could last you for years.

Pore Boy Capper Head Parts and Assembly

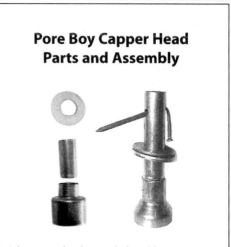

The capper head is made by soldering a 1x½" coupling to a short piece of ½" copper tubing. I included a flat washer on the shoulder to distribute the impact when using it and lessen the likelihood of splitting the wooden block. As shown in the illustration, couplings from different manufacturers have different contours, so you have to file them back so they're just deep enough to seat the cap on the bottle.

straight cuts. You'll end up with 11 pieces of 2"x4", the longest pieces being 26" long. Next, you'll have to drill holes for six ¼" carriage bolts and one bigger hole ½"+ for the capper shaft. You'll also have to plug in 14, 2-½" sheetrock or wood screws which should be drilled to avoid splitting the wood. Now let's build it.

In brief, it consists of a wooden base, a mast of sufficient height to handle even the tallest European bottles, a two-piece lever mechanism, and a cam with the capper head in it. The capper head and shaft must have some slop, wobble, or play built into it. This is necessary because the cam moves in a slight arc, rather than straight up and down. If it's too rigid, the capper meets the bottle at an angle and binds, a little play lets it center and shift and come down over the bottle and cap straight. An engineer could express this more accurately, but I am not an engineer. If you are an engineer, you've probably already noted there is no way to adjust this marvelous machine for bottles of different height. No problem. When you get done making it, you whack off a couple of blocks of scrap wood to put under bottles of different height. If the capper can't come to the bottle, the bottle must come to the capper.

Even if you flunked shop class four years in a row, you can build it in an evening. Final touches: After you get your creation working, tear it all apart and reassemble it using good ol' carpenter's glue. This will make it hell for stout, if not much for pretty. At the same time lubricate all bearing surfaces and bolts by rubbing them with a dry cake of soap. Reassemble and slather on some varnish. A dedication or christening ceremony with friends, family, news media and lots of homebrew is in order.

Holes to be Drilled for "Pore boy" Capper Parts

1. Upper lever/handle – Must have matching ¼ inch bolt holes 4-¾ inches apart. Drill the first hole 1-½ inches from the board ends and then the second holes 4-¾ inches above the first.

2. Cam sides need two matching ¼ inch bolt holes, 1-¼ inches and 4 inches from the top ends. The cam bottom will be attached to the bottom ends with 2-½ inch screws.

3. Again, upper lever/handle – Must have matching ¼ inch bolt holes 4-¾ inches apart. Drill the first hole 1-½ inches from the board ends and then the second holes 4-¾ inches above the first.

"Poreboy" Scales

4. Cam bottom must have ½ inch hole through the center to accept the metal capper shaft. Need to rasp it larger until the shaft is a loose fit with a bit of wobble.

5. Mast – Top of mast requires two matching ¼ inch holes, 2 inches and 5 inches from the top of the mast, centered.

Homemade "Pore Boy" Scales

Accuracy in measuring ingredients is as important as record keeping if you are to improve your skills and reproduce your best beers and wines. Liquid measure is no problem, but weighing ingredients is critical to quality control and a good set of scales can be expensive. A simple set of scales can be cobbled up in no time and at little cost. These will be surprisingly accurate and will do wonders for your self-confidence. They are similar to the ones peddlers used to use to weigh produce. The illustration that follows is pretty self-explanatory, but I'll talk you through making them. You do not have to use a toilet seat for the base, but I think it adds class.

We'll start with a balance bar (straight stick) about two feet long and screw a cup hook in the exact middle to suspend this device from. Next, screw a cup hook into each end to suspend your weights and ingredients from. Install strings on two identical coffee cans to suspend them from the cup hooks. Attach a common string level like carpenters use to the middle of the balance bar with rubber bands. Hang your new scales and adjust them until the bubble on the level is centered. If the cans are not in balance, attach split shot or similar weights to the string until they ride level. Place the desired weight in canned goods in one coffee can and add ingredients like malt or sugar to the other until they balance. You now have a working set of scales, but rather than go scrounging for canned goods every time, you need to weigh something, you should make a set of counterweights.

You can make your counterweights out of anything, but large washers are hard to beat. Buy a couple of pounds of washers and count them to determine how many to the pound. Tape and mark your washers in packets of varying weights, e.g., 1 oz., 4 oz., and 1 lb. If you wish you can verify these weights on your local grocery's scales.

The illustration shows this scale with a wooden base and inverted "L" suspension arm, but you don't really need them. You can just hang this rig from any convenient nail on a length of string. If you play with these scales, you'll be surprised at how accurate they are. You might even want to make a smaller set for weighing hops in fractions of ounces.

Bottle Cleaning

The bane of all homebrewing is bottles. Gathering them, cleaning them and the last minute rush to get everything sterilized are real chores. If you'll dedicate one new, clean 30-gallon plastic garbage can, half filled with a chlorine bleach solution as a bottle collection receptacle, you'll save an enormous amount of time and labor. This solution soaks off labels, kills and loosens yeast and mold in the bottles and kills the bugs in them. When time permits, inspect the bottles and stroke the insides with a bottle brush where necessary. Store your cleaned bottles in sealed plastic garbage bags until bottling day rolls around. Then run the bottles through the dishwasher. As long as you've soaked the labels off, brushed the deposits out of the inside of the bottle and shaken out the big objects, like dead mice, you'll be ready to bottle in the time it takes your dishwasher to run full-cycle.

Tip: A short piece of brass chain such as one from a bathtub stopper shaken in a grungy bottle with bleach solution will clean the worst bottles in seconds, better than brushing.

Don't laugh about the dead mice. It really happens! My old and dear Uncle Bill once found a dead mouse in a half-finished bottle of homebrew. He failed to see the humor in it and has been real particular about "full-bodied" homebrew ever since. Bill was the only one "lucky" enough to get a mouse. All of our n'er do well friends and relatives present were very sympathetic. When Bill started gagging and we all saw the mouse in the bottle, everybody joined him in the rush for the back porch. We refer to the event as The Great Upchucking. We damn near had to call the Coast Guard. Mice, frogs, cockroaches, cigarette butts and other nasty stuff finds its way into bottles, so give each one a visual inspection when you take them out of the dishwasher.

Components of Poreboy Capper

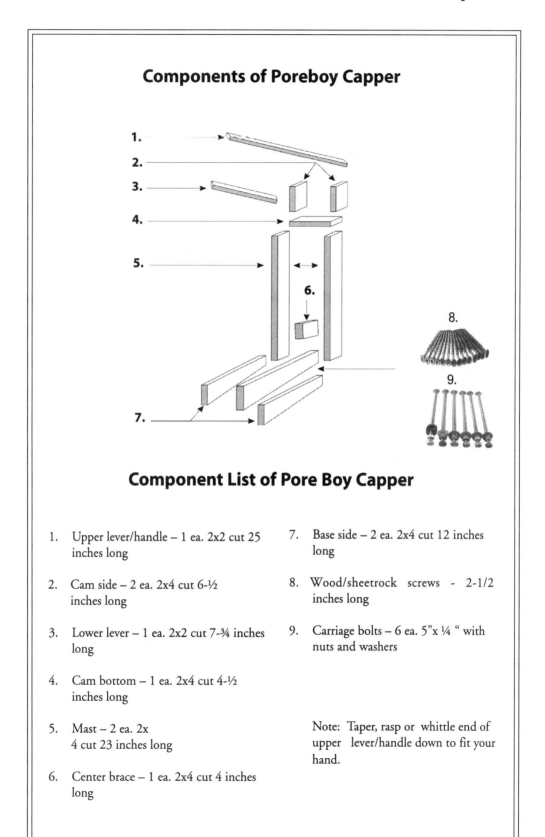

Component List of Pore Boy Capper

1. Upper lever/handle – 1 ea. 2x2 cut 25 inches long

2. Cam side – 2 ea. 2x4 cut 6-½ inches long

3. Lower lever – 1 ea. 2x2 cut 7-¾ inches long

4. Cam bottom – 1 ea. 2x4 cut 4-½ inches long

5. Mast – 2 ea. 2x 4 cut 23 inches long

6. Center brace – 1 ea. 2x4 cut 4 inches long

7. Base side – 2 ea. 2x4 cut 12 inches long

8. Wood/sheetrock screws - 2-1/2 inches long

9. Carriage bolts – 6 ea. 5"x ¼ " with nuts and washers

Note: Taper, rasp or whittle end of upper lever/handle down to fit your hand.

Poreboy Capper Parts

(Specifications & Measurements)

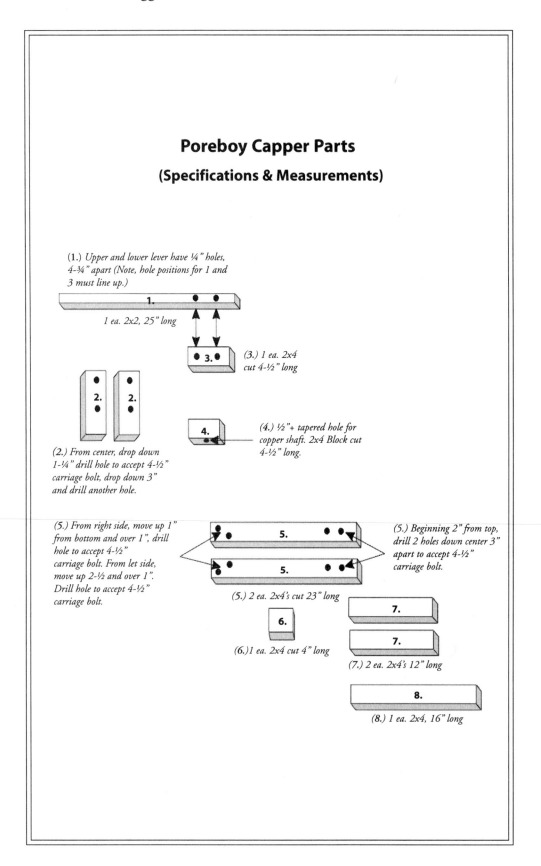

(1.) Upper and lower lever have ¼" holes, 4-¾" apart (Note, hole positions for 1 and 3 must line up.)

1.

1 ea. 2x2, 25" long

3.

(3.) 1 ea. 2x4 cut 4-½" long

2. **2.**

(2.) From center, drop down 1-¼" drill hole to accept 4-½" carriage bolt, drop down 3" and drill another hole.

4.

(4.) ½"+ tapered hole for copper shaft. 2x4 Block cut 4-½" long.

(5.) From right side, move up 1" from bottom and over 1", drill hole to accept 4-½" carriage bolt. From let side, move up 2-½ and over 1". Drill hole to accept 4-½" carriage bolt.

5.

5.

(5.) Beginning 2" from top, drill 2 holes down center 3" apart to accept 4-½" carriage bolt.

(5.) 2 ea. 2x4's cut 23" long

6.

(6.)1 ea. 2x4 cut 4" long

7.

7.

(7.) 2 ea. 2x4's 12" long

8.

(8.) 1 ea. 2x4, 16" long

Grain and Hops Bags

Not one, but several cloth bags in different sizes should be included in your arsenal of brewing equipment. Most commercially made bags are made of nylon and called juice bags, sparging bags and hops bags.

They eliminate a lot of work and frustration, help you make a cleaner product and in the case of wines, can double your production. The store bought ones are nice, but you can make about a dozen out of muslin for the same price and just run them through the clothes washer. I would advise laundering them separately from your clothing as some of the malts and ingredients are very dark brown in color and will turn your whites a dingy beige color, even with bleach. When used as a juice bag, you mash your fruit and berries in them, then squeeze the juice out and/or soak the pulp to extract the good stuff.

Remember, you never get all the good stuff the first time around, so you can make a second batch of good wine out of the bag of pulp by adding some sugar to replace what you've extracted and making what are called second wines. Sparging is brewer talk for running hot water through malted grains to dissolve and extract the sugars such as a big tea bag. A hops bag is the same thing only smaller, just big enough to hold a cup or so of hops and a few glass marbles to make it sink into the hot wort. All these bags contain the solids in the various ingredients, so you're working with an easy to clarify fluid rather than a fermenting mush or porridge.

Making Your Own Malt

Malting your own grain is a natural and simple process. Think of malting as sprouting. If you've ever sprouted seeds like alfalfa, radishes or beans for salads or for oriental cooking, you're well on the way toward making your own malt.

Remember the old moonshiner's trick I told you about where they buried a sack of corn in a manure pile to sprout it. They merely washed the sprouted kernels and broke the sprouts off to arrest growth and often used it in their mash without even roasting or grinding it. That's malting at its simplest, but being a natural process, it's also imprecise. The old moonshiners didn't care. They had corn and grain by the ton, so if a few percent of the starch was not converted, it was no big deal. If there was a starch haze in the wash, no matter either, because distilling would separate it from the whiskey.

If you are the President of Bladderwash Breweries, Inc., however, every percentage point of starch conversion represents profit or loss and a haze in your beer can effect sales. Or worse yet, it could require expensive clarifying chemicals to make the pale, thin, clear brew that made "Burpo" beer heard throughout the land. Forgive me, E.J. Bladderwash, I only used your company to illustrate why commercial breweries strive for maximum conversion in making oceans of cheap beer. You, the homebrewer will strive for quality in your beer, but without an elaborate laboratory and a stable of pedigreed scientists, quality control in malting may seem beyond your capabilities. But there are some old tricks to the malters art that will lend precision to your work and eliminate a lot of guesswork. Let's start with a batch of barley.

First, you'll need whole barley grain, not seed. If you can get your hands on specially bred malting barley, so much the better. The grains should be plump and well filled. *Do not use treated seed barley*. Most commercial seed of all types is treated with chemicals, to deter mold and bugs from deteriorating the seed. Pesticides and fungicides and other poisons have no place in my beer and I'm sure you feel the same.

Tip: You may want to save a few pounds of barley to try growing your own. It's very satisfying to make a batch of grew it myself beer and it's the best way you can be sure you're using organically grown grain. Plant it just like grass seed. A plot the size of a pool table should yield enough for a small batch of beer. If your thumb is greener than mine, you might want to try your hand at growing a few hops vines. Totally homegrown beer, sounds good!

Next, rinse your grain in cool water several times, then let it soak in water overnight. This will help in removing any debris like dead grasshoppers and flushing off any pesticides that might have drifted over from neighboring fields when crops were sprayed. I recently read of a case in which a large field was sprayed with an extremely potent new pesticide and the wind borne contamination encompassed several hundred square miles.

That's scary and ample reason to rinse any whole grains used in brewing thoroughly. It makes you wonder about that half a rack of canned "Burpo" you picked up for the weekend, doesn't it? The soaking begins the growth process and you're on your way to becoming a malter. You should soak the grain for at least two days at between 66° F and 85° F, changing the water each day to keep it from souring. Some advocate soaking for as long as six days, but you risk getting a mash of rotten, sour grain if you overdo the soaking.

The sprouting is a lot like gardening.

You nurture the sprouting seeds until they reach their peak "ripeness" and then harvest them by drying to arrest their growth. "Ripeness" in this case, means the optimum point where most of the starch has been converted or modified in malter's jargon to sugar. The sprout has not grown enough to use up all the residual enzymes that will enable you to modify all the remaining starch and some adjuncts when you go through the mashing and cooking steps.

The now germinating grain should be spread on trays, turned gently daily and kept moist, but not dripping wet. The damp grain should not be layered over an inch and a half deep, because it will generate heat and if it's layered too deep, the grains in the center will sprout too quickly. You want to strive for uniformity in this sprouting process, so all the grains reach the ideal state of modification at the same time. I have malted barley in the bathtub and that works quite well, but since the process can take as long as twelve days, the family with only one bath can get a little gamey before the malt is done.

If you intend to malt in quantity, you might want to cobble up some better equipment. I converted an old refrigerator into a malter and dryer by installing a hotplate and table fan in the bottom, vented it at the top and bottom and made trays out of wood and nylon screen material. It works great and leaves the bathtub free. The screen trays lined with damp paper towels are perfect for sprouting the grain and when it's ready for drying, I just turn the hotplate and fan on. It makes about thirty pounds of pale malt overnight. It's really inexpensive and simple to make.

In two or three days, the damp grain will begin to sprout rootlets. If you nibble on a few grains, you'll find that they are changing from a hard rocklike consistency, to a softer chewable form and the inside will begin to look like flour and taste sweet. Now you need to check a few grains everyday by peeling the husk off and checking the growth of the shoots or acrospire. This is an old-time malter's trick to determine when the malt is fully modified. When the shoot or acrospire inside the husk is two-thirds the length of the grain, it is fully modified. This will give you the optimum of both malt sugar and residual enzymes. Under modified malts are used in some beers to give a fuller body. Over modified malts will produce a more haze free wort, but the total sugar/enzyme yield is reduced because the little barley plant is eating up all the good stuff and before long, your barley tray will turn into a field of grass.

The next old malter's trick I call the sinkers and floaters test. The inside of the barley seed is modified or converted from one end to the other and it becomes porous and less dense as the process takes place. Carefully dry a sample of the sprouting grain at no more than 120° F. A hot air duct, hairdryer or similar device will do. The grains should be dried until the husk will crack. Count out thirty or forty grains and put them in a bowl of water after rubbing the roots and shoots off. The fully malted grains will float level like boats, unmalted grains will sink. Partially malted grains will float end up like fishing bobbers.

Now count your sinkers, floaters and bobbers; and you'll have a mathematical analysis of the status of your malting project almost as good as any laboratory could give you. Keep malting and testing until all the seeds float like boats.

The next step in making malt is probably the most difficult because of temperature control. The basic building block of all

beer making is pale malted barley and if you dry it above 120° F you begin toasting and caramelizing it into darker and less fermentable malt. You can get by with an oven on warm with the door open. The little countertop food dehydrators will work for

Malted Barley, roasted to various degrees, yielding from crystal to black or chocolate malt.

small amounts. If you're a reasonably innovative person, you'll come up with a way to dry, but not toast your first batch of malt.

Winnowing

With your pale malt dried, you now have a bunch of seeds and dried roots you need to separate. Rub, beat, stir or roll around in your newly malted barley until all the rootlets are broken off. Then pour it from a bucket into another container or on a tarp with either a good breeze or a fan blowing all the debris away.

Malt Roasting Temperatures

The temperature range for roasting barley malt ranges from 120° F to 180° F, sixty degrees temperature range. Within that range, there are some 600 degrees or colors of malt recognized by commercial brewers. That works out to ten types of malt per degree of temperature. Obviously, roasting time

Sprouting
Tray with
Barley

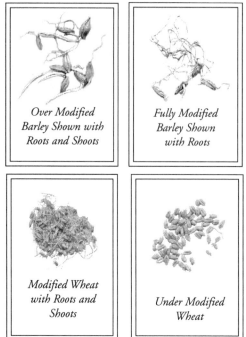

*Over Modified
Barley Shown with
Roots and Shoots*

*Fully Modified
Barley Shown
with Roots*

*Modified Wheat
with Roots and
Shoots*

*Under Modified
Wheat*

is a variable factor here, and you won't match the precision of the professional malters. But, if you record the temperature and roasting time carefully and remove a portion of your malted grain at several stages, you'll be able to produce several types of progressively darker malt from the same batch of grain. Not bad! Aye?

This enables you to make and blend your own malts for a variety of beers. If you keep good records, you'll soon be able to tailor-make your favorite beers from scratch, and inexpensively. At around 170° F to 180° F, you will make black malts. Charred malts do not ferment, but give flavor and body to stouts. At about 160° F to 140° F you'll get brown malts for dark beers. From 140° F to 120° F you'll get amber to pale malts. My last sack of barley from the local feed store set me back a whopping 16¢ a pound. With a little sprouting and roasting, I can make a 5-gallon batch of beer for under two bucks, plus the cost of hops and yeast if I don't have a starter going. That's cheap beer!

Other Tricks

We've covered cracking, grinding, mashing, sparging, boiling, hopping and fermenting earlier. There are a few more tricks or tech-niques that can make you a far more versatile brewer.

The Iodine Test

Iodine turns starch blue. At any point in your malting, mashing, boiling or fermentation, if you put a sample in a white cup and add a drop or two of medical iodine, you'll know if you have starch present if the sample turns blue. Always discard the sample because iodine will kill your yeast.

Malting Wheat

Wheat beers are expensive because barley is tough and easy to malt. Wheat isn't. Threshed barley retains its armored shell or husk. It can be shoveled around by the malter without ill effects and when it's mashed, the husks form a filter bed. The roots are tough and they are not damaged easily. Wheat is delicate and far more difficult to malt. When it's threshed, the husk comes off leaving the

Electric Coffee
"Grain" Grinder

You can grind about 10 pounds of malt in an hour with one of these. They actually grind malt a little too fine, but if you shop at "Sals" Salvation Army Thrift Store, you can be in the malt grinding business for less than the sales tax on the snob models.

Top of the Line Hand Grinding Mill

wheat berry with no husk and very delicate roots, so sprouting wheat is easily killed when handled. When you're working with tons of grain, wheat is a problem because it's so delicate. When you are homebrewing wheat berries are actually easier to malt than barley. You don't turn it. Wait until the sprout is $2/3$ the length of the seed and dry it.

Malting Tips

1. Take a small sample of store-bought malted grain, like pale malt and drop it in a glass of water. Observe the way the grains float. Most should float level, like boats with a few bobbing ends up; none should sink. Your goal should be to modify or malt your barley to get the same results with your finished product.

2. Next, take a random sample (about 5 cups) of the untreated grain you intend to malt and dump it in a flat tray such as a cookie sheet. Spread the sample around to determine if there's a lot of weed seeds, or other foreign material

that should be removed. If so, you may want to screen the weed seeds etc. out through a suitable mesh or a colander from the kitchen. This is about like gold panning. It takes a little practice to get the knack of it, but then you'll be able to clean up a couple pounds of grain in nothing flat.

3. Before you attempt to screen the grain, take a small sample (a couple of tablespoons) and dump it in a pot or large jar of cold water. Stir this sample a few times and observe the results. The well-filled fertile grains will sink to the bottom. The immature, stunted and therefore unmaltable grains will float on the surface. If you are lucky, the species of weed seeds and other debris which may be present will also float so you won't have to screen your grain, only skim it when you begin soaking it.

4. Soaking the grain is the beginning of the malting process. You will have far

better results if you start with a test batch of a couple of cups of grain, take daily samples and record the results. The goal is to soak the grain just enough to get maximum germination. If you don't soak it enough, lots of your grain may not sprout and hence, it will not malt, but remain starchy and give you a cloudy beer. Keep the grain immersed too long and it will turn sour and rot. This, being a natural process, soaking time will vary with each batch of grain. Careful observation and recording will not only give you the optimum soaking time for your grain, but will go a long way toward making you a proficient malter. Understanding under, full and over modification will enable you to tailor malts for the beer you build. Since this will be a scientific experiment, you will need some equipment. Swipe a cupcake pan from the kitchen and number the cups. You may now refer to it as your germination monitor to impress your friends.

5. As you pull your daily samples of soaked grain, you'll wrap them loosely in a damp piece of paper towel and record the date, number and ultimate results on a note card. Keep your germination monitor in a warm, dark place, i.e., a cardboard box at room temperature. As the samples begin to germinate, pull a few grains and peel off the husk to check the growth of the sprout or acrospire. Taste for sweetness and observe the transformation of hard grain into a porous flour-like consistency. When the sprout within the barley husk is $2/3$ the length of the seed, modification of starch to sugar should be complete. Wheat has

no husk so it's easier to tell.

6. After a few days the samples will be achieving nearly 100% germination so you'll now know exactly how much soaking is required for your particular grain, but continue the experiment for several more days. By this time your earliest samples will be look distinctly grassy, with roots and shoots coming out of the grains. When the first fully germinated sample starts pushing shoots out the tip of the husks, your "germination monitor" holds a wealth of knowledge, which will go a long way toward making you a proficient malter. The sprouting part of this test is now complete.

7. Now put your pan of samples in an oven at the lowest heat (about 250º F) for about 20 minutes, then turn the heat off and crack the door until it cools. You have now made a full spectrum of malt from your samples. The samples will be a mixture of under modified (under-germinated) and over-modified grain. The first sample that germinated fully will be over-modified; all of the starch has been converted to sugar, which in turn has turned to sprout and root. This type of malt will yield a clear beer, but with little body and/or enzymes left to convert additional grain in the mashing processes. Subsequent samples will decline from over-modified to the optimum fully modified down through under-modified to unmodified. You now have malted samples of your grain ranging from the good to the bad to the ugly and know exactly how to get the type of pale malt you want. Rub the roots off

each of your dried grain samples. You'll now use a medieval malters test we'll call "the sinkers, floaters and boaters" test with each sample. The modification of starch to sugar progresses from one end of the seed to the other, increasing the porosity of the grain as it goes. When dropped in a container of water, the dense unmodified seeds will sink to the bottom, fully modified seeds will float level like little boats. Under modified seeds will be heavier on one end and float end up like a fishing float or bobber. You will now know exactly how many days to allow your germinated grain to sprout to become fully modified to malt. Any additional sprouting time will yield over modified malt which will produce a clearer, more starch free wort, but sacrifices fermentable sugar which is consumed in the growth process.

8. Sit down! Class isn't over yet. Real malters don't just make pale malt. Real brewers make light beers, dark beers, stouts, bocks and bitters. Just to get your feet wet in making dark malts, start by putting your tray of samples back in the oven for 20 minutes at a time, checking the results and gradually increasing the temperature. The first change you;ll notice is the grain husks get darker, which isn't too astounding. The next change you'll notice when you crack a few grains of thouroughly modified grain is that the floury interior is changing (caramelizing) to a dark crystalline substance that looks and tastes a lot like dried molasses. Congratulations! You just made crystal malt. You can keep this process going until you have chocolate and even black malt (for stouts in small quantities) or until your wife chases you out of the kitchen.

You are now a novice malter, but one with great potential. At about 15¢ a pound, make pale malt to last you for a while, then as you want to build some different beers, toast a pound or two.

The term "Bootlegger" is ancient in origin and meant someone who conceals contraband in their boots. An old friend who worked in a prison boiler plant while a "guest" of the state, told me that the practice still florishes. He said he and his buddies would make pruno at the plant and smuggle it back to their cells by pouring it into the rubber boots they wore and walking through the security checkpoint. Not much different than drinking champagne out of a lady's slipper, I guess.

Making Your Own Malt Factory Out of an Old Refrigerator

I originally conceived of this homemade dehydrator for fruits and vegetables. This cobbled together device has proven to be one of the most versatile and satisfying inventions in a lifetime of cobbling up Rube Goldberg or field expedient equipment. It surpassed my highest expectations in dehydrating fruits and vegetables. Then I found that I could turn moose, caribou and salmon into jerky and "squaw candy" with it overnight (30 lb. at a time.) When I finally got around to using it for malting grain, I was astounded at how easily and efficiently I could make malt with it. I have another book I'm trying to get published on food preservation applications of this rig, but I want to include it here because it makes malting your own grains so easy that it opens up a new dimension to the homebrewer.

In a nut shell, you take an old defunct refrigerator or freezer, gut it, add malting trays, a fan and hotplate and begin making superb quality grain malts, cheap and easy.

Caution: Old refrigerators or freezers are death-traps for little kids. Make damned sure no little ones can crawl into an old one, become trapped and suffocate. Freon gas is now EPA regulated to preclude any ozone depletion. Dispose of any Freon via a reputable appliance firm. You could be fined for improper disposal. Remember, this a homemade device with electrical and fire hazards. Use prudence and common sense in building and using it.

The drawing on page 94 shows the general construction of the device. You vent the old freezer at top and bottom, make trays out of nylon window screen and use a common hotplate and fan to dry the sprouted grain at low temperatures, yielding pale (dried, not roasted) malt.

Sprout the moistened grain on your homemade screen trays, then crank up the fan and hotplate to dry or malt the grain. Toast the malted grain in your oven if you desire darker malt. The following drawing shows you the basics of how to build this device. With a bit of experimentation, you can make any type of malt you desire with it. The dried fruit, vegetables, jerky and fish are a plus.

Malting Your Own Sample Worksheet

Type of Grain - Wheat, Barley, Corn_____

Date:_____

Description:_____
_____
_____
_____

Source:_____
Variety:_____
Quantity:_____
Price:_____

Quality: Chemically treated - Do not use!
            Mold, if yes, do not use!
            Weed seeds - Describe
            Debris - Describe
            Unfilled or immature seeds?
            Other, i.e., broken seeds, age?

Test Data: Dates inclusive_____
                Number of samples_____
                Optimum soak time_____
                Temperature_____

Narrative of results (lessons learned)_____
_____
_____
_____
_____
_____
_____
_____
_____
_____
_____
_____
_____
_____
_____
_____

Malt Factory

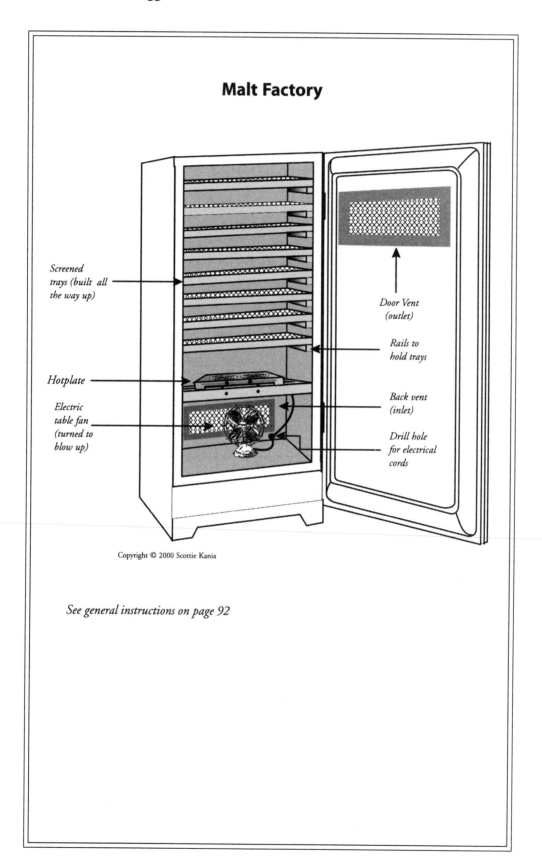

Screened trays (built all the way up)

Door Vent (outlet)

Rails to hold trays

Hotplate

Back vent (inlet)

Electric table fan (turned to blow up)

Drill hole for electrical cords

See general instructions on page 92

Sinkers and Floaters Test

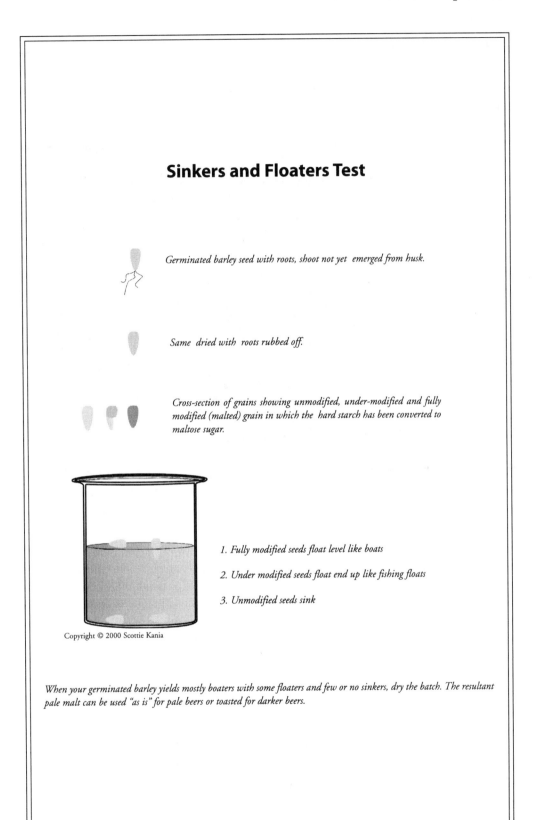

Germinated barley seed with roots, shoot not yet emerged from husk.

Same dried with roots rubbed off.

Cross-section of grains showing unmodified, under-modified and fully modified (malted) grain in which the hard starch has been converted to maltose sugar.

1. Fully modified seeds float level like boats

2. Under modified seeds float end up like fishing floats

3. Unmodified seeds sink

Copyright © 2000 Scottie Kania

When your germinated barley yields mostly boaters with some floaters and few or no sinkers, dry the batch. The resultant pale malt can be used "as is" for pale beers or toasted for darker beers.

Keggin' it (A Cheap and Easy Way to Naturally Carbonated Draft Beer)

A recipe for rabbit stew in an old family cookbook started out with "First you ketch a rabbit." Well, to make your own kegged beer, you first have to "ketch" a keg. We're speaking of a reasonably modern commercial beer keg here, not an antique wooden one (next to impossible to find) nor one of the newest plumber's nightmares with gauges, CO_2 tanks and more lines and tubes than a chicken has guts, that are being marketed to the homebrewer today. What we're looking for is an orphan, a stainless steel, aluminum, or even a plastic keg you can pick up at a garage sale, flea market, or even from a beer distributor.

Kegs are supposed to be returned to the brewery and the customer pays a deposit on the keg to ensure this happens. For various reasons, including brewers going out of business, new types of kegs replacing the old, etc., kegs can be found that do exactly what you want them to do, hold beer under pressure. Metal kegs are made out of either stainless steel or aluminum. You'll need a magnet and a pocketknife to evaluate metal kegs.

The very best kegs are made of high-grade stainless steels. They're very shiny, difficult to scratch with a knife and nonmagnetic. The lesser grade of stainless steel will have a dull finish, be hard to scratch with a knife, but will attract a magnet. An aluminum keg will have a dull finish, be easy to scratch with a knife, probably be scratched and marred on the outside and be nonmagnetic. Plastic kegs are obviously just that, plastic. If you have a choice, go for the stainless steel because it's easier to clean and won't react with chlorine bleach like aluminum will from prolonged exposure.

Also, stainless steel is pretty easy to weld on either for modification of your draft beer set up, or if you are lucky enough to snag two stainless kegs, you modify the second into one or two stainless steel brew kettles. This will save you some bucks because they are expensive and hard to find. Most of these kegs will have three holes or orifices on them, two for valves for dispensing and one, a bung or plug used for cleaning and filling. You,

Fully Reconfigured Keg

the homebrewer are only concerned at this point with the two valve holes. The valves are held in by threaded retaining rings made for a special wrench you probably won't have. Do not despair, merely scrounge a piece of brass brazing rod or similar soft metal about 4" long and stick it in the retaining ring at a shallow angle and tap it to the left with a hammer. Instant wrench! Remove the valves, figure out how the damned things work and then disassemble the one for the bottom of the keg. You should have a cup-like valve housing, a retaining ring with a gasket and a bunch of valve parts. You'll only use the ring gasket and housing.

Caution: A beer keg is a pressure vessel and even though the keg you scrounged might not have any fluid in it and feel like it's empty it *still may contain CO_2 under substantial pressure. Do not attempt to remove the retaining rings until you figure out how the mechanism operates and open and close the valve to ensure any pressure in the keg is bled off. Removing valves from pressurized vessels is like looking for gas leaks with a lighted match, about the only ones who might benefit are florists and undertakers. The hazard is not explosion, but being hit by a valve that blows out when you remove the retaining ring*

The game plan is to replace the valve parts with a common brass faucet. It's about like making a candle, but instead of wax, you'll be working with molten tin. Tin is nontoxic. You can melt it on your kitchen stove and when it hardens, or freezes, just like water, it expands and makes a perfect seal or plug.

Remove all the innards from the brass faucet and fill it with dry sand. Block the hole in the valve housing with a tight-fitting wooden peg, then wire the faucet in place, dead center in the valve housing. Melt enough tin to fill the housing about half full around the faucet. When the new draft beer spigot you've just made cools down, clean out the sand, peg and reassemble the faucet washers and parts.

Tips: Buy a couple packets of tin, not lead, fishing sinkers to melt down for this project. Make sure everything, sand included, is perfectly dry before you pour your tin, wear gloves and safety glasses too, because a little bit of moisture can make the molten tin splatter like heck. Melt the tin in a small cast iron frying pan. Fill a larger frying pan with dry sand and embed the wired together valve housing and faucet in this firmly so you have a stable heat resistant platform when you pour the tin in.

This project is a lot easier to do than it sounds

and when it's done, you'll fall in love with your creation. No more bottle washing! No more capping! You'll just siphon your fermented beer into the keg through the top hole, add priming sugar, seal it up and a week or so later when you open the spigot on the bottom, it's draft beer time.

One additional step vastly improves this rig, simply by putting a flexible hose and float on the rear of the spigot. Otherwise the yeast will settle level with your spigot and you'll always be drawing cloudy beer. If the end of the outlet hose floats above the yeast deposit, you'll get clear beer right down to the dregs of the keg.

Note: Don't over prime with too much sugar (the optimum is ¼ cup of sugar per gallon) because there's no pressure relief valve on this set up, other than opening the top valve or the spigot. I know of only one case of a bung blowing out of a keg and that was because the keg was being rolled up a mountain trail on a hot summer day. The bung broke the fellow's leg that happened to be rolling it when she let go. It could have been a lot worse, so be careful. Prime with ¼ cup of corn sugar per gallon.

Additional Note: As you use this keg of beer up, the CO_2 pressure from the natural carbonation will drop. If the beer ceases to flow, merely open this top valve a few seconds to relieve the vacuum. In olden days, before compressed gas dispensing systems, a tapered wooden plug called a stile (like stylus) was fitted to a hole in the bung. With drawing, the stile would let a little air into the keg so the beer would flow again. This is a sign that your beer is losing its carbonation. You can, either drink it up English style with no head, re-prime the keg with sugar and yeast, drain the keg and bottle what's left, or re-carbonate each pitcher of flat draft by pouring in a bottle of foamy stuff. The next *time you may want to use a little more priming sugar in the keg. Again, this is another example of the importance of keeping a brewer's log book so you get better with each batch.*

Fitting a spigot to a beer keg will make you the envy of all your brewing buddies. Not only does it enable you to have a big batch of naturally conditioned draft on tap, but also it does away with the tedious chores of washing, sterilizing, filling and capping all those bottles. I've been using this 16-gallon keg for over twenty years and normally keg about fourteen gallons at a time, allowing two gallons of headspace in the keg for pressure buildup.

Kegs may vary somewhat in configuration, but this one is typical. It is nice shiny, easy to clean stainless steel. It originally had a wooden bung or plug in the middle, but sometime during the more than twenty years I've been using it, the bung started to leak. As shown (A) I replaced the bung with an expandable rubber test plug available in hardware and plumbing stores. It had two identical valves at either end, one on the side (B inset) the other on the chime or end surface (C) shown here with the spigot installed.

While this "pore boy" keg does have some minor drawbacks, it's simplicity, economy and volume will make it one of your most cherished possessions once you try it.

Thermometers

Most of what I have to say on thermometers is covered in the next section on hydrometers, but the new liquid crystal tape type stick-on brewing thermometers are excellent. The temperatures are even marked for ale and lager. If you can't find one, the aquarium thermometers work almost as well

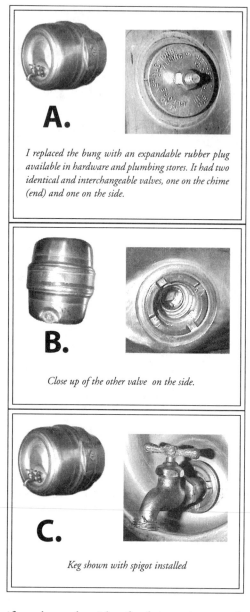

I replaced the bung with an expandable rubber plug available in hardware and plumbing stores. It had two identical and interchangeable valves, one on the chime (end) and one on the side.

Close up of the other valve on the side.

Keg shown with spigot installed

if stuck on the side of a fermenting vessel. The numbers on the tape change color, giving you a temperature reading at a glance without risking contamination by unsealing the vessel.

The Hydrometer

The only other item of equipment we need to talk about is the hydrometer. I have mixed

Shows the spigot retaining ring and the valve body, less internal parts all combined into one assembly by inserting the spigot into the valve body and pouring molten tin in around it.

Shows an optional copper tube pressed into the rear to draw the beer from above the yeast deposits I've experimented with a variety of similar devices to include flexible tubing with floats and feel they're more trouble than they are worth. If you keep the keg tilted so the yeast accumulates away from the outlet and don't juggle the keg, all but the last gallon or two will be clear.

Shows the rear of the valve body. Two holes have been filled with tin, the center one then drilled through to the rear of the valve.

Stick-on Brew Thermometer

emotions about this device because it's the divider between art (fun) and science (work.) A hydrometer is a float that is used to measure the specific gravity, or density of your fermenting fluid as compared to plain water. You don't need one of these damned things, but you should know how they work and if you want to sell your soul to science. Buy one and learn the basics of its use.

Some hydrometers incorporate thermometers, others (cheaper) are only graduated floats and you need a separate thermometer. They work like a fishing bobber with a scale marked on them. In pure water at 60° F, the bobber floats at a certain depth called a specific gravity of 1 or 1,000. As you thicken the fluid by adding malt, sugars and non-fermentables, the float rises, that enables you to estimate the percentages of alcohol that may be produced if everything ferments out.

Close only counts with hand grenades and horseshoes. For the homebrewer, hydrometers only get you close to knowing how much alcohol your fermenting fluids may produce and at what point you should bottle. There are just too many variables like temperature, variance in fermentation, insoluble solids, the phase of the moon and the lack of really sophisticated and accurate analysis equipment that the commercial outfits have at their disposal. The hydrometer at best, will give the homebrewer a rough idea of potential alcohol production. Try it if you must, but follow the "bonfire" steps for bottling and priming. The bubbles don't lie, much. If you are one of those who absolutely must have the cutting edge of technology, go ahead and buy a high-priced thermometer/hydrometer. You don't really need it and it may lull you into a false sense of security.

In the previous sections, we've covered all the brewing equipment you really need vessels, hoses, capper and fermentation locks. There is a great variety of other equipment and supplies available. Homebrew supply is a large and growing industry, comparable to the garden supply industry. I stress the use of minimal equipment, most of it homemade and improvised because one of the attractions of making your own beverages is economy. Regardless of what our leaders in Washington try to tell us, times are hard and they just seem to keep getting tougher.

A lot of gadgets available are so pricey that the aspiring beginner is scared off by the apparent cost and complexity of homebrewing. Grandma was a good gardener too, but she didn't have a $2,000.00 roto-tiller and a shed full of fancy tools. Besides that, I'm a cheap Charlie.

U.S. Proof Spirit and Hydrometer Measurement

Liquor that contains 50% ethyl alcohol by volume is called 100 U.S. proof spirit. U.S. proof is two times the percentage of alcohol by volume. *Specially designated hydrometers are used to determine the alcoholic strength of watery solutions.* They are graduated to indicate '0' for no alcohol, '100' for 50% alcohol and '200' for absolute or 100% alcohol by volume at the standard temperature of 60° F. When you have distilled a volume of high proof alcohol, it is necessary to dilute (cut) it to the desired commercial strength. Do this simply by adding pure, clean water. If you want to exclude the flavor peculiar to some tap waters, then use distilled water.

Distill your own water by running ordinary tap water through your still at a temperature of 212° F, which is the boiling temperature of water.

The homebrewer is concerned with *potential*, rather than *actual* alcohol content of his beers or wines so he'll use a different scale on the hydrometer and calculate percentage rather than proof. It's the same thing, only different.

Use of the Hydrometer

I've discouraged you from using the hydrometer at the outset because brewing is like gardening, without an understanding or feel for the natural processes, you'll never master the art, regardless of the chemicals or fancy equipment you use. I garden organically for the same reason I don't use a bunch of chemical additives in brewing, you get a more wholesome product and greater satisfaction. But modern tools increase your efficiency in both endeavors, so let's take a look at the hydrometer.

The hydrometer is used with two other tools, a thermometer and a hydrometer jar, which is a tall test tube on a stand that you put a sample of your wort in to test it with the hydrometer. A hydrometer is a glass tube, weighted on one end with graduated markings, or a scale on it. It works like a fishing float and is designed to measure the specific gravity, or density of fluids. Pure water at 60° F has a specific gravity of 1 or 1.000 on the hydrometer scale. Using nontechnical terms, anything that makes the water more or less dense (thicker or thinner) will make the hydrometer float higher or lower in the fluid.

Higher or lower temperatures alter the density of water, therefore, you must always know the temperature at which you take your reading and convert or adjust to the equivalent at 60° F. A simple table is included in this section to enable you to correct specific gravity readings to the base temperature of 60° F. So far we've only talked about plain water, so as long as we adjust for temperature correctly, we'll always arrive at a specific gravity of 1.000. *Please note that some people drop the 1 and sometimes zero, writing a specific gravity of 1.060 as 060, or only 60.*

The specific gravity, or thickness of water is also altered by mixing something in it, like malt, fruit juice, or sugar. You should take two readings, one before fermentation and one after, the first called starting specific gravity (starting S.G.) gives you an estimate of how much alcohol might be produced if everything you added to the water was converted to alcohol. The second, or final S.G. reading should tell you how much material did not ferment into alcohol. By subtracting final S.G. from starting S.G. and doing a little calculating, you can arrive at a pretty accurate estimate of the percentage of alcohol by volume in your beverage container. Normally the final S.G. will be greater than that of plain water and this is good because it represents the unfermented ingredients that give body and flavor to our beers and wines.

Now that you've been initiated into the secret order of hydrometer wielders, it's time to draw yours from its scabbard and learn to use it. Most hydrometers have three scales, one marked BRIX or BALLING, another for potential alcohol by volume and a third for specific gravity. BRIX is a measurement of sugar and BALLING is the name of the guy who developed the scale which measures percent of sugar by weight. You should disregard this scale completely. You don't need

it. The next scale for potential percentage of alcohol is deceptively worthless. At first glance, it appears that a before and after fermentation reading will show you how much "kick" is in your "Kickapoo," but we know now that without converting to a base temperature, this scale is about as useless as a cracked crystal ball for predicting anything accurately. I have never seen a temperature conversion table for this scale, so you can disregard it too. The specific gravity scale on your hydrometer is the only one you need and the simple tables in this section will enable you to use it competently, but first a couple of tips.

Hydrometer Tips

1. A small raised collar of fluid will adhere to your hydrometer above the surface level of your wort, must or mash. To get an accurate reading, you must look across the top of the fluid to get the true surface level reading.

2. Rather than muck about in the primary fermenter trying to get temperature and gravity readings and risking contamination, use a sterile dipper to pull a big enough sample to fill your hydrometer jar. The plastic tube the hydrometer comes packed in, is intended to serve as a hydrometer jar.

3. Before you read your hydrometer, spin it in the fluid a couple of times to get rid of any air bubbles that might be clinging to it and cause an inaccurate reading.

4. Record the temperature, S.G. and predicted alcohol content in your record

book.

5. Consider your sample contaminated when you are done with it and discard it, rather than pouring it back in the fermenter.

Specific Gravity to Potential Alcohol Table
(Hydrometer Scale Conversions)

Specific Gravity	Potential Alcohol % by Volume
1.005	.05
1.020	.09
1.015	1.6
1.020	2.3
1.025	3.0
1.030	3.7
1.035	4.4
1.040	5.1
1.045	5.8
1.050	6.5
1.055	7.2
1.060	7.8
1.065	8.6
1.070	9.2
1.075	9.9
1.080	10.6
1.085	11.3
1.090	12.0
1.095	12.7
1.100	13.4
1.105	14.1
1.110	14.9

Specific Gravity Temperature Table

50° F	Subtract .001 from SG reading
60° F	No correction
70° F	Add .001 to SG reading
77° F	Add .002 to SG reading
84° F	Add .003 to SG reading
95° F	Add .005 to SG reading
105° F	Add .007 to SG reading

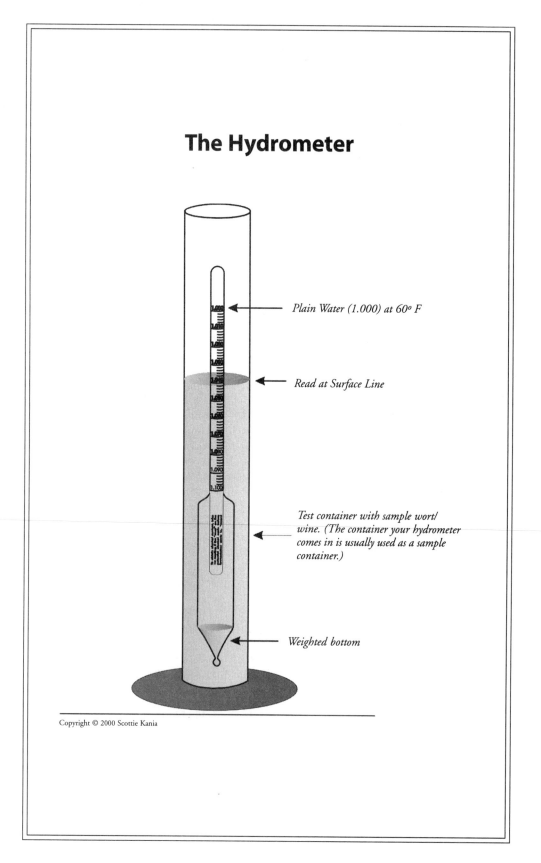

The Hydrometer

Plain Water (1.000) at 60° F

Read at Surface Line

Test container with sample wort/ wine. (The container your hydrometer comes in is usually used as a sample container.)

Weighted bottom

Chapter Five

Whiskey Makin'

In This Chapter

➤   Basics of Mashing for Distillation,
    Distilling, Theory and Dangers

➤   Types of Stills and How They Work

➤   Dangers of Alcohol in Alaska

➤   Effects of Alcohol on Man

➤   Fermentation of Ethyl Alcohol

➤   Still Operation

➤   Cleaning the Still

➤   Safety Factors During Distillation

➤   The Devil, Vodka, Russian Bootlegging
    and Potatoes

The how and the history of making whiskey from laurel thickets and "revenooers," to desert sheikdoms where lose your head meant LOSE YOUR HEAD! Plans and instructions included for a variety of stills.

Caution: While you can make your own beer and wine legally, it is illegal to distill your own spirits in the USA. Even possession of the non-permitted still is illegal. Also, distilling is very dangerous with very real hazards of fire, explosions, scalding and poisoning. If you think you'd like to run off a batch of your own Mountain Dew, think again, you will be breaking the federal law and the "revenooers" will get you. Don't do it! Much of the distilling information in this book came from people that worked in remote, and/or overseas areas and is included as examples of Yankee ingenuity, rather than a blueprint for crime.

Basics of Mashing for Distillation (And Dangers!)

This section reminds me of a cartoon poster I saw at Ft. Benning, GA, the paratrooper training center, depicting a young lad writing home and saying, "Dear Ma, Last month I couldn't spell paratrooper, and now I are one." Well, I'm sure you can spell "brewer" and are well on the way to becoming one by virtue of this book. You may or may not be able to spell "jailbird," but if you choose to put this whiskey making information into practice, you could be one!

With that warning out of the way, let's get to the basics. The lore and information I'll share with you comes from a pretty colorful crew I've known personally, ranging from old-timers who carried muzzle loading rifles and thought Department of Revenue and Department of War were synonymous, to some more modern, but no less interesting guys who made their own whiskey where violating local taboos could get you flogged, imprisoned, or even beheaded. Such a deal, a lifetime haircut for free.

Having never been put up for canonization, indeed never even having been recommended for second assistant to the alternate altar boy, I've enjoyed the company of these "soiled doves" and marveled at their ingenuity. Some of the material presented in this book is extracted from anonymous underground pamphlets that were produced and circulated at great risk in far off lands. My thanks and acknowledgment to those brave, but unnamed souls.

Disclaimer: Much of the following very explicit material has been extracted from underground anonymous and I believe non-copyrighted material that was circulated in Muslim oil producing regions years ago. Clandestine distilling of whiskey was widespread and very sophisticated. Officially, neither the oil companies nor the Muslim regimes knew of these activities. Unofficially, a lot of good booze was made and consumed.

The guys that practiced the arts were brave, smart and more than a little bit crazy, considering what could happen to them if caught. With all credits due acknowledged and with warnings and precautions –which permeate this book reiterated, have a good read!

Mashing for distillation purposes is very similar to mashing for beer, but with several important differences. While the beer maker relies mainly on barley or wheat, the whiskey maker will use just about anything fermentable, including sugar, molasses, corn, wheat, rice, barley, rye, potatoes and even poor quality wines. Since the end product will be extracted from the wort or brew by distilling, the whiskey maker is not nearly as concerned as beer and wine makers about total conversion, starch hazes, clarity, taste and so on.

The prime goal for whiskey making is maximum production of alcohol. We all know that the various distilled liquors have distinctive tastes such as scotch and bourbon, which are imparted by trace amounts of the fermentables that are transferred out of the wort with the alcohol. Here lies the danger, because the same process that lends character or flavor can kill you. Nowadays most seed grains, those intended for planting for next years crop, are treated with various chemicals, pesticides and the like to protect the seed from bugs, fungus, etc. Make sure you use only safe, untreated seeds in any malting or mashing operation (feed gain.)

Additionally, rye seed is particularly susceptible to a fungus called ergot. This fungus forms in the seed head and can cause humans to go mad. In the 1800's a crooked French miller made rye flour out of questionable grain for bread. The ergot contaminated bread caused the entire populace of the region to go violently crazy. Worse yet, when the government sent troops to restore order, the first thing they did when they got off the train was buy bread. Then the maniacs had guns! Do not try mashing or malting your own rye. *The ergot fungus poses a very real hazard to the beginner. Ergot causes a violent deviant sexual behavior. In the incident cited above, peaceful peasants went on a rampage of rape and murder. When armed troops got involved, it was hellish!*

There are two main types or methods of mashing. The more traditional grain mash and the shortcut thin mash or wort method that utilizes manufactured sugars, such as cane sugar, corn sugar or molasses. When mashing grains, you're converting starch via enzyme action into fermentable sugars that the yeast can digest easily. There are numerous types of sugars, some more readily digested by yeast than others and different sugars can be converted into others by various means. It's a very complex subject that there is no earthly reason for us to go into. Results are what count, so all you really need to know is that if you add citric acid as in lemon juice, to a thin mash and heat it, it converts the various types to the ideal invert sugar and increases the speed and efficiency of the fermentation process. Enough theory. Let's start with the simplest mash. This will be a basic recipe for five gallons of thin mash, that should yield 9% to 16% pure alcohol by volume. Pure alcohol or 99.9% is called 200 proof, distilled and cut to 50%, 100 proof. This could yield almost seven quarts of clear 100 proof whiskey.

This recipe is similar to what the old prohibition era bootleggers used. Elliot Ness and his small band of "Untouchables" didn't achieve ultimate victory over Al Capone's criminal empire merely by raiding and destroying illicit stills and breweries, although they did a lot of it. Elliot and his men found the key to victory in tracking sugar shipments. The "Mob" built clandestine stills and breweries with great ingenuity almost as quickly as the "Untouchables" could find them and pay a visit with Tommy-guns, shotguns and axes. The raids were small unit tactics, that hurt the "Mob," but tracking and cutting off the supply of sugar was the strategic master stoke that broke their back!

Thin Mash Whiskey (Moonshine)

The basic recipe calls for two pounds of sugar per gallon, so you would first mark your primary fermenter at the five-gallon level.

Thin Mash Whiskey

5	Gal.	Water
10	Lb.	Cane sugar
2-½	T	Yeast nutrient or tablets for 5 gal.
5	T	Lemon juice
5	Ea.	Campden tablets
1	Cup	Dry bakers' yeast or vigorous wine yeast starter. (The more yeast, the quicker the fermenting is done.)

Boil water, sufficient to fill your fermenter to the 5-gallon mark. Put the sugar and lemon juice in the primary fermenter, add boiling water to five-gallon mark and stir until the sugar is dissolved. Cover and let cool to room temperature, then add yeast and the remaining ingredients. Cover mash, or better yet, fit with a fermentation lock. Keep fermenter at 78-90° F until fermentation ceases and yeast settles. (Approximately two weeks.) The fluid, now called wash, no longer mash or wort, is now ready to be siphoned off the lees or yeast dregs and distilled into whiskey. The old-timers also called it beer.

Grain whiskey mashing for distilling is far simpler than for beer making because it's not critical to get a completely starch-free wort. The starch will make beer cloudy, but distilling will separate the solids from the fluids. The malted grain is crushed or coarsely ground with a rolling pin or coffee grinder. The grist, as it's called, is now boiled for at least an hour to convert the starch. Do this at a rate of two pounds of grist per gallon of wort or mash, e.g., 10 pounds for a five-gallon batch. Proceed as with the basic batch

of thin mash by filling the fermenter to the five gallon mark, add yeast and other ingredients then ferment and distill as for thin mash or wort. The terms mash and wort are used interchangeably when working with thin mash that is basically a sugar water mixture. Obviously you can combine methods and materials by converting and fermenting blends of sugars, malted grain, un-malted grain, fruits, berries, herbs and vegetables and even using poor quality wine in the wash.

We've only covered two very simple mashes so far and don't want to get into recipes here. You'll get them galore in later sections. Just as an illustration of the art though, let's look briefly at bourbon. Bourbon grist is made of barley, rye and corn in a 1:1:3 ratio. Only the barley is malted however, because barley has enough enzymes to convert the starches in the other grains to fermentable sugars. If you desire sour mash bourbon, you will use the lees or yeast dregs from a previous batch to ferment your wort, rather than fresh yeast. Just like a sourdough starter in bread making, this old recycled yeast culture will impart a distinctive taste to the end product. Sour mash, "sippin' whiskey," drink it straight or mix it with a little branch water. Makes me so thirsty, I'm starting to spit dust. Pass me the jug, Henry, and pick the one about the egg suckin' dawg again.

Bathtub Gin

Like unicorns, Bathtub Gin appears to be mythological. There are no living witnesses, nor are there chronicles to support its existence, yet the legend persists that during prohibition a wicked, illicit form of gin was commonly made in bathtubs. There are wicked, illicit things you can do in a bathtub, but making gin is not one of them. You can ferment a thin mash, or sugar wine in a tub, distill it and make gin out of the alcohol and this appears to be what gave birth to the legend. A bathtub is actually a pretty good fermentation vessel and since gin is only alcohol and water flavored with juniper berries, it's the easiest of the commercial boozes to imitate. The evil reputation of this stuff was not caused by the bathtub, but by the shortcuts taken by the bootleggers.

Good whiskey is distilled several times, charcoal filtered or aged in charred barrels to remove impurities, including the headache, nausea and diarrhea producing fusel oils. Single run whiskey from a sugar water mash will be crystal clear, 80-120 proof and just loaded with fusel oils. Drop a couple juniper berries in it or boiled extract and you could have it bottled and in a speakeasy while it was still warm. "23 Skidoo" and be sick tomorrow too. The old-time rustic American moonshiners called this first run whiskey pop skull for good reason.

Bathtub Gin #1

1	Pint	180 proof ethyl or grain alcohol
1	Pint	Distilled water
5 to 10	Ea.	Juniper berries

Steep, soak or simmer the juniper berries to extract the flavor. Mix the above ingredients and age for thirty minutes. Put on your fedora, "zoot suit" or flapper dress, blow the dust off your Tommy gun, rouge your kneecaps and roll your stockings. Charleston! Charleston! Oh you kid!

Bathtub Gin #2

1	Pint	180 proof alcohol
1	Pint	Distilled water
3	Drops	Noirot Gin Flavor

You needn't age this one as long as the previous recipe. It is best consumed from a hip flask in the back seat of a Model "A" Ford in the company of an attractive companion of the opposite sex. I still have a Model "A" Ford of my youth, unfortunately, it's a pickup truck in which I hauled things like pigs and manure, but damned few attractive companions.

Rum "White Lightening" 40 Rod

5	Gal.	Water
10	Lb.	Brown sugar, molasses, sorghum syrup, corn syrup or cane sugar
1	Cup	Vigorous wine yeast starter

Flavoring or additives optional (See Appendix) Proceed with basic thin mash procedure. This is an all sugar-based whiskey, that utilizes the darker types of sugar and syrups, that are either residual from sugar refining or home produced sweeteners. The product can vary in color and flavor, dependent on the composition of the ingredients and additives. One of the traditional favorite additives to this type of whiskey was sassafras and in the case of red sassafras, added both coloring and flavor. These are thin mash whiskeys, but can be augmented with grains, fruits or berries or even spices like cloves or cinnamon.

Corn Whiskey (Corn Likker, Moonshine, Splo, White Lightening, Tanglefoot, Mountain Dew, Loudmouth, and a lot of other names)

Corn whiskey is distinctly American and played a significant part in our history. Not only a beverage for our ancestors, it was actually a medium of exchange, that enabled the farmer to convert his corn into an easily transported value-added product. The moonshining and "revenooers" lore is part of our national fabric, but "real" corn whiskey is seldom encountered today. The definition of "real" corn whiskey varies from region to region and even from person to person, so we'll look at several variations.

Real Corn Whiskey #1 – With or Without Horse Turds

10	lb.	Corn, whole kernel, un treated with any chemicals
5	gal.	Water
1	cup	Yeast, champagne yeast starter
10	lb.	Horse Manure, dried and pulverized (optional)

The corn is placed in a feed sack and buried in the warm moist center of a manure or compost pile for about ten days. When the sprouts are about a quarter inch long, the corn is fully "modified" or malted. Wash the corn in a tub, rubbing the shoots and roots off in the process, then skim them off. Transfer the fresh malted grain to the primary fermenter, mash it with a pole, add five gallons of boiling water and when the mash cools down, add the yeast.

Since fermentation was usually done in open vats or barrels, the alcohol tended to evaporate. When the vigorous fermentation slowed down to the "glowing embers" stage, a layer of powdered manure or bran was spread on the surface of the mash. This acted as a vapor barrier to retard evaporation. If you're one of those finicky types who don't

relish horse turds in your whiskey, a plastic sheet would serve the same purpose today. The manure would have to lend some unique character to the end product, but on the whole, I'd say this stuff might be just a bit too organic for most tastes

The fluid was dipped out of the fermenter, leaving the fermented grain behind, of which we'll have more to say after the next recipe. Distillation of the fluid or beer was done when the mash stopped bubbling. Unlike the prohibition era bootlegger and their bathtub gin, old time moonshiners took pride in their product, drank it themselves and therefore distilled it several times. An old-timer told me one of the ways he judged whiskey was whether the guy he bought it from would take a drink of it himself. The first distillate was called single run whiskey or "pop skull" and the first stuff to come out of the coils or worm was often discarded because it had the highest content of the volatile fusel oils. The second time through the still, it was called doublings, or double run whiskey. There were many other simple, but ingenious techniques that were used to test and purify what was usually a high quality and wholesome product. Sadly, this part of our heritage is nearly a lost art today.

Real Corn Whiskey #2

6	Lb.	Cornmeal
4	Lb.	Dried sprouted corn.
5	Gal.	Water
1	Cup	Champagne yeast starter

By now, if you've read from page one, you're knowledgeable enough to take this recipe and run with it with no further instructions. This is a malted whiskey, but not an all malt whiskey. Assuming you've sprouted and dried four pounds of corn (now malt) you'll proceed much like you were making beer from grain malt. Crack or grind the malted corn and mix it with the cornmeal. The grist as it's now called, should be mixed with hot (about 180° F) water and kept at about 150° F for several hours. The resultant mash or cornmeal mush is not something that will pour through the spout of a mash tun or beverage container, nor can you sparge it. The simplest way to mash the mush is to set the pot in a tub full of hot water and replenish the hot water periodically, Stir this mixture occasionally to help the mashing or conversion along. This is not a precise process, nor is it necessary to get a complete conversion as in mashing for beers. Put the mash in the fermenter and add boiled water to the five-gallon mark. Stir in the yeast when the mixture cools and proceed as with the previous recipe.

Preachers Whiskey (Also Free Whiskey or Sneaky Pete)

2-½   gal.   Boiled, cooled water

This was made from the residue in the vat or fermenter after all the thin beer or mash was dipped out. It's similar to second wines in that the yeast rich leftovers will still have a lot of fermentables in it. Add one half the original amount of water boiled, but cooled to around 50° F so you don't kill the yeast and let it ferment

Distilling Theory (or Mother Nature is a Moonshiner)

If someone was to ask me, What's the biggest still in the whole world? I'd have to answer, the whole world. Planet earth is in fact, one big still. A simple definition of distillation is the separation of the components of a mixture by partial vaporization of the mixture and separate recovery of the vapor and the residue. I don't mean to imply that Mother Nature has "Mob" connections, but she is the biggest distiller there is and without her distilling, most life on Earth would soon cease. I'm talking about the natural evaporation of our oceans into naturally distilled rainwater, of course, and that's what a still is basically, a little puny man-made rainmaker.

When I say puny, I only do so in comparison to nature. A still is basically a scarcely under control bomb. When distilling you're obviously dealing with heat, steam and pressures that pose readily apparent hazards of fire, scalding and explosion from the cooking process. What is not so obvious and therefore even more dangerous, is that alcohol compares very closely to gasoline in flash point, or flammability and explosiveness. We all know this because we all know we can drive our cars on gasoline and alcohol. What most of us don't know is that pound-for-pound gasoline has more explosive energy than TNT. This is fact, not fiction. Gasoline, like alcohol burns fiercely as a liquid and to get the maximum explosive force out of either, they must be vaporized before ignition. People who use gasoline as a cleaning solvent often meet St. Peter prematurely when the vapors ignite. Sometimes they take family members and innocent bystanders with them as a result of their stupidity. You wouldn't cook gasoline or TNT on your stove, I'm sure, but distilling alcohol is just as hazardous. Remember, distilling, like the sea, is terribly unforgiving of carelessness, incapacity or neglect.

There's a paradox here, because I introduced Mother Nature, whom we think of as benign as a distiller, then blasted you with all the dire hazards of distilling. Mark Twain once said, "There are lies, damned lies and statistics" and the same holds true for definitions. Another definition of distilling is, a method of separation based an differences in volatility. Volatility describes a substances tendency to be transformed into a vapor, or cloud, and both water and alcohol are volatile, but alcohol is explosive!

All stills, those in this book included, are designed to capture produced vapors and condense them into liquids before they escape into the atmosphere. They may fail to function as intended due to many causes, chief of which are human error, negligence or plain stupidity. I knew a guy who made gunpowder in an electric blender and got away with it, at last report, but I don't think it's the final report. The volatile and explosive alcohol produced from any still could make your final report brilliant, widely noticed and one that leaves a lasting impression. Be reel keerful!

Types of Stills and How They Work

The first stills were marvelously simple, but very inefficient. State-of-the-art modern stills are marvelously efficient, but awesomely complex. All work according to the principles or theory of distilling, that we covered. We will look at a variety of ingenious stills in this section, to include construction and operation, but first, some general characteristics.

All distilling apparatus must as a minimum include the following:

1) Heat source

2) Vessel, pot or kettle to heat the wash, or alcohol bearing fluid in.

3) Condenser to capture, cool, and condense vapors.

4) Receiver to collect and contain the distilled fluids.

Note: The four necessities cited above are for feasibility, the minimum it would take an old-time hillbilly to make whiskey. The modern-day practitioners of the art insist on two additional items for control and safety.

5) Thermometer

6) Fire extinguisher. (We might also include a rabbit's foot, four leaf clovers, and a Tarzan type swing in case something goes wrong)

The Retort Still

The Retort Still is so like a watering can that you'd use on your flowers, that the same guy probably invented them both. Made out of glass, clay or metal, a Retort Still has a small sealable hole on the top for filling. The long, thin spout, actually the condenser, comes out of the top and angles downward, The vapors condense as they travel through the long condenser and the fluids (alcohol and water) drip into the receiver vessel.

The Retort Still is only marginally efficient for distilling small amounts because the whole thing tends to heat up and the cooling efficiency of the condenser drops off rapidly. The addition of a water cooling jacket or even wrapping the condenser with water soaked rags will improve its efficiency, but it

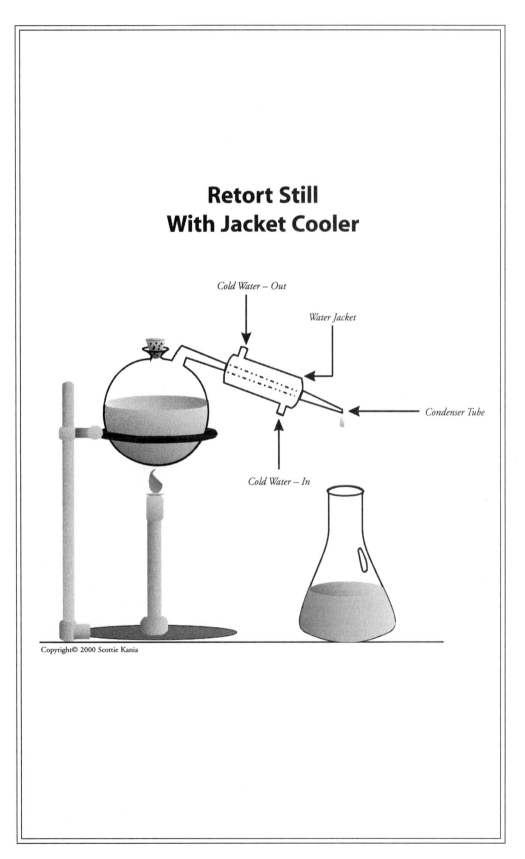

Retort Still
With Jacket Cooler

Cold Water – Out

Water Jacket

Condenser Tube

Cold Water – In

still leaves a lot to be desired. Other than inefficiency, the Retort Still has two main drawbacks, both in regard to safety. First, most retorts encountered today are made of glass, for laboratory use and are fragile. Second, the outlet or tip of the condenser is relatively close to the heat source.

If you run your distilled fluids through several times to increase their strength, the increasingly flammable fluids and vapors that are produced may result in a Molotov Cocktail. If the cocktails you desire are the sipping kind, not the fire bomb kind, beware simple glass retorts.

The next still up the evolutionary ladder from the Retort is the Pot Still. This is the one we all visualize when we think of the traditional old-time American moonshiner. I think more of the old-fashioned copper wash boilers were used for stills than were used for laundry. But a lot of them were real works of art. Lost art, in that our ancestors actually cut, formed and soldered them out of sheet copper.

Traditional Pot Still

The traditional old Pot Still shows it's retort ancestry, but Grandpa put in a few new wrinkles. The Pot Still was to the Retort what a Boeing 727 is to a hang glider. I believe if I made one of these from scratch and some "dern revenooers" hacked it up with axes, I'd be inclined to give them a "whiff" of buckshot, just like Grandpa did.

The Pot Still was made of copper in almost its entirety. The seams and joints were done with lead solder so it would never pass muster today. The kettle often had a retort styled cap, but sometimes a much plainer style was used. With a wood fire as a heat source and no thermometer controlling the

temperature and boiling rate, it was literally a matter of playing it by ear. Consequently, the kettle tended to boil over at times, which would send un-distilled fluids and solids into the condenser and not only contaminate the distilled liquor, but could block it with solids and possibly blow the still up. Therefore the slobber box evolved which basically was a pressure relief and debris-catching chamber installed between the still and the condenser coils.

When the still boiled over, or "slobbered," the slobber box retained the fluids and debris, but let the distilled vapors pass on to the coils. The box has a drain on it and was emptied periodically and the contents were saved for distilling in the next run. Ingenious, wasn't it?

The condenser consisted of coiled copper tubing immersed in a barrel of cold water. Stills were usually sited on a hillside near to a "branch" or small stream. By means of wooden trough or pipes, water was diverted to flow into the barrel keeping the coils icy cold. Now, the coiled tubing, or copper worm of the condenser was the most difficult to make and expensive part of the whole set up. If a still was raided, the operators tried to save it above all else.

It's interesting to note that while we usually think of the U.S. Federal government as the raider and confiscator of stills, they weren't the worst or the first. The Confederate government was by far, the most aggressive still buster. At the outbreak of our Civil War, the Confederate States were desperately short of all types of war material. One of their most dire needs was for percussion caps for the muzzle-loading guns of the day. Percussion caps are made of copper and there was little to be had in the South, so Richmond decreed that every country still and

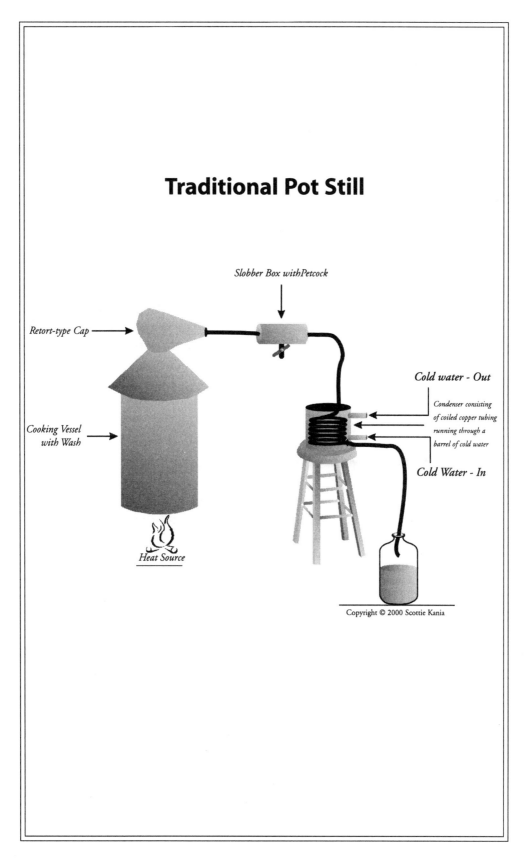

Traditional Pot Still

Slobber Box withPetcock

Retort-type Cap

Cold water - Out

Condenser consisting
of coiled copper tubing
running through a
barrel of cold water

Cooking Vessel
with Wash

Cold Water - In

Heat Source

worm that could be found, be confiscated. I imagine, there were more than a few old moonshiners that damned Rebels, damned Yankees and damned damn near anybody else that crossed their path for awhile.

The Modern Pot Still (From a Pressure Cooker)

Damned if the Pot Still isn't still with us, almost anyway. If one were shopping for a modern-day Pot Still and found something that "looks like a duck, walks like a duck and quacks like a duck," you'd be looking at a stainless steel pressure cooker, preferably one with its own electric heating element and temperature control. Quack! Quack! Remember the six things we said we need for a modern still.

Let's score it on a 6-point score sheet:

1. Heat source. Electric, with temperature control no less +1 point

2. A vessel. Stainless steel. Designed with lid for heat and pressure +1 point

3. A condenser. No, but the pressure gauge just screws off so you simply replace it with a threaded fitting and copper or stainless steel tubing. You're half way home with this one. +½ point

4. A receiver. No problem. This is just an empty jug. +1 point

5. A thermometer. No big problem. The simple weight that acts as a pressure valve screws off. Find a candy thermometer that's a press fit in the hole and gasket. If you get a pressure build up, it pushes

the thermometer out just as it would the weight, except the thermometer will pop completely out of the hole, venting the pressure. It shouldn't be this easy. +½ point

6. Fire extinguisher. Use the one you should already have in the kitchen or the garage. +1 point

Score 5 Out of a Possible 6 Points

The condenser and the "slobber box" are the main challenges here and they aren't big ones. You could get a welder to fabricate a stainless steel "slobber box." This would just be a canister with threaded fittings for your inlet and outlet tubes and a drain valve or vent on the bottom. An easier, but less professional looking method is to use a stainless steel teakettle with a spring loaded flapper cap/whistle. Block the little whistle hole with a wooden plug, making the kettle a pressure vessel with a manually operated flapper valve. You'll mount your new "slobber box" teakettle upside down, so the flat side becomes the top and the spout drain is on the bottom. Connect your inlet and outlet tubes on opposite sides about an inch down from the flat side.

Hooking up the tubing to the various components may seem like a daunting task but there are a great variety of easy to use, off-the-shelf fittings available to make this a simple chore. You could use copper tubing and flared fittings, but far better to use is stainless steel tubing and stainless steel Swage-Lok fittings. The Swage-Lok fittings are designed for high pressure, (5,000 PSI) high temperature and they come in incredible variety. They're a mainstay in the petroleum and gas industry where one leak or mistake gets you enrolled in Harp Playing 101, Pearly Gates School of Music. They are very reliable. You should only need four fittings.

The Swage-Lok fittings are compression fittings, meaning that they slip on the tubing and through the holes in your containers easily, but once they're tightened they grip and seal with enormous force. Buy the fittings to match the diameter and type tubing you use. You'll need one coupling to match the threads of the pressure gauge you removed from the pressure cooker. You'll need three bulkhead fittings that are designed to connect tubing to the metal walls of tanks or vessels. Two of these will attach the condenser tubing to your "slobber box" teakettle and one will secure and seal the end of the condenser coil protruding from your metal bucket/Water jacket. Easy, ain't it?

A. Pressure Cooker – Remove weighted pressure relief valve (1) and pressure gauge (2) Dial-type thermometer (3) should press-fit into valve hole.

B. Stainless Steel Tea Kettle – Converted to slobber box by drilling holes for condenser tube (4,5) and plugging whistle (6.)

C. Metal Bucket (Condenser) – Drilled to allow condenser tube to protrude from lower side (7.)

D. Copper or Stainless Steel Tubing – With four fittings to connect condenser tube to cooker, slobber box and metal bucket.

E. Receiver Jug

F. Four fittings mentioned in D.

The Modern Pot Still Components

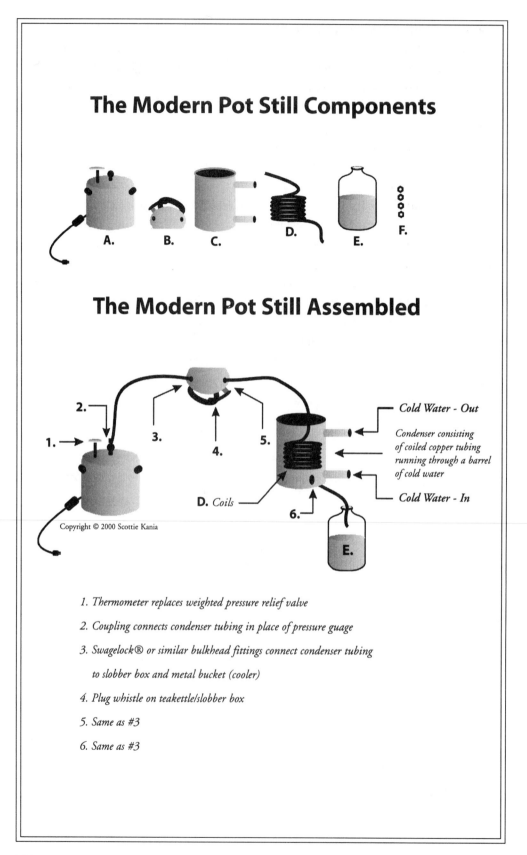

A.   B.   C.   D.   E.   F.

The Modern Pot Still Assembled

1.
2.
3.
4.
5.
6.

Cold Water - Out

Condenser consisting
of coiled copper tubing
running through a barrel
of cold water

Cold Water - In

D. Coils

E.

Copyright © 2000 Scottie Kania

1. *Thermometer replaces weighted pressure relief valve*

2. *Coupling connects condenser tubing in place of pressure guage*

3. *Swagelock® or similar bulkhead fittings connect condenser tubing*
   to slobber box and metal bucket (cooler)

4. *Plug whistle on teakettle/slobber box*

5. *Same as #3*

6. *Same as #3*

The Reflux Still, or Don't Lose Your Marbles (Reflux Column Still)

The next great leap forward in distilling was, and is the Reflux Still, sometimes called the Column Still. Like most great inventions, it's stunningly simple. It has many variations, but it boils down to putting a couple of buckets of marbles in the top of your still, between the cooking vessel and the outlet to the condenser. This feature doubles the efficiency of the best Pot Still. We all know heated vapors rise, but alcohol and water vapors are almost equally volatile. If we think of the alcohol and water molecules as little mountain climbers and the alcohol molecules as just a little bit better climbers (more volatile) then the Reflux Still starts to make sense.

Instead of just letting them all shoot out of the top of the still together, we put a mountainous obstacle (a column of marbles) in their path. The marbles sap away heat (strength) from both teams. The stronger climbing team (alcohol) begins to lead while the weaker team (water) loses strength (heat) and either stops or starts sliding down hill, back to the kettle (refluxes.) The obstacle can be numerous things, marbles, stainless steel scouring pads or even broken glass. It all serves the same purpose, to separate the strong from the weak. Pot, same as used in simple pot still.

The Compound Still

With the Reflux Still we simply added a column of marbles between the kettle and the condenser outlet as an obstacle to the water molecule's climb. Now we compound their difficulties by adding a small cooling coil at the very top of the marble column. This coil is filled with circulating cold water and serves to eliminate most of the remaining water molecules. It almost makes you feel sorry for the little guys because just as the strongest (hottest) climbers claw their way to the top, you stomp on their fingers with the cooling coil and send them screaming (refluxing) back down into the kettle.

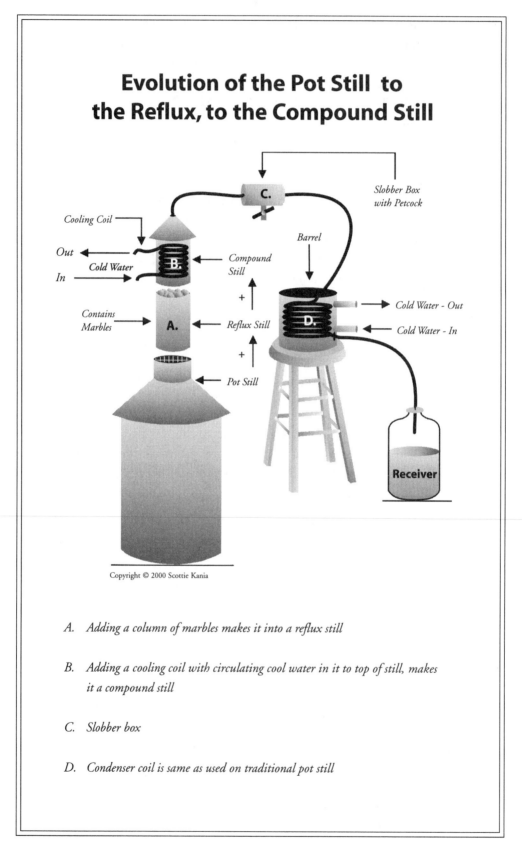

Evolution of the Pot Still to the Reflux, to the Compound Still

Slobber Box
with Petcock

Cooling Coil

Out

Cold Water

In

Compound
Still

Barrel

Contains
Marbles

A.

Reflux Still

Cold Water - Out

Cold Water - In

Pot Still

Receiver

Copyright © 2000 Scottie Kania

A. *Adding a column of marbles makes it into a reflux still*

B. *Adding a cooling coil with circulating cool water in it to top of still, makes it a compound still*

C. *Slobber box*

D. *Condenser coil is same as used on traditional pot still*

The Two-Dollar Still or Get Crocked on Your Crock Pot

I call this one the Two-Dollar Still because it can be made for less than two dollars worth of materials at current U.S. prices (less the crock-pot, of course.) When they started putting plastic, instead of glass lids on crock pots, the Two-Dollar still became a reality. For about two bucks or less, the newer crockpots with plastic lids can be converted to stills in minutes. The only additional materials you need are a piece of nontoxic metal tubing and a plastic milk jug, a blob of bread dough and a glue gun.

The first step in making the Two-Dollar Crockpot Still is to drill a ⁵/₁₆" hole dead center in the top of the plastic lid. ⁵/₁₆" It is the exact outside diameter of the common ¼" (inside diameter) copper tubing. Then bend the first four or five inches of one end into a 90° arc. Press-fit the end into the top of the crockpot lid.

Now we get high tech, making a cooling jacket out of a plastic milk jug. Bend the rest of the tube so it points downward at about 45° then stick it into the mouth of the milk jug until it touches the side about ⅓ of the way from the bottom. Mark this spot and drill a ⁵/₁₆" hole in the jug. Slip the copper tubing through the hole in the side of the jug so about six inches protrudes. Bend the tubing so it protrudes straight out of the side, then rises about ¼,"then drops downward. This slight curve in the tubing serves as a drip catcher. You'll tie a little piece of rag here later, just in case your milk jug/cooling jacket leaks, this feature will prevent the water from running down the outside of the tubing into the receiver. If you do the next step well, you won't have any drips or leakage to worry about. Taking your trusty hot glue gun, seal the tubing to the milk jug with lots of hot glue. Your Two-Dollar Crockpot Still is now complete. If you want to enhance the efficiency of this one, just add a couple more milk jugs.

To use this creation, one would next fill the milk jug cooling jacket with ice water, seal the crockpot lid with bread dough (1 cup flour, ½ teaspoon sugar, a pinch of bakers' yeast and enough tepid water to make a dough) and secure the lid with a couple of heavy rubber bands or bungee cords. Remember, this is a "how-to," not a "have-to" book and while you can make this still for two dollars, it is illegal to do so, and might cost you much wampum, if you do. Ugh! Heap big trouble! ATF no likeum home still.

At a certain point, dependent on the composition of your wash, the flow of distillate through your condenser will probably stop. This means, that's all she wrote for that particular batch, due to the limited fixed temperature range inherent to a crockpot. Different crockpots and mixtures will give varying results, but all should reach a point of diminishing return where *most, but not all* the highly volatile alcohol has been removed. Just consider this still a cream separator that removes most of the richest product from the wash and leaves behind a weak skimmed milk fluid.

You've probably noted that I've made no mention of a thermometer for this still. A thermometer is always desirable to monitor what's happening in the pot. You can incorporate one in this still by drilling a small hole in the lid and installing it as we described for the modern pot, or pressure cooker still. On the other hand, there are only two heat settings on a crockpot, so all you can do is set it on high and let'er cook.

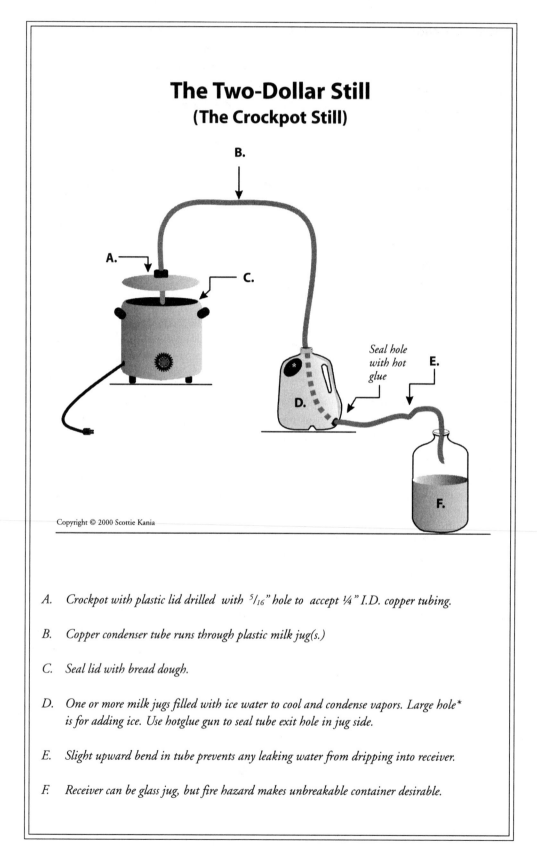

The Two-Dollar Still
(The Crockpot Still)

B.

A.

C.

Seal hole
with hot
glue

E.

D.

F.

A.   Crockpot with plastic lid drilled with ⁵/₁₆" hole to accept ¼" I.D. copper tubing.

B.   Copper condenser tube runs through plastic milk jug(s.)

C.   Seal lid with bread dough.

D.   One or more milk jugs filled with ice water to cool and condense vapors. Large hole*
     is for adding ice. Use hotglue gun to seal tube exit hole in jug side.

E.   Slight upward bend in tube prevents any leaking water from dripping into receiver.

F.   Receiver can be glass jug, but fire hazard makes unbreakable container desirable.

The Disappearing Still or Two Woks and a Pot

This is my favorite for ingenuity, simplicity and uniqueness of operation. This still so intrigued me, that I actually did a patent search on it with the U.S. Patent Office. Nothing quite like it had been patented and I had visions of wealth and glory to be mine by filing a patent on a still using the same principles. Unfortunately, a little further research revealed that a similar device had been around long before there was a U.S. Patent Office. It was called a cone still and was a common household item back in colonial times. Housewives used it to extract the essence from herbs like mint and chamomile. Easy come, easy go.

Anyhow, this still is unique in several ways It works very efficiently at relatively low temperatures. Just as nature dries up puddles, or even the ice on your sidewalk without boiling temperatures and clouds of steam, this still sublimates the fluids in the kettle directly from the liquid state to a vapor or gas. There's no steam in between, at least not much. Without the high temperatures and steam, there is consequently very little pressure build up in the vessel or pot. The lid of the still is the condenser and the receiver is located in the pot, so the whole process or separation of fluids, condensation and collection take place in the pot.

This is also the only still I know of that can be built out of items commonly found in the kitchen with no modification or fabrication. You put it together, use it and put the components back in the cupboard. That's why I call it the Disappearing Still. The drawings and materials lists shown in the illustrations detail how to build one of these disappearing stills out of common items.

To illustrate, or explain its workings in the "bare nekked" basics, I'll draw you a word picture using two Chinese woks and a pot. We'll start with a big pot containing a couple of inches of heated fluid in it. Then we take a big wok full of ice water and set it in the mouth of the pot. Almost immediately the rising vapors will begin to condense on the bottom of the wok, roll down to the bottom and drip back into the pot. We are now distilling, but it's fruitless because what goes up just drips right back down into the original fluid. But, if we suspend a smaller wok (receiver) a few inches below the big one, we capture the distillate. Just like the little beekeeper, you lift the lid off your hive, or pot periodically and harvest the nectar.

All the precautions for other stills apply doubly to this one, because when you open it up to harvest, you'll be venting the flammable vapors in the pot. Any open flame, or hot heating element could ignite the vapors and the nectar. Used with a bit of common sense, this is a slow, but very efficient still.

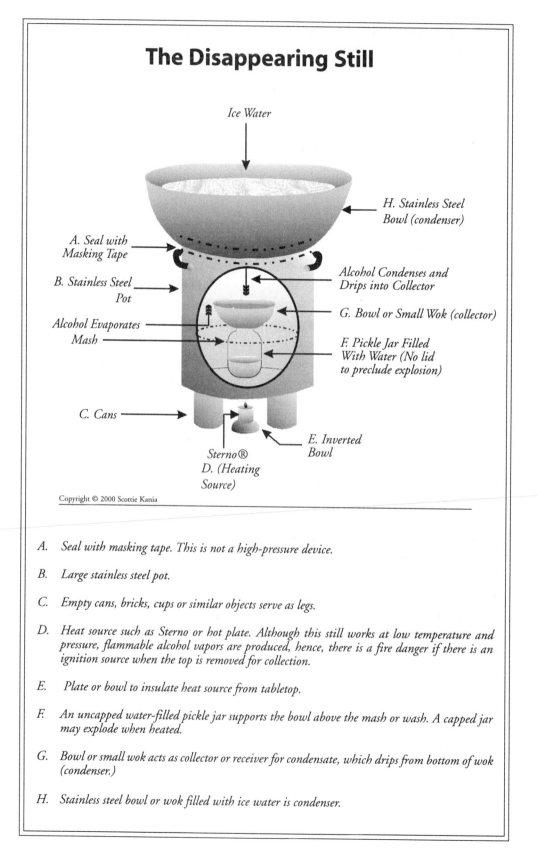

The Disappearing Still

Ice Water

H. Stainless Steel Bowl (condenser)

A. Seal with Masking Tape

B. Stainless Steel Pot

Alcohol Condenses and Drips into Collector

G. Bowl or Small Wok (collector)

Alcohol Evaporates Mash

F. Pickle Jar Filled With Water (No lid to preclude explosion)

C. Cans

E. Inverted Bowl

Sterno®
D. (Heating Source)

Copyright © 2000 Scottie Kania

A.   Seal with masking tape. This is not a high-pressure device.

B.   Large stainless steel pot.

C.   Empty cans, bricks, cups or similar objects serve as legs.

D.   Heat source such as Sterno or hot plate. Although this still works at low temperature and pressure, flammable alcohol vapors are produced, hence, there is a fire danger if there is an ignition source when the top is removed for collection.

E.   Plate or bowl to insulate heat source from tabletop.

F.   An uncapped water-filled pickle jar supports the bowl above the mash or wash. A capped jar may explode when heated.

G.   Bowl or small wok acts as collector or receiver for condensate, which drips from bottom of wok (condenser.)

H.   Stainless steel bowl or wok filled with ice water is condenser.

The Desk Drawer Still (No Home or Office Should Be Without One)

There are several variations of this still that I know of, but someday I would like to meet the guy that built the first one. And we should all be thankful he chose to design stills, instead of weapons, because he'd probably have designed a nuclear derringer. The still proper, is about the size of a bicycle tire pump and would easily fit in the middle drawer of most desks. Heck, you could carry this one around stuck in your waistband. We know you can get in trouble for having a non-permitted still. Just imagine the trouble you could be in if you got caught carrying a concealed still! Awesome, ain't it?

Equally awesome is the fact that this little derringer of stills is a continuous feed column still. You can run many gallons of wash through it, nonstop. You may already have guessed that this baby is also a barely under control bomb. Your guardian Angel will probably develop ulcers and a nervous tic, if you even think of building one. The heart of this still is an electric soldering iron, as the heat source. You remove the soldering iron tip and replace it with a stainless steel or copper tube (pot/column) sealed on one end, open on the other to accept a cork and thermometer. Near the top, or open end, you weld or silver solder (nontoxic, no lead solder) a 2-$\frac{3}{8}$" outlet tube which leads to the condenser.

The top third of the tube is packed loosely with stainless steel scouring pads, making this a Reflux Still. A $\frac{3}{8}$" feed tube enters the pot or column about midpoint and delivers the wash (the wash must be very clear, no solids or junk in it) right to the very bottom. This serves to preheat the wash and delivers it right to the face of the heating element of the soldering iron. It's sort of like spitting on the hot stove, instant evaporation of the most volatile fluids (alcohol) and the rest boils and bubbles. About two inches above the soldering iron heating element, you fit a $\frac{3}{8}$" outlet tube to let the less volatile fluid (expended wash) flow out of the pot.

What we have now, is like a chain reaction started by dribbling liquid on a small, but very hot stove and the only means of keeping the whole shebang from turning into a bomb is to keep the fluid input rate exactly in balance with the boiling/evaporation rate. This diabolical device is fed either by direct gravity flow (best) or by siphoning (risky.) If the siphon flow stops because of a bubble or debris in the line, this still can overheat quickly. A direct gravity flow is more reliable. You must have an adjustable valve on the feed line, because this is the only way you can control this monster other than pulling the plug on the heat source. (The fire extinguisher and the Tarzan swing may come in very handy also.) The thermometer is a necessary instrument, if for no other reason than it will tell you when to run. Give that angel another glass of Pepto Bismol bartender!

Since this is a continuous run still, you will need a continuous flow of water through your condenser. Hook it up directly to the faucet, so you can increase the flow if things start getting out of hand. Remember, this is an ingenious still, but it only operates in the red line or danger zone. The difference between booze and boom is very small with this one.

The Deskdrawer Still - Components

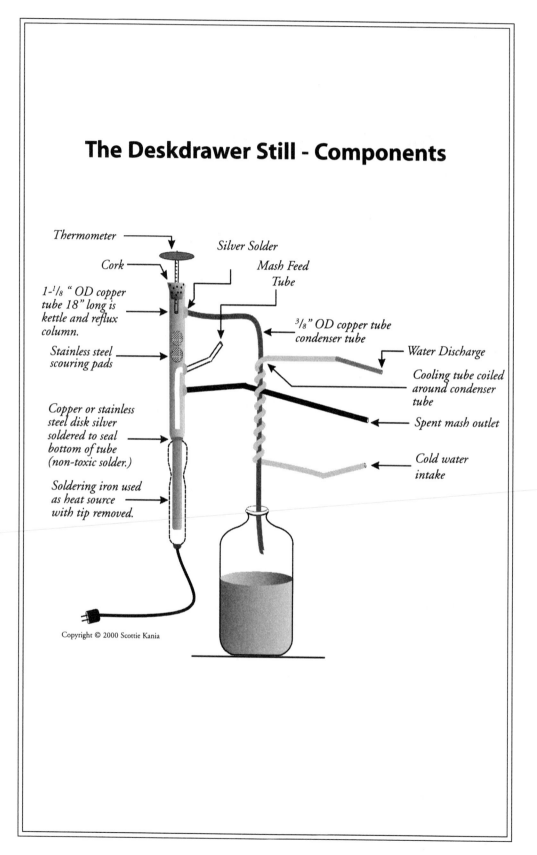

Thermometer

Cork

Silver Solder

Mash Feed Tube

1-1/8 " OD copper tube 18" long is kettle and reflux column.

Stainless steel scouring pads

³/₈" OD copper tube condenser tube

Water Discharge

Cooling tube coiled around condenser tube

Copper or stainless steel disk silver soldered to seal bottom of tube (non-toxic solder.)

Spent mash outlet

Cold water intake

Soldering iron used as heat source with tip removed.

Copyright © 2000 Scottie Kania

The Deskdrawer Still - Operation

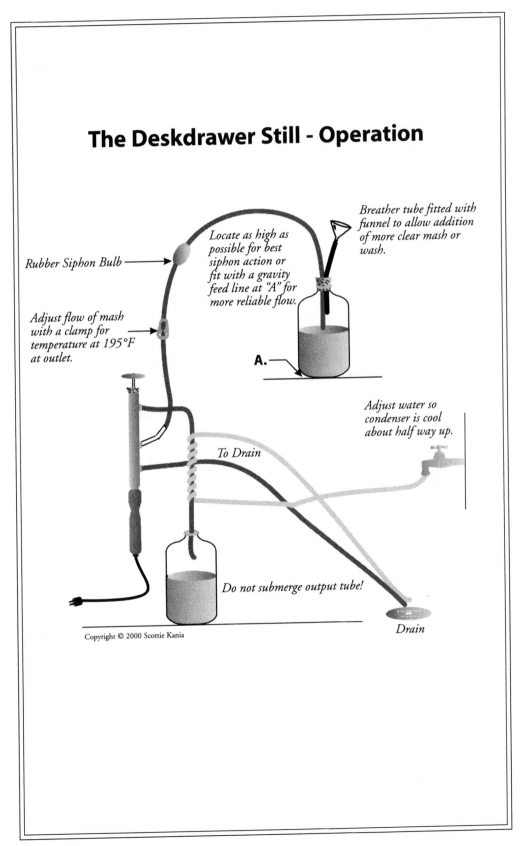

Breather tube fitted with funnel to allow addition of more clear mash or wash.

Rubber Siphon Bulb

Locate as high as possible for best siphon action or fit with a gravity feed line at "A" for more reliable flow.

Adjust flow of mash with a clamp for temperature at 195°F at outlet.

A.

Adjust water so condenser is cool about half way up.

To Drain

Do not submerge output tube!

Copyright © 2000 Scottie Kania

Drain

Properties of Alcohol

Liquor includes all alcoholic beverages made by distillation, as distinguished from those made by fermentation, such as beer and wine, but even distilled liquors begin with a fermented alcoholic solution. Any carbohydrate source, such as sugar, properly fermented and distilled, can produce a potable spirit, e.g., ethyl alcohol, more or less diluted with water and carrying volatile essences that gives it a characteristic flavor.

If distillation is done efficiently, and the distillate redistilled, the final product is colorless, flavorless, pure ethyl alcohol, and no testing analysis can reveal whether its source was wine, beets, potatoes, fruit, grain or sugar. It's chemically the same, no matter what its source. Pure ethyl alcohol is a colorless liquid, having a mild agreeable odor and a burning taste. It very easily mixes with water, thereby reducing its strength, and will absorb moisture from the air. Many names are applied to ethyl alcohol, such as grain alcohol, ethanol, spirits of wine, or cologne spirits. Pure ethyl alcohol boils at 172° F. It readily burns in air with an almost colorless, smokeless flame producing water and carbon dioxide, at a heat a little over half as hot as burning gasoline.

Cold Weather Hazards of Alcohol

Hypothermia – We're all familiar with the image of a big cuddly St. Bernard coming to travelers rescue with a warming keg of brandy around its neck. Unfortunately, for the legend and the traveler, a shot of brandy is about the worst thing possible for someone suffering from what we now recognize as hypothermia (exposure.)

As a person's body temperature gets dangerously low, their body tries to preserve the vital or core body temperature by reducing the flow of warm blood to the extremities. Shivering and numbness of the extremities are the first symptoms that your body is fighting back against hypothermia. If heat loss continues, a person becomes disoriented and a sort of euphoria sets in. Having experienced this near fatal condition and survived mainly because a friend luckily came along and helped me. I can best describe the effects as similar to being pleasantly drunk. I was disoriented, realized that something was happening to me, but was unable to think clearly or help myself.

Alcohol temporarily reverses the symptoms, but hastens the body's heat loss. By increasing the flow of blood to the extremities, your fingers and toes may get warmer, but the core body/brain temperature drops even further and you quickly become even more incapacitated. It's not my intent to teach a cold-weather survival course here, just to caution you that alcohol aggravates, rather than alleviates hypothermia and the combination of the two can be fatal.

The Dead Trapper, Soldier, Miner, Bootlegger

I've heard several versions of this tale in Alaska, in all of which a young man is killed in his prime by a single gulp of whiskey. Unless you guzzle a lot in Arctic regions, it's not a hazard you need to worry about, but since this is an Alaskan book, I'll tell you the story.

First, let me say that when it gets really cold, strange and sometimes horrible things happen. I've seen little kids get their tongues frozen to metal dumpsters trying to lick the frost. Gear shifts snap off in your hands and a cup of hot coffee thrown in the air will explode into a cloud of ice crystals at -20° F. Really cold to the old miners was when the mercury they used in recovering fine gold froze to a solid silvery metal (happens around -40° F.) They'd stop work and stay in their cabins. High proof whiskey doesn't freeze even when mercury does. It gets syrupy like the stuff you put on pancakes, but still pours. (Alcohol freezes at -170° F.)

As one version of the story goes, a young soldier delivered some whiskey to the officer's club by dogsled, of course. He also swiped a bottle of whiskey, which he hid in a snowdrift. When he recovered the bottle, he took a quick drink of the hideously cold booze, which seared his throat about like molten lead and killed him on the spot. As I said, I've heard several similar stories and seen whiskey that was so cold, it had to be dangerous. Just stick to hot toddies and you'll be okay.

Fermentation of Ethyl Alcohol

When yeast, a living fungi, grows in sugary solutions in the virtual absence of air, most of the sugar is converted into ethyl alcohol and carbon dioxide gas. The alcohol and carbon dioxide formed almost equal in total weight and quantity of carbon, hydrogen, and oxygen, the sugar consumed. Common bakers' yeast is a mass of tiny plants akin to bacteria that reproduces by budding. The living bodies of the yeast produces enzymes (sucrose and zymase) that in turn, breaks up sugar (or starch) into alcohol and carbon dioxide.

The formation of ethyl alcohol and carbon dioxide uses up almost 95% of the sugar present, and are the chief products of fermentation. However, the remaining 5% of sugar contributes to the simultaneous formation of several by-products (impurities in very small proportions, such as glycerol, volatile acids, fusel oils or higher alcohols, ethers, aldehydes and esters. It is these substances that enhance ethyl alcohol with its many peculiar flavors, color and the seemingly ever-present "hangover." More about this quality under the heading of Distillation.

Incidentally, poisonous methyl alcohol is not produced by the fermentation of pure sugar. It is manufactured in the fermentation of starch or cellulose, such as found in wood, hence it is called wood alcohol. The addition of fruit juices in home wine making may yield some methyl alcohol. The pectins, or starch, compounds contained in fruits are generally insufficient to yield methyl alcohol in significant quantifies, but from the view of eliminating hangover effects, any methyl alcohol is undesirable. Among the commercial liquors, brandy has the highest per cent of methyl alcohol.

The several general conditions required for efficient fermentation of a satisfactory alcoholic yield are:

1) A favorable temperature specific proportions of sugar, water and yeast, a fertilizer, inhibition of vinegar formation and sufficient time.

2) Temperature: High temperature kills the yeast plants, whereas low temperatures decrease their rate of activity. The higher the temperature, the faster the rate of fermentation, but the lower the alcoholic yield. The optimum temperature is 78° F. Never exceed 90° F.

3) Sugar and water: The optimum ratio of sugar to water is 2 lb. to one gal.

4) Yeast and time: The usual proportion of yeast is 1 cup to 5 gal. of water. At this ratio, other conditions being optimum, the yeast will, in plus or minus 14 days, have manufactured enough ethyl alcohol to kill themselves and stop fermentation. Since the yeast will reproduce rapidly in sweet solution, using less than one cup of yeast is satisfactory. However, active fermentation will take a little longer to get going. Nevertheless, in plus or minus 14 days, as the presence of alcohol increases, fermentation will stop. Let experience be your guide.

5) Vinegar inhibition: The solution of mash or wine, upon exposure to oxygen, will tend to promote the growth of another fungi that will manufacture vinegar.

6) When fermentation is complete, the mash or wine will be turbid and must be allowed, to settle. The sediment contains precipitated organic matter, yeast bodies and potassium tantrate. The settling may take several days or a week, or even months in the case of wine. Chilling the fermented mash and/or filtering will shorten the time it requires to settle. Siphon or decant the clear solution and discard the sediment. Try not to aerate the mash or wine unnecessarily, thereby encouraging the formation of vinegar.

7) The resulting mash or wine now will be no more than 16% and not usually less than 3% ethyl alcohol by volume. Thus, it is a very dilute alcohol solution, akin to most wines that must be concentrated by distillation if you are to have a high proof spirit.

Basic Mash for Distilling Neutral Spirits

In 5 gallons of ordinary tap water, dissolve 10 lb. Granulated sugar. Add 1 cup of Champagne yeast starter culture. Allow the mash to ferment at about 78° F for 14 days, or until the fermentation stops. Provide for the release of CO_2 gas and keep air out. Let the mash stand until clear of sediment and siphon and decant. It is now ready for distillation. Yield: *½ gal. Of 190 proof alcohol*

Distillation of Ethyl Alcohol

Distillation is simply boiling a mixture to separate the more volatile (having the lowest boiling point) from the less volatile fluid, and then cooling and condensing the resulting vapor to produce almost nearly pure liquid. The nonvolatile impurities will remain in the residue, which in this case is discarded. Direct distillation of alcohol can yield at best only by the constant boiling of a mixture of alcohol and water (172° F) containing 97.2% alcohol by volume (194.4 proof) because this mixture boils 18° F lower than pure alcohol (172.9° F) hence, do not expect more than 190 proof alcohol from your home still.

If ethyl alcohol is redistilled several times to 170 proof or better, it will be a neutral spirit and all but free of any hangover producing components, such as the volatile acids, fusel oils, ethers, aldehydes and esters mentioned under the heading of Fermentation. Commercial whiskey is distilled out at a much lower proof specifically to retain these components pulled from the grain of which it was made, to impart a desired flavor to the liquor. It is because of these by-products (impurities) that you get a hangover. The ethyl alcohol produced as described in this book and flavored alcohol to make duplicate the liquor you want, is the best you will ever drink.

The simplest distillation apparatus, often used in high school chemistry laboratories, consists of six basic parts, as does any still:

1) a heat source

2) a boiler to heat the mash

3) a thermometer to observe the vapor temperature

4) a condenser to cool and condense the vapor and

5) a receiver to collect the distillate.

6) a fire extinguisher

The usual home "pot" is just a variation of the glass apparatus described elsewhere, but far safer. The pot should be made of stainless steel throughout to prevent corrosion by the hot acids produced during distillation. All fittings must be airtight to prevent leakage of alcohol or its vapors and possible explosion and fire. The tubing extending from the pot can be of almost any metal, such as copper, but not of iron, which corrodes too easily. The condenser should be made of metal and not glass. It is a cylindrical metal box with copper tubing coiled up inside of it. The best heat source is an electric stove. A gas stove or an open flame of any type are quite dangerous, due to the ever present alcohol vapors. Immersion heaters are satisfactory, but they court disaster if through mishandling, they become exposed and ignite the alcohol or its vapors. The simple Pot Still requires three or four consecutive time consuming distillations (runs) to produce a wholly pure, hangover proof distillate.

Brandy is distilled from wine, either grapes or other fruit. Fermentation of fruit not only produces ethyl alcohol, but also methyl, or wood alcohol and lots of fusel oils, the stuff that makes you sick. Aging brandy in charred kegs for a few years colors it and mellows it by absorption and chemical breakdown of the more wicked components. A good percentage of the initial product is also lost in the process, so the aged end product (cognac) is far more expensive, but a lot more humane.

First Run

Start Collecting at 170° F to 180° F Through 205° F, Then Stop.

Gradually heat the 5 gallons (or more) of clear mash in the pot and expect the first condensate to begin dripping in the receiver in about an hour between 170° F and 180° F. Collect all that comes over on this first run. About 2 hours later when 205° F is reached, stop collecting. You should have about 1-¼ gallons of distillate that will be about 40 to 60% and by-products (80-120 proof.) Throw away the residue in the pot, rinse it out and flush out any solids that may have boiled over into your tubing.

Caution: Too high heat will cause the mash to boil over through the tubing, clouding the distillate and possibly clogging the tubing. The more slowly you heat, the less impurities will go over and the better your product will be. Remember; this is a "how-to," not a "have to" book. These are explicit instructions from a Moonshiner that operated overseas. If you do this in the U.S., it is a federal offense.

Second Run

Start Collecting at 160° F to 172° F Through 204° F, Then Stop.

Gradually heat the first run distillate in the pot and begin collecting the condensate in the receiver between 160° F and 180° F. In about an hour, when 204° F is reached, stop collecting. You should have about a gallon of 70% alcohol plus by-products. Discard the residue from the pot as before.

Caution: Your 70% alcohol is 140 proof and has a flash point of 40° F. The product is now very flammable.

Third Run:

Start Collecting at 170° F Through 184° F, Then Stop.

Gradually heat the second run in the pot. Action is fast. The temperature moves rapidly to about 170° F. Discard whatever distillate comes over before 170° F or that which comes over before the trickle steadies into a solid stream. Stop collecting at about 184° F in about 45 minutes. You should have about $1/2$ gallon of about 85% alcohol. Throw away any residue in the pot.

Caution: Your distillate is about 170 proof and extremely flammable.

If you make one more run, purifying the

product even more, you will have hangover-proof alcohol.

Fourth Run

Start Collecting at 170° F Through 180° F, Then Stop

Gradually heat third-run stock in the pot. The temperature will rise to 170° F very quickly. As before, discard what comes over before 170° F and keep what comes over between 170° F to 180° F. It should take about $1/2$ hour, and you will have about ½ gallon of 90-95%, almost pure ethyl alcohol.

The Reflux or Fractional Distillation Still (Reflux Still)

This is a refinement of the preceding Pot Still, but is more efficient and more complex in design, therefore it produces in one run what the above stills may require three runs to do. A tubular metal reflux column packed with glass marbles, stainless steel scouring pads, or a system of baffles and sieves is attached just above the pot. The column or tower may or may not be combined with a second reflux condenser at its top.

In fractional distillation, the point is to achieve the closest possible contact between rising vapor and descending pre-condensed liquid within the reflux column, and thus permit only the most volatile vapor to continue through to the second condenser while returning the less volatile vapor as a liquid toward the pot. The purification of the more volatile vapor by such counter current streams of vapor and liquid is known as sectification and the descending liquid is know as reflux, hence the name "Reflux Column." This system may yield a first run of about 170 to 180 proof alcohol, double that of the first run of the simple Pot Still.

The efficiency of the reflux system depends upon the length and diameter of the reflux column. A column of about 6 inches high and 3 inches across may require two runs, whereas a column 18 inches high and 4 inches across may require only one run to produce 170 to 180 proof alcohol. Heat control is accurate because of the controlled water flow through the reflux condenser in the top of the column. The incorporation of this additional cooling coil turns the Reflux Still into a Compound Still. Also, you can control the temperature by raising or reducing the heat source as in the simple Pot Still, but it is not so critical.

Keep the temperature between 172° F to 176° F for optimum results. This run should be sufficient and yield pure spirits, but if yeast flavor or odor is present, run the distillate a second time at the same temperature range.

Cleaning the Still

Immediately after each distillation, while the metal is still warm, thoroughly rinse and with a cloth, wipe out your still. Flush out all tubing with clear water. If washing is indicated, use a weak detergent solution, but not soap. Soap may impart an undesirable odor.

Caution: Do not store 15% or better alcohol, even temporarily, in plastic containers. There are many types of plastic and unfortunately some of them will dissolve in alcohol.

Safety Factors During Distillation

Recognize the fact that when distilling alco-hol, we might just as well be distilling gasoline. From a fire and explosion/hazard point of view, alcohol is almost as dangerous as gasoline and what moron would cook gasoline on his stove? The mash is not flammable, however, the vapors from the first and successive run distillates certainly are. The flash points or the temperatures above which alcohol produces vapors which will ignite and below which it will not are:

A. 51° F for 100% or 200 proof ethyl alcohol (pure)

B. 57° F for 94% or 190 proof ethyl alcohol (uncut)

C. 78° F for 45% or 90 proof ethyl alcohol (Bourbon)

When you are distilling, the temperatures of the alcohol will be well above these flash point temperatures, so be careful.

Memorize the following common-sense rules:

1) Do not smoke while running a still.

2) Do not use an open flame if you can avoid it.

3) Ensure proper ventilation. Alcohol diffuses readily in air and will explode very easily with a spark or a flame.

4) Avoid using glass containers. Use metal or plastic only.

5) Never fill a pot while it is on the stove or near any heat source. Alcohol spilled on an electric stove burner may explode.

6) Never leave a still unattended. Hose lines may fail or the receiver may overflow, spreading dangerous vapors.

7) Keep the receiver and its vapors low on the floor, away from the heat source. Use a small-necked receiver, then if a fire starts, it will burn at the small- necked opening, that is easily extinguished. A damp cloth wrapped loosely around the tubing where it enters the receiver will keep the vapors in the receiver.

8) Never store uncut alcohol unless it is in the refrigerator. It is a potential bomb at room temperature.

9) Be sure all fittings are tight, thus avoiding vapor leaks in your still. If a leak develops, stop all sources of heat first, then fix it.

10) Have a CO_2 (Carbon Dioxide) fire extinguisher on hand, and know how to use it.

11) Four leaf clovers, rabbits foot and Tarzan swing are optional.

The Devil, Vodka, Russian Bootlegging and Potatoes

My Grandmother used to tell me stories about the hell-raising Cossacks who occupied Poland in her youth. She said she'd seen them get so drunk they'd pass out with their eyes open and when flies would walk across their eyeballs, they wouldn't even blink. She also said she'd seen a drunken Cossack who, going through mounted exercises with the saber neatly sliced his horses ear off. I didn't believe Grandma then, but after working in Russia on several projects, I sure do now.

You can't talk about vodka without talking about Russia. Russian consumption of vodka is staggering, no pun intended, because it's not funny. Not only is the populace heavily dependent on it, but the government derives a large part of its revenue, as much as one third in Soviet times, from alcohol production and taxes.

Almost like a pact with the devil, everything the Russian government tries with vodka, has evil results. Increasing production to meet popular demand (15-20% of all retail trade, 14% of family income spent on alcohol under the old regime) caused profound social, health and economic problems due to decreased production of everything due to drunkenness. Gorbachev's anti-alcohol campaign reduced consumption, but was hugely unpopular, reduced the tax base very significantly and prompted increased production of illicit sa*mogon*, or moonshine.

What is germane to this book is that much of this bootleg *samogon* is deadly. 90,000 cases of alcohol poisonings in 1997, estimated 43,000 deaths. State revenue from alcohol *pyanye dengi* (drunken money) has fallen to 3% of the national budget, yet the country is awash in booze.

Now, most of the bootleg stuff comes from organized crime, but a lot also comes from traditional home stills and methods, using potatoes. The point I'm getting at is something is killing a hell of a lot of people and it seems to come from potatoes. In making vodka, I know potatoes are boiled, mashed (physically) and mashed (converted) with malted grain or industrial enzymes, fermented and then distilled. Yield per sack of potatoes is said to be thirty-some bottles of 100 proof vodka. That sounds good, but knowing that there are lethal pitfalls to making potato spirits, I can only say, don't attempt it!

Distilling For Reasons Other Than Whiskey Making

Many people concerned with distilling their own drinking water and alternative fuels for their vehicles have purchased stills from a foreign supplier via the internet. If you feel you just have to have a still for the above or other reasons, contact your local office of the Bureau of Alcohol, Tobacco and Firearms (BATF) regarding getting a legally permitted still. *Having a non-permitted still will get you in a lot of trouble.* Getting a legally permitted still will probably be far more trouble than it's worth.

Back in the 60's, Castro and his guerillas fueled their vehicles with alcohol distilled from sugarcane with a couple of mothballs (naphtha) added to each barrel. Granted that this was ingenious, but the really amazing thing is that they're still driving the same vehicles. Also, bear in mind that the vehicles that Fidel and crew ran on alcohol were far simpler than current day vehicles with all the sensors, computer chips and emission control systems. The fact remains, even if you got your vehicle to run on homebrewed fuel, you'd probably still be in trouble with the authorities because of all the systems you'd have to override or disconnect. Get a horse, they don't have to have emission controls, yet.

Chapter Six

Concocting Your Own Liqueurs

In This Chapter

➢ Flavoring and Making Liqueurs

➢ Recipes

➢ Recipes Using Flavors for Preparation
   of Cordials & Liqueurs

➢ Recipe for Spirits (Brandy, Run, Gin,
   Rye, Etc.)

➢ Homemade Liqueur Recipes

How to make your own fancy liqueurs, using both homemade and store bought flavorings

My special thanks to Mr. Gunther Anderson for his assistance in this chapter. For information about liqueur-making you can go to his web site on the internet:

www.guntheranderson.com

Liqueurs

Liqueurs are the most sensual of alocholic beverages. They are a blend of alcoholic and non-alcoholic ingredients to give pleasure and in many cases to have tonic or even aphrodisiac affects. Most, like traditional eggnog are mildly alcoholic, good tasting and good for you; such as the many liqueurs made by rosy cheeked monks for centuries in Europe.

Some are not so appetizing, such as traditional Asian concoctions that steep fresh bloody deer horn and ginseng roots in alcohol to extract the "goodness" from the ingredients. They are said to have great restorative powers and the ingredients are so hightly prized that they sell for more per ounce than gold in the orient. In fact, Alaska has had its share of dealers in legal reindeer (domesticated caribou) and wild caribou (illegal) antlers who cater to these demands. True Perod is banned in most of the civilized world today because two of its original ingredients, opium and wormwood, caused addiction and madness.

We'll focus on the more benign, or appetizing liqueurs, first teaching you how to make them from scratch yourself and then using readily available commercial flavoring. "Commercial" is the keyword here because we will be imitating, but not duplicating beverages whose names and recipes are closely guarded and legally protected. In all the following recipes "similar to" applies to commonly recognized names

and used only to categorize them. We wouldn't want to make all those rosy cheeked monks mad at us, would we?

Flavoring and Making Liqueurs

Liqueurs are made by mixing and steeping flavorings, sweetners and coloring ingredients with liquors, wines and things such as cream to make pleasing and usually mildly alcoholic beverages.

There are three stages to making a liqueur. Steeping, filtering and ageing. You will find there will be differences depending on the type of fruits. Cranberries need no aging whereas others such as orange peels need up to three months just ageing. Many of the flavors, primarily all the dry spices, roots and beans and prepackaged liqueur extracts such as Noirot® need almost no steeping and will be ready for filtering in anywhere from several hours to a week.

1.   For fleshy fruits such as apples or peaches, steep from 2 weeks to a month and age for 1 month.

2.   For berries, steep 2 weeks to a month and age for a month

3.   For oils such as citrus peels, steep a month and age for 3 months. Use only the zest or colored part of peels.

4.   For whole spice, steep from 4 to 7 days, no aging.

5.   For powdered spice, steep a day or two, bottle and serve.

6.   For artificial flavorings, such as a liquid additives, no steeping or ag-

ing. It's usually ready to bottle and serve. **(1)**

Steps:

1. Combine all flavorings in a con
tainer.

2. Add alcohol.

3. Seal container and let steep in a dark place.

4. Shake container periodically to keep flavorings from massing to
gether.

5. Strain and filter.

6. Add syrup.

7. Seal in another container and age

8. Filter once more.

9. Bottle and serve. **(1)**

Simple Syrup for Liqueurs

It is one of the basic ingredients of many of these recipes, It is made by simmering equal volumes of water and sweetener for about five minutes. Sweeteners can be cane sugar, brown sugar or honey. Powdered, or confectioners sugar is not suitable because it has a starch filler and will make a cloudy syrup.

(1) You may double the amount of water for a less sweet liqueur.

Homemade Recipes

Crème de Menthe I

Dissolve 2 cups of sugar in 2 cups of water; add 2 tbs. of white Karo® syrup and boil for 10 minutes. When cool, add ½ qt. of

100 proof, 1-½ to 2 tsp. of peppermint flavoring and green vegetable coloring to your satisfaction. *Yield: About 1-1/2 quarts*

Crème de Menthe II

2	Tsp.	Peppermint extract
2	Cups	Simple syrup (cane sugar) (P. 139)
3	Cups	90 proof vodka
1	Tsp.	Glycerin

Mix and store for 1-2 weeks in a sealed container.

Fresh Mint Liqueur

12-14	T	Fresh crumpled mint (peppermit or spearmint) leaves or
6	T	Dried mint or
3	T	Mint extract
3	Cups	Vodka
1	Tsp.	Glycerine (optional)
1	Cup	Simple sugar syrup

Steep leaves (fresh or dried) in vodka for 10 days, shaking occasionally. Strain and filter.

Note: Be sure to squeeze as much liquid from leaves as possible and age for 2 weeks.

If using extract, just combine all ingredients and mix thoroughly. Age at least 2 days. As with most liqueurs the longer the age, the better the flavor. **(2)**

Bailey's Irish Cream

1	Can	Sweetened condensed milk
1-¾	Cups	Irish whiskey
4	Ea.	Egg whites
1	Cup	Heavy cream
1	Tbsp.	Chocolate syrup

1	Tbsp.	Instant coffee
1	Tsp.	Vanilla extract
¼	Tsp.	Almond extract

Combine ingredients in a blender and blend until smooth. Bottle and steep in the refrigerator for one week. Will last up to 1 month refrigerated.

Irish Crème I

1	Tsp.	Almond Extract
1	Can	Sweetened condensed milk
2	Cups	Rye Whiskey
1	Tsp.	Instant coffee

Mix ingredients. Age in refrigerator 3-4 weeks.

Irish Crème II

1	Cup	Cream
½	Cup	Honey
1-½	Cup	Irish/Rye Whiskey
1	Tsp.	Instant coffee

Mix and age in refrigerator for two weeks. (4)

Creme De Cacao

Thoroughly mix 1 pint of chocolate syrup, 1 pint of Karo® syrup, 1 quart of 120 proof and 1 oz. of vanilla extract. *Yield: About 2 quarts*

Coffee Liqueur (Kahlua)

Boil 1 lb. of drip grind coffee in 1-¼ quarts of water and simmer 40 minutes. Strain liquid (for grounds) through cheesecloth. Dissolve 3-lb. sugar in 1 quart of water and boil 5 minutes. Add coffee concentrate and cool. Add 1-¼ quarts of 180 proof and 2 oz. of vanilla extract.

Yield: About 2-½ quarts.

Coffee Liqueur

2	Cups	Water
1-½	Cups	Brown sugar
1	Cup	Cane sugar
½	Cup	Instant coffee
2	Tbsp.	Vanilla extract
3	Cups	90 proof alcohol (Vodka)

Simmer sugars and water 5 minutes. Mix in coffee. When cool, mix with vodka and vanilla. Store in sealed container for two weeks. (4)

Drambuie I

To one pint of simple syrup, add 4 ounces of Karo® syrup and 25 drops of Noirot Scotch essence. Bring to boil and cool. Add to one pint of 180 proof and let stand for one week.

Yield: About 1-½ quarts.

Drambuie II

3	Cups	Scotch
1	Cup	Honey
¼	Tsp.	Rosemary

Add rosemary to scotch and let stand overnight. Strain scotch and mix with honey. Age two weeks. (4)

Amaretto

¾	Tsp.	Almond extract
3	Cups	80 proof vodka
½	Cup	White sugar
½	Cup	Brown sugar
1	Cup	Water

Simmer 5 minutes (1)

Cointreau No. 1

Pour a quart of 180 proof in a wide mouthed jar; suspend a well colored orange from a string, about ¼" above the alcohol and cap tightly. Let stand quietly, unopened for 14 days. Oils from orange peel will drip into the alcohol, flavoring and turning it yellow. Mix 12 oz. of sugar in 16 oz. of water. Slowly boil this mixture until the syrup will almost thread when poured from a spoon and not spatter. Pour this hot syrup slowly into the orange treated alcohol and stir slowly until thoroughly mixed. Pour your finished Cointreau into an appropriate bottle.

Yield: About 1-½ quarts.

Cointreau No. 2

Dissolve 3 cups of sugar in 2 cups of water and mix well in 1 qt. 150 proof Add the outermost peelings of 2 well-colored oranges and ½ lemon and a little pulp of both. Allow to marinate for two weeks. Shake every other day. Strain the Cointreau® into an appropriate bottle.

Yield: About 1-½ quarts.

Anisette

Add 1-½ oz. of Anise Flavoring to 2 quarts of vodka and sweeten to taste (the drink will turn milky white when served with water.)
Yield: About 2 quarts

Grand Marnier

3	Cups	Brandy
1-½	Tsp.	Pure orange extract
1	Cup	Honey
½	Tsp.	Glycerine
1	Dash	Cinnamon (ground)
1	Dash	Coriander (ground)

Combine all ingredients and steep for one month. Clarify and bottle.

Rum Shrub

6	Ea.	Medium sized oranges
1	Pint	Cold water
2-3	Lb.	Sugar (cane)
2	Qt.	Dark or light rum

Peel oranges very thinly using only the zest or colored part, no white part, and place peelings in a gallon container. Squeeze and add the juice of the oranges with a pint of cold water close container tightly and let stand for 3 days, stirring or shaking occasionally. Strain into an enamel pot, add sugar and bring to a boil. Add a pint of the resultant orange mixture to the rum, strain and bottle. Age for at least a week.
(3)

Almond Shrub

1	Qt.	Rum
2	Cups	Orange juice
		Zest of one whole lemon
¾	Lb.	Sugar (cane)
2	Cups	Milk
5-10	Drops	Almond extract

Combine ingredients except the milk and almond extract in a container. Add the almond extract (to taste) to the milk and mix thoroughly and add to the container. Cover with a lid and place in a warm place approximately. **(3)**

Kümmel

2	Tsp.	Caraway seeds
1	Qt.	Vodka

Crush seeds and add to the vodka. Steep for 2 weeks and filter. This is supposed to be drunk after meals. Carraway is said to aid in digestion and preventing flatulence.

Orange Peel Liqueur

4	Ea.	Medium oranges (the peels only scraped for the zest, no white pulp)
3	Cups	Vodka
1	Cup	Simple sugar syrup (P. 139)

Combine all ingredients in a container and steep for 3 weeks. If you should decide to add extra peels, make sure the white pulp is removed. Strain and filter, add syrup and age for at least up to 4 months.

Whole Orange Liqueur

3	Ea.	Whole oranges pierced
½	Ea.	Lemon pierced
2	Ea.	Whole cloves
3	Cups	Vodka
1	Cup	Simple sugar syrup (P. 139)

Combine oranges, lemon, closves and vodka in a container (make sure vodka covers the fruit) and steep 10 days. Strain, filter and add simple syrup. Age 3 to 4 weeks.

Tangerine Liqueur

5-6	Ea.	Whole tangerines
4	Ea..	Whole cloves
3	Cups	Vodka
1	Cup	Simple sugar syrup (P. 139)

Pierce fruit liberally with a fork or knife. Place cloves in some of the holes. Steep 10 days using just enough of vodka to cover fruit. Strain and filter. Add syrup and age at least a month, remembering the longer the aging, the better the liqueur.

Tangerine Liqueur (made with peels or the zest)

6	Ea.	Medium peels scraped and cut
½	Ea.	Medium lemon peel scraped and cut.
3	Cups	Vodka

| 1 | Cup | Simple sugar syrup (P. 139) |

Combine ingredients and steep for at least 3 weeks. Strain, filter and add simple sugar syrup. Age for at least 2 months.

Peach Liqueur

9	Ea.	Peaches
3	Cups	Vodka
1	Cup	Simple sugar syrup (P. 139)

Skin, pit and slice peaches. Combine all ingredients and steep for 1 week. Strain, squeeze and filter. Add syrup and age at least one month.

Peach Brandy (Canned Peaches)

1-½	Cups	Peaches (canned)
1	Cup	Sugar
1	Ea.	Cinnamon stick (not ground)
3	Cups	Vodka

Combine ingredients in a 1-quart container and fill with vodka, steep 2 weeks, strain, squeeze and filter, age one month.

Nectarine Liqueur

5	Ea.	Nectarines
1-½	Cups	Vodka
½	Cup	Simple sugar syrup (P.139)

Skin, pit and slice nectarines. Combine all ingredients except syrup and steep one week. Strain and filter, add syrup, bottle and age at least one month.

Apricot Liqueur

2	Lb.	Dried apricots
2	Qt.	Vodka
4	Cups	Sugar (cane)

Combine all ingredients in a container and seal tightly. Steep for at least 3 months in a dark place. Strain, filter and bottle.

Note: the resultant apricots are great to eat or be used in a favorite recipe for baked goods.

Apple Brandy

Add 1-lb. Dried apples to 2 qt. of 100 proof, let stand 2 days, then strain. Sweeten if desired. *Yield: About 2 qt.*

Apple Liqueur

3	Ea.	Large Granny Smith or other tart apples, cored and sliced.
1	Ea.	Lemon peel zest
2	Ea.	Cloves
2	Cups	Sugar (cane)
1	Pinch	Nutmeg
2	Cups	Vodka

Combine all ingrediets and steepat least one week (the longer, the better) Strain, squeeze and filter. Age 1 month.

Cranberry or Alaskan Watermelon Berry Liqueur

1	Lb.	Cranberries or Alaskan watermelon berries
1-½	Cups	Vodka
1-½	Cups	Simple Syrup (P. 139)
½	Ea.	Lemon or lime peel (zest)
¼	Ea.	Peel of orange (zest)

Process cranberries/watermelon berries in a blender until coarse and place in a container with zest of lemon/lime and orange and vodka. Combine sugar and water in a sauce pan, bring to a boil and simmer until sugar is completely dissolved. Let cool and combine 1-½ cups with the rest of ingredients. Seal the container tightly and place in a cool dark place to steep for one month. Shake lightly occasionally. After steeping, strain and bottle and serve.

Plum Liqueur

1	Lb.	Fresh plums (cut up or whole)
3	Ea.	Cloves
1	Pinch	Cinnamon
1	Cup	Sugar (cane)
2	Cups	Vodka

Place plums in a container with flavorings, sugar and vodka. (If using whole plums, be sure to pierce the skins)Make sure vodka covers the plums completely. Steep for 3 months, shaking occcasionally. Strain andfilter. Age approximate 3 months.

Rhubarb Liqueur

4	Cups	Fresh rhubarb
3	Cups	Sugar (cane)
3	Cups	Vodka

Clean and trim rhubarb. Slice about ¼" thickness. Place in container and add sugar and stir, add vodka and mix again. Cover and let steep at room temperature for about 3 or 4 weeks, mixing occasionally. After aging strain and press juice out of rhubarb. Strain again and filter. Bottle and age one more month.

Elderberry Liqueur

4	Cups	Elderberries
2	Cups	Sugar
1	Tsp.	Lemon zest (fresh)
1	Ea.	Lemon
1	Cup.	Water
3	Cups	Vodka

After cleaning, crush elderberries and sugar in a container. Let stand for 1 hour. Add lemon zest and juiceof lemon, vodka and water. Age for one month in a cool, dark place, shaking occasionally. Strain and filter, age for one more week. Filter again and transfer to final container. Age for one month more.

Caution: Native Alaskan Elderberries are toxic. Use only domesticated berries.

Raspberry Liqueur

4	Cups	Raspberries (mashed)

½	Ea.	Leomon peel (scraped)
3	Cups	Vodka
¾	Cups	Simple surgar syrup (P. 139)

Steep 3 weeks, strain and filter, add syrup and age about 5 or 6 weeks.

Pineapple Liqueur

2	Cups	Pineapple
½	Tsp	Vanilla
2-½	Cups	Vodka
½	Cup	Simple sugar syrup (P. 139)

Combine ingredients and steep for 1 week, strain, squeeze and filter. Add syrup and age 1 month

Blackberry or Other Berry Cordial

2	Cups	Berries, crushed. (You can use many kinds of berries like raspberries, salmon berries, strawberries, etc.
3	Cups	Brandy
1-½	Cups	Simple syrup (P. 139)

As with wine making, don't crush the seed or you'll let the nasty stuff out. You can use a juice bag or filter this later.

The wild yeast on the berries may start a fermentation, so it's a good idea to soak the berries in a campden tablet solution before you crush them.

Caution: Once you've mixed all ingredients, age this one for about 1 week in a covered, but not tightly sealed container. If you get a ferment going, it may burst the container and the mess you'll have will not be very cordial. Strain bottle and enjoy after two weeks.

Spiced Rum

2	Cups	Bacardi light rum
2	Tsp.	Vanilla extract
½	Cup	Simple sugar syrup (P. 139)

Combine ingredients in a container. Shake to mix. Other than letting it settle, this can be served right away.

Egg Nog

This is a basic recipe which you can vary the strength of. Makes about one gallon.

12	Ea.	Eggs (separated)
1	Lb.	(2-½ cups) sugar, cane or confectioners.
½ to 4	Cups	Brandy, cognac, rum, bourbon or rye whiskey.

You may blend the above, or even use fruit flavored brandies, but take note of the strength of what you use. Some rye whiskey runs to 110 proof and 4 cups in a gallon may give you "Nuclear Nog."

2	Qts.	Whipping cream
1	Tsp	Nutmeg or nutmeg and cinnamon (½ tsp of each.)

Beat egg yolks and gradually blend in sugar, cream and liquor. Beat egg whites until stiff, then blend into other ingredients. Refrigerate for 3-4 hours, then serve sprinkled with nutmeg/cinnamon or blend in before refrigerating.

Noirot® Liqueur Extracts

Noirot® liqueur extracts can be found almost all over the world. There are over 70 extract flavors in the Noirot® line. Most of these flavors are made using 100% natural ingredients. They contain no artificial preservatives or stabilizers. While there are other liqueur extracts on the market, Noirot® are the best and the easiest way to make liqueurs at home. In making your liqueurs, sugar and alcohol (Vodka or other tasteless spirits such as grain alcohol) are the standard components. The most critical element being the flavoring.

Note: The source for Noirot® liqueur flavoring concentrate is given in the appendix F of this book.

The following are some of the Noirot® flavoring extracts available:

Noirot® Flavoring Extracts

Amaretto – Aromatic, reddish brown liqueur with a nutty Almond flavor

Apricot Brandy – A rich fruit liqueur made from Apricots

Banana – Banana liqueur

Café sport (Tia Maria) – Coffee liqueur with a hint of chocolate

Chocolate Menthe (Vandermint) – Chocolate liqueur with refreshing mint flavor.

Couvent Jaune (Yellow Chartreuse) – Herbal liqueur with slight spice and honey flavor

Couvent Verde (Green Chartreuse) – Herbal liqueur with a stronger taste that the yellow version

Genepy (Galiano) – Soft Licorice liqueur with golden appearance

Grenadine (non-alcoholic) – Red syrup, very sweet. Non-alcoholic with raspberry taste. Used in cocktails.

Irish Glen (Irish Mist) – Sweet herbal liqueur with honey taste. Drier than Lorbuie.

Kirsch – Unsweetened, clear cherry drink. Also used a lot in cooking

Lorbuie (Drambuie) – sweet, heather-honey liqueur with golden color. Ideal base Scotch whiskey.

Mocha (Kahlua) – sweet Coffee liqueur with Cocoa and vanilla taste

Noisette (Frangelico) – sweet Hazelnut liqueur

Noix de Cocoa (Malibu) – sweet Coconut liqueur

Orange Brandy (Grande Marnier) – medium orange liqueur with a hint of herbs

Pastis (Pernod) – unsweetened aniseed flavored drink. Much stronger than Sambuca.

Reverendine (Benedictine) – Medium herbal liqueur with a powerful aroma.

Sambuca – Medium Anisette flavored clear liqueur. Strong flavor and aroma.

Sambuca Nera (Opal Nera) – Medium dark Aniseed liqueur with strong flavor and aroma.

Recipes for the Use of Flavors in the Preparation of Cordials and liqueurs

Anisette, Apricot, Blackberry, Creme de Cacao, etc.

Sugar	¾ lb. (12 oz.) approx.
Water	¾ pt. (12 Fl. Oz.)

Alcohol	¾ Pt. (12 Fl. Oz.) approx.

Noirot® Flavor Per label instructions

Dissolve sugar in warm water. When cool, add alcohol in which you have previously dissolved the necessary flavor. Shake well and let it stand for a few days, or longer.

Recipe Spirits (Brandy, Rum, Gin, Rye, etc.)

Alcohol	1 Pt.
Water	1 Pt.
Noirot® Flavor	Per label instructions

Dissolve flavor in alcohol, add water and shake well. One teaspoon of chemically pure glycerin makes a smoother beverage. In beverages such as brandy, rum and all types of whiskeys, an aged-like taste can be obtained by adding a small quantity (about a tablespoon) of specially toasted oak chips. Let stand for 10 or more days and then filter.

Any Cordial or Liqueur

¾	lb. (12 oz.)	Sugar
12	Fluid oz.	Water (boiled or distilled)
¾		Pint (12 oz.) 190 proof alcohol

Use Noirot® flavoring per maker's instructions. Dissolve sugar in warm water; cool. Add alcohol in that you have dissolved the desired flavoring. Shake well and let stand for several days or longer.

Any Grain Alcohol (Using Noirot® Flavors)

1	Pint	190 proof
1	Pint	Water
21	Drops	Any flavor, such as bourbon

Vermouth

¾	gal.	White Wine
½	lb.	Sugar
½	pt.	Vodka
1	oz.	Flavor cognac, rum etc. (except 3 drops gin flavor)

Dissolve flavoring in alcohol; add water and shake well. One (1) tsp. of chemically pure glycerin may be added to one quart of prepared beverage, producing a smoother liquor.

Aging - To age beverages like brandy, rum and all whiskies, add about a tablespoon of toasted oak chips. Let stand for 10 or more days, and then filter.

n the earlier printings of this book, we failed to show proper credits for a number of recipes in this chapter. We have provided footnotes and a bibliography at this chapter end to rectify our ommission.

Sources for More Information

The following books and web sites contain more recipes, instructions and perspectives on liqueur making. Some of the books may be very hard to find, but well worth the effort.

(1)www.guntheranderson.com/liqueurs.htm

More recipes and more detailed instructions about liqueur-making.

(2) Meilach, Dona Z., The Best 50 Homemade Liqueurs, San Leandro, CA: Bristol Publishing Enterprises, 1996 [ISBN1558671412]

(3) Jagendort, M.A. Folk Wines, Cordials and Brandies, New York, NY: The Vanguard Press, 1963 [Library of Congress Cat. Card No.: 63-21854

(4) Linda Cunningham
www.guntheranderson.com/liqueurs

Crosby, Nancy and Sue Kenny, Kitchen Cordials, Westport, MA: Crosby and Baker Books, 1992

Henley, Katrina and Loreena Bloomfield (The Slosh Sisters) Falling Off the Top Shelf. East Malvern, Victoria, Australia: Self-published. [ISBN: 064628163]

Long, Cheryl and Heather Kibbey, Classic Liqueurs, Lake Oswego, Oregon: Culinary Arts Ltd., 1993 (Revised) [ISBN 0914667114]

Meilach, Dona and Mel Meilach, Homemade Liqueurs, Chicago, IL, Contemporary Books, Inc., 1979 [ISBN: 0809275821]

Morris, Mary Aurea, Ed. Glorious LIqueurs, New York, NY, Lake Isle Press, 1991 [ISBN: 0962740314]

Thomas, Charles, Sweet Sips 2, Vancouver, WA, Charles Thomas Publications [ISBN:0965264319]

Vargas, Pattie and Rich Guling, Cordials From Your Kitchen, Pownal, VT, Storey Publishing, 1997 [ISBN: 0882669869]

Walton, Stuart and Norma Miller, Spirits and Liqueurs Cookbook, New York, NY, Lorentz Books, 1997 [ISBN: 1859674151]

www.liqueurweb.com/-Recipes, techniques and plenty of links to other sites.

Characteristics of Alcoholic Beverages
(Beer)

Description

Fermented mash of various malted grains, notably barley flavored with hops	Alcohol %
Lager, pale, dry	6%
Ale, pale to dark, bittersweet	6%
Stout, dark ale, strong malt flavor, bitter	6%
Porter, like stout, but not as strong. Dark, bitter	6%
Sake, rice beer, white, dry, still	14-16%

Types and Characteristics of
(Other Spirits)

	U.S. Proof	Alcohol %
Vodka distilled at 190 proof from grain or Potatoes. It is not aged. White, usually cut with water.	90	45%
Brandies distilled at 140 proof from wine or fermented mash of fruit juice.	96-108	48-54%
Cognac, brown, dry	84	42%
Calvados (applejack, brown, dry)	100	50%
Kirsch (cherry brandy) white, dry, bitter almond	96	43%
Quotach (plum brandy) white, dry	100	50%
Van der hum, tangerines (mandarins)	70	35%
Anisette, aniseed, white	54	27%
Apricot liqueur	60	30%
Blackberry liqueur, dark, red, sweet	86	43%

Types and Characteristics of Other Spirits Continued

	U.S Proof	Alcohol %
Cherry Liqueur, black cherry, red, sweet	60	30%
Crème de Ananas, pineapple	60	30%
Crème de Cacao, chocolate, vanilla	60	30%
Crème Cassis, black currants, red	36	18%
Crème Fraisers, strawberries	60	30%
Crème de Menthe, peppermint	60	30%
Curacao, green orange peel	60	30%
Sloe Gin, wild plum, red, sweet	80	40%
Triple Sec, a white curacao, sweet	80	40%
Peach Liqueur	60	30%
Maraschino, wild cherry, white	60	30%
Absenth, aromatic plants brandy, yellow-green, liquorice	136	68%
Benedictine, secret blend of herbs, plants, etc., spicy, sweet	60	30%
Chartreuse, secret blend of herbs, plants etc., spicy, sweet	86	43%
Cherry Heering	110	55%
Drambuie, secret blend of scotch whiskey and honey golden, spicy sweet	60 to 80	30 to 40%
Kümmel, caraway and cumin seed	60 to 80	30 to 40%
Liqueur d'or, lemon peel, herbs, plants	86	43%

If we think of malt as what gives beer its body and strength, then hops is what gives it character, or personality. The hops we use in brewing are the cone shaped blossom from a perennial vine. The paper-like cone, when picked looks a lot like a pine cone, is pungent smelling and sticky with oils and resin.

The essence from hops gives the bitter flavor and aroma to beers, helps to preserve it and aids in clarification. The processing and storage of hops is a brewing related art which directly affects the quality of the brew and you should strive to obtain the freshest possible and preserve that freshness. The availability, variety, packaging and preservation of hops for the homebrewer today is light years ahead of where it was just a few years ago. Today, instead of a dried out brick of compressed hops that may have been packed during the Crusades, we have hermetically sealed packets, pelletized hops and liquid extracts; all dated and kept under refrigeration. Short of growing your own hops in the backyard, it can't get any better. To date, I've had no luck growing hops in Alaska, but since I've finally succeeded with asparagus and kiwis, I'll keep trying.

There are many varieties of hops, but only two main types or more appropriately, uses. The first type called boiling, bittering or flavoring hops is stronger flavored and is boiled with the wort. They are normally used at around 2-2-½ ounces per five gallons. The second use of what is usually a milder flavored, more fragrant variety is called aromatic hops, which is added at the end of the cooking process to preclude its volatile oils from being boiled away. They are used at a rate of around ½ oz. per five gallons, but remember, this is a matter of taste. You're the brewmaster.

Some people get "chemi-crazy" about hops, citing acid ratings and chemistry terms to forecast flavor. They probably do it for apples and tomatoes too. There's nothing like biting into a nice juicy #37 or a good bacon, lettuce and A-186 sandwich. Without a bunch of numbers, the following table attempts to describe the characteristics of some common hops. To further your education, you should sniff and taste some hops

Common Hops Table

Variety	Bitterness	Flavor - Aroma, etc.
Brewer's Gold	High	Strong full-bodied bitter hops - stouts, dark beers
Bullion	High	Strong, full-flavored bittering - ales, stouts, barley wines (best not used alone, but blended with other hops)
Eroica	Very High	Strong bittering - Use sparingly - Dark beers, stouts
Fuggles	Low	Spicy, aromatic - mild English style ales
Galena	Very High	Strong bittering - use sparingly - ales and steam beers
Hallertauer	Low	Pungent, spicy, aromatic - continental lagers
Northern Brewer	High	Flavorful bitter hops, can also be used as an aromatic - good for all dark beers
Nugget	Very High	Strong bittering - use sparingly - dark beers, stouts - use with other hops
Saaz	Low	Distinctive, spicy, aromatic - traditional pilsner hops from Czechoslovakia, also wheat beers
Styrian Golding	Medium	Mild, spicy - pale ales and bitter
Talisman	Medium High	High quality bittering
Tettnanger	Medium	Bittering hops - can be used as an aromatic - continental lagers
Willamette	Medium	Similar to Fuggels - ales

Leaf Hops

Pelleted Hops

➠ Adding chips or shavings of beechwood or hazelnut is an ancient and organic way of clarifying beer.

➠ Adding lightly charred oak chips to distilled spirits is an excellent way of aging them. If left to soak for a week or so, this accomplishes the same thing as aging in charred wooden barrels. The charred wood adds color and flavor while absorbing the lighter hangover producing fusel oil and methyl alcohol that may be present.

➠ A short length of brass chain (1 to 2 feet) can be used in cleaning-really grubby bottles. Just shake it around inside the bottle with a little detergent or bleach solution.

➠ Primitive, but effective, scales can be improvised easily from a wood stick, three cup hooks, some string and two coffee cans. Screw one cup hook in the top at exact center or balance point of a uniformly dimensioned wood strip like doweling or 1x 1's. Screw the other two hooks into the ends. Suspend your new balance beam from a string and hang two coffee cans on the ends. Use a combination of full cans of soup or whatever with the net weight marked on the container as the counter balance, or desired weight in one can, then put malt, sugar, etc. In the other can until the balance beam (stick) is level. When you're filthy rich, you can buy a set of scales, until then, this "pore boy" scale will get you by. If you want to be a show off, then cobble up a set of counter weights using metal washers. Tape a carpenters string level to the balance beam if you want to get fancy. With a little practice, you can weigh to small fractions of an ounce accuracy with this rig. Crude? Primitive? Yep. Does it work? Yep. Cheap too (See Chapter 4)

➠ A little bit of "The Hobo's Friend," chlorine bleach solution, goes a long way. Watch it when using it in your fermentation locks. If you dribble just a bit in your fermenting fluids, it will shut down the works quick. With beer you can re-boil the wort to evaporate the chlorine. With wine warm, don't boil the must in a loose lidded pot, then hit the must with a big, strong yeast starter. Best of all, don't get sloppy in the first place.

➠ Replacing a wooden bung in a keg is just about a lost art. Expandable rubber test plugs sold in industrial supply stores work very well to replace a missing or leaking bung. They come in various sizes and have an expansion bolt in them that swells the plug up when you tighten it. They are easy to remove for cleaning and draining the keg.

➠ To protect your carboy and make it easy to handle, make a stand or carrier for it from two stackable plastic milk crates. Cut a hole for the neck in the bottom grid out of one crate and epoxy glue it into the top of the other. Make the joint fail-safe by reinforcing it with wire or strapping tape. The carboy will fit nicely into the crates with enough spare room to slip a cardboard carton over for padding and light exclusion.

➨ Smoked beers are a high point in the brewers art, but malting and smoking your own grain is more of a task than the average homebrewer wants to undertake. There's an easy way to make smoked beer, but first let me interject a point on types of smoke. Regardless of what we're led to believe, the fish smoking industry has found that it is a rare individual that can actually differentiate between the type of smoke used in fish smoking. Hickory, alder, beech, apple or corncob smoke all tastes the same. Now if you use something like Christmas trees or outhouse shingles, you probably will get a distinctive taste that you probably won't like. To make an easy smoked beer that you probably will love, just use the liquid smoke® seasoning sold for bar-b-Queing. This stuff consists of natural smoke concentrate and water only. A little bit goes a long way, so go lightly. I suggest you use $1/8$ ¼ and ½ tsp. per 12 oz. bottle on a portion of your next batch and then adjust to your taste.

➨ Stuck ferments are usually due to your yeast being shocked into dormancy, by too high or too low of a temperature. You can cure it by moving your must or wort to a cooler or warmer spot, but sometimes the recovery is slow. It's best to add a new vigorous yeast starter to a stuck ferment and add some yeast nutrient tablets to help jump-start the ferment.

➨ You'll accumulate paraphernalia and ingredients as time goes by and staying organized can become a chore. Early in the game, it's a good idea to dedicate a footlocker or trunk for brewing stuff, except yeast and hops that should be kept in the refrigerator.

➨ Charcoal is wood that has been heated (charred) in the absence of oxygen. Moisture and other components of the wood are cooked out as vapors and gasses leaving behind a porous, rather pure form of carbon that looks something like petrified wood. Its porosity and chemical properties make it a good filter and absorbent of fusel oils.

➨ Bar-be-Que briquettes are made out of ground charcoal and clay, compressed into shape and not suitable for filtering. Whiskey makers make their own charcoal out of hardwoods like maple and oak. You can do it too on a small scale. You'll need a safe, non-toxic metal container with a sealable lid, some hardwood and an outdoor heat source.

➨ Using a cookie tin with a tight-fitting lid, punch a small nail hole in the lid and save the nail (non-galvanized.) Fill the tin with small chunks or slivers of hardwood, not pine or resinous woods. Seal the tin and cook outdoors until no more gasses come out the nail hole. Remove the tin from the heat and let it cool. Spraying the tin with a garden hose will help. Cool things off. Replace the nail in the lid to keep air from getting to the hot charcoal so it doesn't burn. If you do this too soon atmospheric pressure will crush your cookie tin, due to the vacuum inside.

- Yeast (brewers and bakers' yeast) can yield up to 10% alcohol. Wine yeast up to 15%. Some proprietary yeasts are said to produce up to 21% alcohol. In all cases the yeast dies because it can't tolerate alcohol above a certain level.

- Flashpoint, in nontechnical terms, is the temperature at which a fluid is giving off flammable vapors, which can be ignited readily by a spark or open flame. Gasoline and alcohol are at their explosive best when mixed with lots of air in a confined space, e.g., an empty gasoline drum or a fume-filled room. The risk of explosion is a deadly hazard inherent to distilling. Flashpoints for distilled alcohol range from 78º F (90 proof) to a mere 51º F (200 proof.)

- Putting graduated markings on your fermentation containers to show the number of gallons eliminates a lot of guesswork.

- Rousing means aerating must or wort to get a strong ferment going. There are obvious airborne contamination hazards, but it may become necessary because boiling tends to drive the dissolved air out of water. If your yeast just doesn't want to get going, this may be your problem. To cure or prevent this problem, incorporate some air into your must or wort by stirring or shaking it up or just make it a practice to pour it into the fermenter slowly so it splashes, rather than one quick dump. (Look at causes and cures for stuck fermentation in this tips section.)

- The ideal temperature range for mashing malted grains is from 140º F to 170º F. This is best done by gradually increasing temperature over several hours to attain maximum conversion of starch to sugar. The boiling water/insulated container method described elsewhere in this book is a compromise method for the homebrewer; less efficient, but cheap and simple.

- Bakers' yeast or old outdated beer and wine yeast can be used as yeast nutrient. Just boil them in a little water to kill off the original yeast and use the fluid in your next starter.

- Old stills found in the attic or barn are likely to have been made with lead and would be toxic and cause brain damage. Don't use them!

- A common electric heating pad underneath a carboy and a blanket wrapped around it will keep a batch of wine or beer at a constant temperature. This works especially well if you also stick one of those liquid crystal tape thermometers to the side of the carboy.

- Plastic milk or juice jugs make good fermenting vessels for small batches like a gallon or two of dandelion wine. Fit them with the fermentation locks I show you how to make in Chapter 4.

- $15/_{64}$ and ¼" drill bits will make press-fit airtight holes for most plastic straws when cobbling up fermentation locks as detailed in Chapter 4.

Causes and cures for stuck fermentation

1. You were a cheapskate and used old outdated yeast – add new fresh yeast.

2. You added yeast before the wort cooled and killed it – add new yeast.

3. Wort or must is too warm or too cool – check temperature, move to cooler or warmer location.

4. You got sloppy and left some bleach in the fermenter or dribbled it out of the fermentation lock – reboil wort, warm and stir must to drive out chlorine, cool, add new yeast. Vow, as I have never to use bleach solution in fermentation locks again after killing the same batch twice.

5. Boiled wort or water needs rousing or aeration. Aerate by shaking up or stirring. Add fresh yeast to be safe.

6. You have angered the brew spirits – There is no hope, take up golfing.

These are not standard weight and measurement tables, but more helpful rules-of-thumb that I have compiled over time.

For priming beer, use either corn or cane sugar at the ratios of:

5-Gal.	1-¼	Cups
1-Gal.	¼	Cup
1-Qt.	1	Tsp.
1-Bottle	¼	Tsp.

Pounds of sugar by cup

2-½	Lb.	6-½	Cups
1	Lb.	2-½	Cups

5-lb. Dry malt extract equals 6-lb. Liquid or syrup malt extract

The Shape of the Grape formula for wine making with different forms of whole and processed grapes:

14-Lb. Fresh grapes = 1-Gal. 100% juice = 32 Oz. Frozen concentrate = 10 Oz. Canned concentrate = 6-Lb. Raisins = 1-Gal. Wine.

Optimum Temperatures:

Fermentation	50° F - 60° F
Add yeast	55° F
Mashing	150° F 8-12 hours, start with 175° F water to compensate for lower temperature of the grain and heat loss if using an insulated beverage container for mashing.
Sparging	170° F - 180° F
Distilling	173° F - 205° F
Aging	The cooler, the better as long it's above freezing.

5-gal of beer using 6-lb. total of various malt, cane, or corn sugar, etc. will yield a weak beer around 4% alcohol. Work up from this to develop your own recipes.

Safety – Distilling and Temperature Control

The fluids in a wash vaporize, or cookout at different temperature ranges, e.g.

Methanol	64° C
Ethanol	78° C
Propanol	82° C
Water	100° C
Butanol	116° C

Methanol, propanol and butanol can make you sick, blind, dead or brain damaged. Temperature control is obviously necessary to control what you produce. The old timers often threw away the first and the last fluids from a run for safety. Ignorance is *not* bliss, but deadly in distilling!

2-½ Lb. of sugar is the maximum that will ferment in a gallon of water, yielding around 14% alcohol. More yields a sweet wine, less, a dry wine.

Commercial breweries use a pressurized gas (CO_2) bottling system to purge air from bottles because air can degrade the beer's quality. The homebrewer can accomplish the same thing by priming his beer in bulk the night before bottling. The beer will then foam up when the bottles are filled, thus purging the air. It's a bit messy, but it works and gives you a better quality beer.

Bottle Table (rounded off to the next highest bottle)

	U.S. 7 Oz. Ponys	U.S. 12 Oz.	European 17 Oz.	European Green 22-24 Oz.	U.S. 40 Oz. Screw Tops	Import 2-Liter Containers
1 Qt. 32 Fl. Oz.	5	3	2	2	1	
1 Gal. 128 Fl. Oz.	19	13	8	6	4	2
5 Gal. 640 Fl. Oz.	92	54	38	27-29	16	10

Rather than mess with mathematic formulae, just use a straight edge on this illustration to convert Celsius and Fahrenheit temperatures.

Since it is the main ingredient in all wine, beer and whiskey making, quantitatively at least, we should look at the part water plays in brewing. Water is the stuff of life, the benign medium necessary for fermentation to take place. But in its chemically pure form, water or H_2O, like distilled water is not a good medium for fermentation, it is lacking in dissolved minerals or salts. We describe water as being hard or soft, meaning it has lots of, or lesser amounts of dissolved minerals, respectively, dissolved in it.

Some "authorities" say, hard waters make better light beers, like Czech Pilsner and soft waters make better dark beers, like Irish stouts, other "authorities" say exactly the opposite. Earlier we said that regional brews evolved by trial and error and passing down yeast cultures that gave the best results. This evolution of beers and wines was a process of learning what worked best with local materials, water included.

The characteristics, or chemical composition of water vary greatly, not only from region-to-region, but also from season-to-season. For example, when reservoir levels are high from rain fall and snow melt, the water might be classed as soft, but in the dead of winter as freezing captures the pure water in a layer of ice, the salt concentration in the water of the same reservoir will increase it's hardness. Furthermore, the character of the local water will change as you boil it. Chalk or calcium will precipitate, or solidify and settle out. Chlorine will boil out and it will acquire hardness from the ingredients of your brew.

The strain of yeast you use and probably the color of socks you are wearing will all influence the character of your brew. In short, as a homebrewer, you are just like the little old brewmaster of bye-gone days trying to make the best product possible with local ingredients. You will find many recipes that include water treatment additives that I wouldn't put on my garden, let alone put in my beer. The potable water which you drink every day, if it is not settling up into concrete in your bowels, will make any type of beer or wine you desire. You might not make a world class pilsner, ale or stout with your first batch, but you will have, with good records, established a base recipe to work from. Who knows? You may make a classic brew. If you shovel in a bunch of plaster of paris, salts and junk trying to duplicate the water of "Bilge Water by the Sea" or "Dead Horse Springs," you will have departed from both art and science into imitative magic. If you choose to go this route, you should put on some feathers, beat a drum, burn incense and dance around a fire in your skivvies chanting to the brew spirits. On the other hand, if you use your local water, sound brewing procedures and keep good records, you will not fail and in time will excel in whatever brew you're striving for.

In summary, "hard" and "soft" are only relative terms for the amount of "stuff" in your water. It's what that stuff is that affects the characteristics of your beer. The chemistry is complex and even the experts can't agree on what does what. As a homebrewer, you can soften your water by diluting it with distilled water or rainwater, or you can harden it by boiling it down to concentrate the "stuff." If you keep good records, you'll soon be able to tailor your beer to your wants.

Thee Auld Scotsman
Homebrew Supplies
P.O. Box 170
Paola, KS 66071
Free Catalog

Big Basin Brewing
Homebrew Supplies
Supplies in the Redwoods
Santa Cruz Mountains Area
13180 Hwy 9
Boulder Creek, CA 95006
(800) 509 BREW Visa/MC
Brew pub quality at home

Great Fermentations of Marin
87 Larkspur
San Rafael, CA 94901
(800) 570-BEER

Belgian Candi Supply
Homebrew Supplies & Equipment
Full line of beer and wine books
319 1/2 Milburn Ave.
New Jersey 07941
(201) 376-0973

Winemaker's Supply
4386 N. Essex Ave
Springfield, MO 65803
(417) 833-4145
Free Catalog

Country Wines
3333 R Babcock Blvd.
Pittsburgh, PA 15237
Large inventory brewing supplies.
Free Catalog (412) 336-0151

Just Hops
335 N. Main

Mt. Zion, Il. 62549
Free Catalog
(217) 864-4216

Freshops
6180 Kings Valley
Philomath, OR 97370
(800) 460-6925

Arklatex's Best Homebrew
Homebrew Supplies
(318) 858-2219

The Flying Barrel
Homebrew Supplies and Equipment
Serving Baltimore, Maryland &
Washington
111 S. Carrol
Frederick, MD 21701
(301) 663-4491
(Mail orders welcome)

Third Fork Homebrewing
Homebrew Supplies
690 Walnut
Union Star, MO 64494

DelFalco's Homebrewing Supplies
Homebrew Supplies
Free Catalog
5611 Morningside
Houston, TX 77005
(800) 216-2739

Wild West Homebrew Supply
Catalog and Recipes
(800) 786-5141
Wildbrew@sioux.sodak.net
Free catalog
(800) 659-9870

Fort Below Products
Graham, WA USA
Brewing Equipment
Free Catalog
(206) 846-2081
Custom bottle labels
Designs full color labels with your photo or artwork.
(800) 232-LABEL

F.H. Steinbart Company
Wine & Brewing Supplies
Wide variety of supplies
234 S.E. 12th Ave
Portland, OR 97214
(503) 232-8793
*Source for Noirot Liqueur Flavorings

Williams Brewing
Home beer making catalog & newsletter
703 Castro St. #2
San Leandro, CA 94577
Write and get on the mailing list for this informative catalog/newsletter.

Alaska Mill Feed
Beer and Wine Making Supplies

Bush orders welcome
1501 E. First Ave
Anchorage, Alaska 99501
Stocks a delightful inventory of supplies, ingredients and books.
*Also supplies Noirot flavoring extracts
(907) 276-6016

Arctic Brewing Supply
Alaska's Largest Selection of Beer and Wine Making Supplies
5915 #3 Lake Otis Parkway
Anchorage, Alaska 99507
(907) 561-5771
1 800 770-BREW
*Supplier of Noirot Flavor Extracts

Pine Tree Garden Seeds
Box 300
New Gloucester, ME
Tel: 207-926-3400
Fax: 1-888-52SEEDS
Email: superseeds@worldnet.att.com
Sells the book "The Homebrewer's Garden" - How to grow, prepare and use your own hops, malts and brewing herbs.
$14.95

Brewing Log

Type of Beer or Wine _____

Start Date _____

ID # or Code used on Bottles _____

Ingredients (type malt, fruit, yeast and additives   **Quantity**

Processing Notes (boiling, sparging, type containers, juice, or fruits)

_____
_____
_____
_____
_____

Fermentation Notes (time, problems, yeast production and type)

_____
_____
_____
_____
_____

Evaluation

_____
_____
_____
_____

Lessons Learned

_____
_____
_____
_____
_____
_____
_____

Glossary

Adjuncts - Fermentable ingredients used in beer making in addition to malt. Corn, rice and various other grains and sugars are common adjuncts used to vary the body, flavor and alcohol content of the end product.

Bakers' Yeast - Can be used for making beer and wine but, is not very satisfactory because it doesn't settle out well and has a distinctive taste. When pouring, the yeast residue in a bottle usually gets stirred up and makes the beverage murky.

Beer - A low alcohol beverage fermented from malted grain, water, hops and yeast. The many variants include, ale, lager, pilsner, porter, stout and barley wines. Adjuncts, or additional fermentable ingredients are often used, such as sugars and un-malted grains to vary the character of the brew and for economy.

Beer (when making whiskey) - A mixture of fluids and solids which is fermented for distillation of alcohol. Also called mash.

Brewers Yeast - Falls into two main types, lager yeast which settles to the bottom of the fermenting vessel and ale yeast which forms a cake of dead yeast on the surface of the wort, which should be skimmed off. Both types will produce around seven percent alcohol by volume before the alcohol kills them off. Both types form a stable residue on the bottom of bottles making it easy to carefully pour your homebrew without making it murky. While you may discern subtle differences in flavor, either type can be used interchangeably.

Campden Tablet - Potassium meta bisulfate tablets which release a sterilizing gas (sulfur dioxide) when dissolved. Used to sterilize ingredients and equipment used in fermenting. Advantage over bleach is that it doesn't kill beer or wine yeast.

Capper - A device used to squeeze metal caps on to bottles. There are several types commonly encountered ranging from a simple one you tap over the cap with a hammer, to far more efficient types which use levers to seat the cap.

Carbonation - CO_2 bubbles in your beverage. Best achieved by adding a small amount of sugar to a beverage when bottling to encourage natural fermentation and carbonation in the bottle.

Carboy - Large glass jug, such as you see on old-fashioned water coolers. Really fine for fermenting beer and wine as long as you don't use the cap forming or top fermenting ale yeasts.

Chlorine Bleach - AKA "The Hoboes Friend." Unscented Chlorox or similar product, diluted at about one tablespoon per gallon , is an excellent sterilizing agent for bottles and equipment. Its disadvantage over campden tablets is that if not thoroughly rinsed from equipment, even a small amount will kill the yeast in your fermenter.

Clarification - Newly fermented beers and wines are murky due to the presence of suspended solids, mainly yeast. These solids will settle naturally to the bottom of a vessel or bottle in time. The settling or clarification process can be speeded by adding various substances to the brew near the end of fermentation. Unflavored gelatin is the clarifying substance recommended in this book.

Crown Caps - Common metal caps used to seal beverage bottles by being crimped or squeezed on. Available from any homebrew supplier.

Fermentation - The natural process by which yeast converts sugars and starches to alcohol and CO_2

Fermentation Lock - Also called air lock bubbler, thumper. There are many types of homemade and store-bought devices, all of which work sort of like a snorkel letting carbon dioxide produced by yeast escape from the fermenter while excluding air and airborne organisms.

Hops - The resinous Cone-shaped blossom of the hops vine adds bitterness to, aids clarification and helps preserve malt beverages. The two main types or uses are bittering and aromatic hops. The first is used throughout the cooking process; the second, more delicately flavored type is used after cooking to add the gourmet touch to hand-crafted beers.

Hydrometer - Instrument for measuring specific gravity or density of a fluid. Used before and after fermentation to determine potential and actual alcohol content. It's use is covered in Chapter Four of this book.

Malt - (Malt extracts, malting, hopped malt) Malt, the main ingredient of beer is grain which has been sprouted, thereby beginning a natural process of converting its starches to sugar (maltose sugar.) This process is called malting and also includes toasting the malt to varying degrees to change its color and flavor and ultimately give us a wonderful variety of light to dark and heavy beers. Malt extracts are derived by dissolving the sugars and good stuff from the grain and concentrating them as is done with milk by dehydrating into condensed syrup or powdered form. Most, but not all malt syrups prepared for the homebrewer contains hops extract, also for flavoring and preservative purposes.

Mash - (Wort, must, mush, beer) The mixture of water, malt, fruit, grain, etc., used in fermenting alcoholic beverages is called respectively. Beer, mash, then wort when solids are removed and fluids boiled with hops. Wine - must, which may include crushed fruit and sugar or just the juice or fluid. Whiskey - mash or mush, refers to all the fermenting ingredients while beer refers to the fluids separated for distillation. Mashing converting the starch in malt to sugar via action of

natural enzymes. Done by gradually heating a mash of cracked malt and water.

Must - Raw wine. The mixture of fruit juice, sugar, water and yeast which eventually ferments into wine.

Priming - Adding a small amount of sugar to beer (or wine) when bottling to promote natural carbonation from fermentation in the bottles. Several methods of priming are covered in this book.

Proof - The alcohol content of beer and wine is normally described in percent by volume. With spirits or distilled products the percentage multiplied by two, i.e., whiskey that is 50% alcohol is 100 proof. Now you know.

Racking - Siphoning fermenting beer or wine carefully to another container in order to leave the lees or dregs of dead yeast, fruit pulp, hops, etc., behind.

Sparging – Extracting the sugar from a mash of cracked malt by running hot water through it.

Starter - A vigorous yeast culture prepared in advance to ensure a strong initial ferment. Also describes reserving and nurturing a sample of yeast for future use.

Trub - The protein and other junk (dregs) deposited in the bottom of your brew kettle when you boil the wort. Discard it when you transfer the wort to the primary fermenter.

Vinegar Bugs - Airborne bugs which are the enemy of all beer and wine makers. Sterilize all ingredients and equipment and use a fermentation lock to exclude them from your must or wort.

Index

A

A Fresh Grape-Raisin Wine 26
acids 36
acrospire 87
additives 2, 21
adjuncts 64
adverse affects of light 12
aging 155
aid clarification 31
air space in all bottles as a safety factor 20
airborne contamination 19
airborne yeast 14
Al Capone Beer 60
Al Capone Speakeasy Beer 60
Alaska Bush Beer 58
Alaskan Currant or Cranberry Wine 30
Alaskan Fireweed Blossom Wine 39, 40
Alaskan wild elderberries 28
all malt beers 64
Amaretto® 146
Any Beer Using Malt Extract Syrup 61
Any Cordial or Liqueur 147
Any Grain Alcohol (Using Noirot Flavors) 147
Appendix A Tips 152
Appendix B Tables 155
Appendix C Hops
   hopstables 150
Apple Sherry 30
Apple Wine 28, 29
Applejack 8, 44
Applejack Recipe 44, 45
apricot 29
aquariums and battery cases 12
aromatic hopping 54

B

bakers' yeast 10, 15 59
Balkans 46
BALLING 101
Banana liqueur 146
baneberries 27
barley 67

Barley Wine 7, 65
Barley Wine (Pearled Barley) 38, 39
Basic Grape Wine Recipe 26
Basic Potato Wine 35, 36
basic procedures and common pitfalls 17, 18
basic recipe for just about any other fruit. 31
basic wine making steps, recipes and instructions 20
"Beary" Berries 30
Beech smoke 66
beechwood chips 21
Beer
   adjuncts 64
      rice 64
   aging 55, 62
   aluminum containers 55
   aromatic hopping 54
   artificial carbonation 52
   Basic Beer Making 52
   beachwood 152
   Blue Ribbon Malt 58
   bottling 55, 62, 71
   break 53
   brewer's log 56
   Causes and cures for stuck fermentation 155
   Cooking 53
   crown caps 55
   dark heavy-bodied stouts 64
   dark malts 64
   exposure to light 55
   filling the bottles 55
   German law 52
   hazelnut chips 152
   heading agents 52
   hopped malt extract 54
   hops 54
   labels 56
   light malts 64
   light-bodied beers 64
   liquid smoke 153
   malt extracts 58
   mashing 52
   nutrient tablets 153
   "off" tastes from aluminum 53
   organic way of clarifying beer 152
   powdered concentrated malt extract 53
   priming 58, 62, 155
   priming beer 155
   rousing 154

Index

smoked beer 153
sparging 155
spruce needles 54
sterilization 54
storing 55
stuck ferments 153
trub 53
wort 52
yeast 154
yeast nutrient 154
Beer Making
    beer 52
Beer Recipes
    Al Capone Beer 60
    Al Capone Speakeasy Beer 60
    Any Beer (using malt extract syrup) 61
    Aromatic Hopping All-malt Beer 62
    Barley Wine 65
    Basic Lager 69
    Basic Wheat Beer 68
    Chicha #1 72
    Chicha - Corn Beer 71
    Corn Beer #2 73
    Oatmeal Stout 64
    Pale Lager Pilsner 64
    Pilsner Style with Rice 64
    Prohibition Style Beer 58
    Smoked Beer (The Easy Way) 66
    Smoked Stout 66
    Steam Beer 61, 65
    Steam Beer - All Grain 61
Beer yeast 15
Beet Wine (red beets) 35, 37
beets 35
Birch Sap Wine 43-44
blackberries 27
Blossom Wines 39
Blossoms you can use to make wines are: 40
Blue Ribbon Malt 58
Blueberry Wine 27, 28
Boiling 70
bottles 12
bottles that take a twist-off cap 12
Bottling homemade wine 19-22
bottom fermenting yeast 15
brandy 8
Brandy, Apple 143
Brandy, Apricot 146
Brandy, Peach (Canned Peaches) 143
brewers flour. See See ground malted wheat
BRIX 101

bubbles 19
bull's blood 21

C

Café (Tia Maria) 146
campden tablet 2, 14–16
cane fruits 27
canned concentrates 26
cappers 22
carboys 11, 77
carnation 40
Carrot Wine (Carrot Whiskey) 35, 37
Casa De San Josè Monastery 46
champagne 19. See also sparkling wine
Champagne bottles 12
champagne-like cider 33
Cheating for Better Grain Wines 38, 39
chemical additives 23, 36
cherries 27, 73
Cherry Wine 29
Chicha 71
Chicha #1 72
chlorine bleach 13. See also hobo's friend
Cider (Apples) and Perry (Pears) 31-32
Cider vinegar 32
citrus fruits 36
clarification 21, 53, 68, 70, 150 See also
        Racking
classes of grape wine 25
cleaning bottles 152
clear plastic tubing 11
CO2 gas 6
color of bottle 12
commercial additives 68
Commercial sweet cider 32
Compound Still 120
conversion
        52, 53, 62, 67, 71, 85, 107, 111. See
        also See mashing
"conversion" 65
conversion of the milk sugar 46. See also
        lactose
conversion of wheat 68
cooling 70
copper 10
corks 22
corn beer. See Chicha
Corn Beer #2 73
Corn Likker 110
Corn Squeezins 8, 49
corn whiskey 8

Corn Wine 34
cowslip 40
Cranberries 138
Cranberry Alaskan Watermelon Berry
        Liqueur 144
Crème, Irish II 140
crown caps 12, 19, 21
culture for future use 20
Currant Wine 30
cut. *See* See dilute

D

dandelion 40
dark beers 64
dark malts 64
dead yeast 21. *See also* lees
desirable acids 36
developing your own wines 23
diastase 67, 68
dilute. *See* See cut
Diocese of Whitehorse, Yukon Territory 46
distillation
    mashing 107, 155
distilled liquors 128
distilled moonshine 8
distilled spirits 8
Distilling
    40 Rod 109
    aging 152
    aging bandy 131
    alcohol 129
    aldehydes 131
    barley 106
    Bath tub gin
        prohibition 109
    Bathtub Gin
        juniper berries 109
    Bathtub Gin #1 109
    Bathtub Gin #2 109
    bourbon 107
    bourbon grist 108
    brandy 131
    butranol 156
    cane sugar 107
    carbon 129
    carbon dioxide 129
    charcoal 153
    charcoal filtering 109
    charred oak chips 152
    chilling 130
    cognac 131

commercial whiskey 131
commonsense rules 133
conditions required for efficient fermenta-
        tion 129
converting starch 107, 111
corn 106
Corn Likker 110
corn sugar 107
Corn Whiskey 110
dangerous vapors 134
Elliot Ness 107
enzymes 129
esters 131
ethers 131
ethyl alcohol 128, 129, 131
explosion/hazard 133-134
Federal Law 106
fermentable sugars 107
filtering 130
fire 133-134
first run whiskey 109
flash point 132-133, 154
Free Whiskey 111
fruit juices 129
fusel oil 131, 152
glass containers 134
grain whiskey mashing 107-108
hangover 129, 131-132
Hydrogen 129
Loudmouth 110
mashing 106, 111
metal containers 134
methyl alcohol 131, 152
molasses 106, 107
Moonshine 110, 134
Mountain Dew 110
must 130
neutral spirit 130
non-permitted still 106
Optimum ratio of sugar to water 130
optimum temperature 155
oxygen 129
pectins 129
plastic containers (storing) 133-134
"pop skull" 109
potassium tantrate 130
potatoes 106
Preachers Whiskey 111
propanol 156
proper ventilation 134
pure ethyl alcohol 132

Index

Real Corn Whiskey #1 110
Real Corn Whiskey #2 111
rice 106
Russia
  samogon 134
rye 106
  ergot fungus 107
scotch 107
seed grains 107
single run whiskey 109
sippin' whiskey 108
smoking 133
Sneaky Pete 111
sour mash 108
Splo 110
starch 129
starch hazes 107
sucrose 129
sugar 106
Tanglefoot 110
temperature 129, 133, 154
thin mash 107
  wort 108
Too high heat 132
total conversion 107
turbid 130
un-cut alcohol storage 134
vinegar formation 129
vinegar inhibition 130
vodka 135
volatile acids 131
wheat 106
White Lightening 109, 110
wood alcohol 129
wort method 107
yeast and time 130
zymase 129
distilling 85
  cellulose 129
  ethyl alcohol 130
  mashing 154
  methyl alcohol 129
dregs 18. *See also* lees
drinking Chicha 72
dry cider 33
Dry Strawberry Wine 28
dry wine 23
dynamite 9

E

e-coli bacteria 32, 33
Easy Grape Wine 27
egg whites 21
Elderberry Wine 27, 28
Elliot Ness 107
enamelware 10
enzymes 36
ergot fungus 107
ethyl alcohol 128, 130
European style beer bottles 12. *See also*
    European style beer bottles. *See also*
    flip-tops
excessive heat 13-14
extraction 32, 53. *See also* See sparging

F

Father Emmett Engel 46
Feast and Famine Fermentation Method 31
Federal law 106
Federal law permits 3
fermentable sugar 46 *See* fructose
Fermentation 36, 70
fermentation lock 18, 77
fermented mare's milk 46
fermenting containers 11
filling your bottles 22
final fermentation for carbonation 22
fining 21
flaked corn 67
flaked maize 71
flavoring, Noirot® extracts 146
flip-tops 12
Flower and Honey Wine (sweet) 41
flower wines 39
food grade plastic 11, 77
fortified wines 15
fractional crystallization 44, 46
Frangelico 141
Free Whiskey 111
freeze-dried yogurt starter 46
frozen concentrates 26
fructose 46
fruit beers 73
fruit sugar 52
fruit wines 28
fruits and berries 27
fusel oil 10, 46

G

galvanized metal containers 10
gelatin 2, 21, 71, 162
Gin 147
glass 11
Gooseberry Wine 27, 28
Grain, Any Alcohol (Using Noirot® Flavors)
    147
grain wines 38
grapa 7. *See also* additives
grape wine 25
Great Cider 32, 34
gristing 69
ground malted wheat. *See* See brewers flour
ground up eggshells 21

H

hangover 10, 131
Hard Cider 34, 45
hawthorn 40
heavy-bodied stouts 64
herbs 42
high starch content 36
hobo's friend 13. *See also* chlorine bleach
honey 41
Honey and Fruit Juice Wine (sweet) 41, 42
Honey and Fruit Wine (medium dry) 41
Honey Wines (Mead) 41. *See also*
    mead; melomel; metheglin; pyment; sack
honeysuckle 40
Hopping 70
Hops, 38
  aromatic 150
  flavoring hops 150
  liquid extracts 150
  pelletized 150
Horse Turd Whiskey, 110
Hot Pepper Beers 74
Hydrometer 31
  100 US proof spirit 100
  before fermentation 101
  commercial strength 100
  density of fluids 100
  density of water 101
  density of your fermenting liquid 99
  distilled water 100
  final S.G. reading 101
  higher temperatures 101
  hydrometer jar 100

hydrometer scale 100
  lower temperatures 101
  percentage of alcohol by volume 100
  percentages of alcohol 99
  potential alcohol production 99
  potential alxohol by volume 101
  readings 101
  Scales
    BRIX 101
  specific gravity 99, 100. *See also* See
    thickness of water
  starting specific gravity 101
  temperature 101
  thickness of water. *See* See specific
    gravity
  US proof 100
  US Proof and Hydrometer Measurement
    100
  variables 99

I

initial ferment 15
iodine 89

J

jacking 45
Jaune, Couvent (Yellow Chartreuse) 146
juices 26

K

kefir 46
koji 68
koumiss 46. *See also* fermented mare's milk
Koumiss - Kefir Recipe #1 (the easy way)
    46, 47
Krausening 71
Kriek 73
Kvass (bread wine) 42, 43

L

lactose 46
Lager 15
Lager - Basic Recipe 69
Lambic 73
latent ferment 16
lead 154
lead in the booze 2
lead solder 10
lees 18, 21

Index

Less fermentables 23
light malts 64
light-bodied beers 64
lime 40
liqueur 138
Liqueur, Apple 143
Liqueur, Apricot 143
Liqueur, Elderberry 144
Liqueur, Nectarine 143
Liqueur, Noirot® Extracts 146
Liqueur, Peach 143
Liqueur, Pineapple 145
Liqueur, Plum 144
Liqueur, Rhubarb 144
Liqueur, Tangerine 142
Liqueur, Tangerine (made with peels or the zest) 143
live yeast 16
logbook 20
Loudmouth 110

M

making spiced wines 25
malt sugar 35, 46. *See also* malt sugar
malted barley 38
malting 85
   acrospire 87, 90
   black malts 88
   brown malts 88
   caramelizing 87
   charred malts 88
   clear beer 91
   cloudy beer 90
   countertop food dehydrators 87
   dark beers 88
   hazy beer 90
   maximum germination 90
   over modified malts 87
   over-modified grain 90
   pale beer 88
   pale malted barley 87
   roasting temperatures 88
   roasting time 88
   sinkers and floaters test 87
   soaking time 90
   stouts 88
   temperature 88
   temperature control 87
   threshed barley 89
   toasting 87
   total sugar/enzyme yield 87
   under modified malts 87
   unmaltable grains 90
   unmodified grain 90
   wheat beer 89
   wheat berry 89
   winnowing 87
maltose 7, 46
Mangel Wine 35, 38
Mango Wine 28
Marnier, Grand 141
mashing 52-53, 67, 71, 88. *See also* See conversion
mead 41
medium dry wine 31
melomel 41
Menthe, Chocolate (Vandermint) 146
metal kegs 96
Methanol 156
metheglin 41
Mideast 46
milk sugar 46.
milk wine 46. *See also* kefir; koumiss *See also* lactose
Milk Wine Recipe #2 (the more traditional way) 46, 48
Mint Wine 23, 24
Modern Corn Squeezins 49
Moonshine 110
more fermentables 23
More Full-Bodied Blossom Wines 39, 40
Mountain Dew 110

N

natural full-strength vinegar 32
natural ingredients 36
natural sugar 31
natural yeast 14, 25
Naturally Improved Potato Wine 35, 36
naturtian 40
nectarines 29
nitroglycerin 9
Noirot® 146
non-permitted still 2, 106
non-treated barley 36
noncarbonated wine 19. *See also* still wines
nontraditional wines 21
nutrient tablets 9

O

Oatmeal Stout 64
Old Time Cider From Apples 32, 33
older potatoes 36
Optimum temperature for fermentation 155
Optimum Temperatures
    Distilling 155
Optimum temperatures
    Add yeast 155
    fermentation 155
    Mashing 155
    sparging 155
Orange Peel Liqueur 142
Orange, Whole Liqueur 142
Orange Wine 28, 29
Other Wines 42
over carbonating 16
oxalic acid 34
oxidation 22

P

pale beers 7
Pale Lager Pilsner 64
Parsnip Wine 35, 37
parsnips 35
pasteurization 32
Pea Pod Wine 42
Peach, Plum, Prune and Apricot Wine 27, 29
penny bubbler 20
percent of sugar by weight 101
perry 32
pewterware 10
Pilsner Style with Rice 64
Pitching the Yeast 70
plumcots 29
plums 27, 29
pokeweed 27
Pore Boy Equipment 76
Pot Still 120
potassium metabisulfate 14
potatoes 35
Pounds sugar by cup 155
Preachers Whiskey 111
preservation of fruits and berries 27
prime fermenting stage 36
Priming 62, 71
primrose 40
Prohibition Style Beer 58
promote a stronger fermentation 31
proprietary mixtures 21

prunes 27, 29
Pruno – Jailhouse Wine 48-49
pungent spices 41
pyment 41

Q

no entries

R

racking 21
raisin 26
raspberries 27, 73
raw whiskey 10
re-capable beverage bottles 19
records 20
red wine 25
Retort Still 113
reusing the bottle 12
Rhubarb leaves 34
Rhubarb Wine 34, 35
Rice Wine 38, 39
rolled oats 67
Root Wines 35
roots 35
rose 40
Rose Hips Wine 42
Rum 147
Rum, Spiced 145
rye 67, 107, 147

S

sack 41
Safety 12
Safety Distilling and Temperature Control
    156
Salmonberry Wine 27
Sambucus Racemosa – Pubens 28
samogon 134
scale for potential percentage 101
screw cap container 21
second wine 25
Second Wine Recipe (grape) 26
Secondary fermentation 21
secondary fermentation container 19
Shape the Grape formula 155
Shrub, Almond 142
Shrub, Rum 142
Sieben Brewery 60
silo 9

Index

simple apple cider 44, 45
Simple Dandelion Wine 23, 24, 39
Simple Malting to Augment Wine 35, 37
Simple Syrup for Liqueurs 139
Simplest Flower Wine 40
Simplest Honey Wine 41
Siphoning 11, 21
Smoked Beer (The Easy Way) 66
Smoked Stout 66
Sneaky Pete 58, 111
sodium bisulfate 13
Some Simple Wines 23
sparging 67, 85. *See also* See extraction
sparkling wine 19. *See also* champagne
specific gravity 19
specific gravity scale 101
Spirits
    Anisette 141
    Blackberry Cordial 145
    Coffee Liqueur 140
    Coffee Liqueur (Kahlua) 140
    Cointreau No. ! 141
    Cointreau No. 2 141
    Creme De Cacao 140
    Creme de Menthe 139
    Creme de Menthe II 139
    Drambuie 140
    Drambuie II 140
    Irish Creme 140
    Vermouth 147
Spirits, Recipe (Brandy 147
Splo 110
stainless steel 11
starch and sugar levels in a potato 35
starch conversion 36, 85
Steam Beer 61, 65
Steam Beer – All Grain 61
sterilizing equipment 13
sterilizing your equipment 14
still. *See* noncarbonated wine
still wines 19
Stills
    efficiency of the reflux system 133
    Still fittings 134
stills, Old 154
Stone Fruit Wines 29
Stone fruits 27-29
strength and safety of the bottle 12
stuck ferment 9
sugar 46
Sugar Beet Wine 35, 37

sugar beets 35
sugar cane 35
sugar content of the fruit 31
Sugar Wine 23
sweet cider 32
Sweet Potato Wine 35, 38
Sweet Strawberry Wine 28
sweet wine 19, 23
sweeter cider 33

T

Tanglefoot 110
tannic acid 27
tannin 36
tape type aquarium thermometers 98

The Crockpot Still 122
The Deskdrawer Still 126, 127
The Disappearing Still 124
The Modern Pot Still 118
The Two-Dollar Still 122
Tomato Wine (red or green) 34
top fermenting yeast 15
Traditional Pot Still 115
treated seed barley 86
Two-Dollar Still 122
two-liter Japanese beer containers 13

U

un-permitted still 8
unfermented sugar 16, 19
Universal Recipe Made With Store-Bought 100% Fruit 25
Unorthodox and Stunningly Simple Wine Making 24
unwashed apples 32

V

Vegetable Wines 34
vinegar bacteria 10, 14, 31
violets 40
Vodka 35
    alcohol poisoning 134
    potatoes 135
    samogon 134
volatile acids 131

W

Water
    calcium 158

chalk 158
chemical composition 158
chlorine 158
Czech pilsner 158
dark beers 158
distilled 158
hard 158
Irish stouts 158
light beers 158
pure 158
soft 158
treatment additives 158
Watermelon Wine (any type of melon is fine) 34, 35
wheat beer 67-68
  wheat beer tips 67
wheat berries 36
Wheat Wine 38
whey 46
whiskey barrel 10
white grape concentrate 36
White Lightening 110
White raisins 36

White wine 25
whole barley grain 86
Wine From the Vine, Fruit Trees and Berries 25
wine yeast 38
Wine yeasts 15
wooden kegs 10
woodruff 40

X

no entries

Y

yeast, Bakers' 154
yeast culture 15, 17, 18, 20, 68
yeast nutrient 20
Yogurt First (Miss Muffet's favorite) 46, 48

Z

Zinc-coated or galvanized metal containers 10

Order Form

Happy Mountain Publications
Leon Kania
3401 E. Naomi Ave
Wasilla, Alaska 99654
Tel/Fax 907 376-2610

e-mail: leon@happymountain.net

Name_____

Address_____

City_____ State_____ Zip_____

Telephone_____

e-mail address_____

Please send me_____copies of The Alaskan Bootlegger's Bible

@21.95 USD each. (Price subject to change.)

US Shipping $4.00 for first copy, $2.00 for each additional copy.
International shipping $8.00 for first copy, $3.00 for each additional copy.

Books (total number) $_____

Shipping $_____

Total $_____

For volume discount (10 or more copies) for clubs or dealers, inquire at above address or Tel/Fax 1-907-376-2610 (e-mail: leon@happymountain.net)

Visit our web site at: www.happymountain.net

Order Form

Happy Mountain Publications
Leon Kania
3401 E. Naomi Ave
Wasilla, Alaska 99654
Tel/Fax 907 376-2610
e-mail: leon@happymountain.net

Name_____

Address_____

City_____ State_____ Zip_____

Telephone_____

e-mail address_____

Please send me_____copies of The Alaskan Bootlegger's Bible

@21.95 USD each. (Price subject to change.)

US Shipping $4.00 for first copy, $2.00 for each additional copy.
International shipping $8.00 USD for first copy, $3.00 USD for each additional copy.

Books (total number) $_____

Shipping $_____

Total $_____

For volume discount (10 or more copies) for clubs or dealers, inquire at above
address or Tel/Fax 1-907-376-2610 (e-mail: leon@happymountain.net)

Visit our web site at www.happymountain.net